HAZARDOUS HOME-BASED
SUB-CONTRACTED WORK
A STUDY OF MULTIPLE TIERED EXPLOITATION

HAZARDOUS HOME-BASED SUB-CONTRACTED WORK

A STUDY OF MULTIPLE TIERED EXPLOITATION

SHAHRUKH RAFI KHAN

SABA GUL KHATTAK

SAJID KAZMI

SUSTAINABLE DEVELOPMENT POLICY INSTITUTE
ISLAMABAD

OXFORD
UNIVERSITY PRESS

OXFORD

UNIVERSITY PRESS

Great Clarendon Street, Oxford OX2 6DP

Oxford University Press is a department of the University of Oxford.
It furthers the University's objective of excellence in research, scholarship,
and education by publishing worldwide in

Oxford New York

Auckland Cape Town Dar es Salaam Hong Kong Karachi
Kuala Lumpur Madrid Melbourne Mexico City Nairobi
New Delhi Shanghai Taipei Toronto

with offices in

Argentina Austria Brazil Chile Czech Republic France Greece
Guatemala Hungary Italy Japan South Korea Poland Portugal
Singapore Switzerland Thailand Turkey Ukraine Vietnam

Oxford is a registered trade mark of Oxford University Press
in the UK and in certain other countries

ISBN 0 19 597838 2

Typeset in New Century Schoolbook
Printed in Pakistan by
Kagzi Printers, Karachi.
Published by
Sustainable Development Policy Institute,
#3, UN Boulevard, Diplomatic Enclave 1,
Islamabad, Pakistan
and
Ameena Saiyid, Oxford University Press
Plot No. 38, Sector 15, Korangi Industrial Area, PO Box 8214
Karachi-74900, Pakistan.

CONTENTS

PREFACE

Not much, based on qualitative and rigorous work, is known about sub-contracted home based work (home-based work) even though it is assuming increased importance in terms of the workforce it absorbs. The limited research done on this subject indicates that it is highly exploitative, entails low wages, require long and irregular hours, and is repetitive and often quite hazardous. Furthermore, there is a concentration of women and children, particularly girls, in the work force. This book adds to the conceptual and empirical base of this limited knowledge.

Our focus is both on macro and micro issues at the national level and also on the value chain. On a micro level, we investigate the contribution of the children to total family income, and the impact of the increased earnings on improving household education, nutrition and health. Other consequences are also explored, such as the possible neglect of children and a worsening of women's health as they attempt to shoulder a double burden of home-based work and housework and childcare. In particular, we focus on the hazardous nature of home-based work for women and children. The power dynamics within the household due to the start of home-based work are also explored. Finally, we attempt to locate the household production within the international value chain. In order to understand the nature of bargaining power and exploitation, the allocation of surplus across the different tiers of the chain are also explored.

On a macro level, we explore the importance of rising transaction costs, poor labour-management relations, deregulation, demand uncertainty, competitive pressures and regulations that may be constraining the formal sector and leading to informalization. In addition, we explore some inherent advantages of home-based work such as greater flexibility in responding to demand variations, pushing overheads on to contractors and the lack of enforcement of regulations.

The criteria of sector selection were that women and girls be involved in the work, that the work be hazardous to health and that some insight must be forthcoming at least from one of the selected sectors regarding exploitation across the international value chain.

In a nutshell, this is a study about the multi-tiered exploitation this work entails. Exploitation is not defined in the strict Marxian sense of appropriation of surplus value, although we come closest to this in Chapter 4 when reviewing the distribution of revenue across the national and international production or value chain. In the remaining chapters of the report, the reference is to social exploitation where the weaker party is taken advantage of in work or domestic relationships. This can occur in relations between contractors and home-based workers, between men and women and between adults and children within households.

The relevant debates pertaining to home-based work including research methods, child labour, informal sector, globalization and structural adjustment, gender discrimination, exploitation, and empowerment are dealt with in context in the various chapters. In Chapter 1, we provide the Pakistan specific macro-context, situate home-based work in the broader context of the informal sector and review the literature on home-based work in Pakistan. In Chapter 2, we provide the legal context with a review of the legislation pertinent to the protection of home-based workers. In Chapter 3, we describe the study design and survey method in the broader context of research methods utilized to generate quantitative and qualitative data. We also provide a review of Karachi city in which we surveyed the various localities where home-based work was being conducted and a profile of the home-based work sectors. In Chapter 4, we review the extent of worker exploitation by documenting the distribution of surplus across the value chain.

In Chapter 5, we analyze the qualitative data including field reports, case studies and focus group discussion reports. The approach is a sectoral analysis with a focus on work and socio-economic conditions and the cultural norms of the communities the work is located in. Quantitative data analysis is used to substantiate and provide support to the arguments. The findings in Chapter 6, based exclusively on quantitative data analysis, complement those in Chapter 5. We address issues of why home-based work was opted for, work conditions, women's double burden, nutrition, health and child schooling and other activities. Gender comparisons for children and comparison of the home-based workers with a control group of non home-based workers provide important benchmarks and contrast throughout the chapter.

It is often argued that women become more empowered from earned income. We explore this issue in Chapter 7 which takes into account the qualitative and quantitative findings of Chapters 5 and 6 in this regard, and re-examines the initial assumptions of the study with regard to women's empowerment. The conclusion is that empowerment is a highly complex and contextual issue and not amenable to change based on simple indicators or checklists. We end the book with a summary and policy recommendations.

This study is part of a regional set of studies on sub-contracted home-based work carried out with the financial support of Innocenti Research Center UNICEF, Florence, Italy. The other countries in the set include India, Indonesia, Philippines and Thailand. An earlier and shorter draft of the Pakistan study, and other country studies, are available at www.unicef.org/orc. Also relevant are two other papers available on this website which contain a cross-national analysis. These include 'Social Protection in the Informal Economy: Sub-Contracted Home-Based Work and Outsourced Manufacturing in Five Asian Countries,' by Santosh Mehrotra and Mario Biggeri, Innocenti Working Paper (2002), and 'The Subterranean Child Labour Force: Home-Based Manufacturing Work in Low and Middle-Income Asian Countries,' by Santosh Mehrotra and Mario Biggeri, Innocenti Working Paper (2002). Innocenti is editing each of the five country studies in the research project into a paper of around 15,000 words. These country papers will be included in an edited book as well as appear on Innocenti's website.

We, therefore, owe a particular debt to Santosh Mehrotra of Innocenti who is leading the cross-country project and was involved in the participatory conceptualization of the study from the inception and Shiona Hood is acknowledged and thanked as the project manager based in the UNICEF country office in Pakistan.

SDPI was able to undertake this work due to its previous involvement in looking at the interconnections between the global economy and home-based work. That research provided insights and initial cues that we were able to explore in greater detail in the present study. We, therefore, owe thanks to Radhika Balakrishnan who had conceptualized that research.

This book benefited a great deal from extensive and valuable comments from Gunseli Berek of the University of Utah, and from comments on the first draft provided by Santosh Mehrotra and Shiona Hood. Extensive comments were also provided by the book referee.

Many thanks are also due to the keen and motivated field team, led by Sajid Kazmi, including Nadia Maleeha Assad, Azmat Ali Budhani, Taqdees Fatima, Aamir Habib, Ayesha Khurshid, Samina Maitlo and Sadaf Naz. Thanks are also due to our key informants Muhammad Ismail, Hafeezur Rehman, Zaitoon, Safia, Raheema and Maryam. The Pakistan Institute of Labour Education and Research (PILER) facilitated our fieldwork and we thank the Director, Karamat Ali, and Joint Director B. M. Kutty, and in particular,

Muhammad Nawaz and the driver Nasir Khan and the rest of the
PILER Staff. Finally, many thanks are due for word processing
assistance to Irshad Tabussum and Mahjabeen Hussain.

Chapter One
BACKGROUND: CONCEPTUAL ISSUES AND MACRO-CONTEXT[1]

1.1 INTRODUCTION

We begin this chapter with a discussion of some conceptual issues in section 1.2, following which, in section 1.3, we review the macroeconomic situation to highlight the macro-micro linkages i.e. to explain the increased pressures on the informal sector to absorb extra workers. Globalization, liberalization and structural adjustment have generated unemployment as the public sector and the large-scale protected industrial sector has shrunk. The loss of livelihoods has created pressures on non-household heads to supplement household income through home-based sub-contracted work in the informal sector. Worldwide trends indicate a rise in informal sector work coupled with a rise in women and children's share of work in this sector. The definition of 'informal' as opposed to formal sector has been extensively questioned over the past decade as the informal sector has begun to contribute a larger share to national economies.[2] We discuss the dimensions of the informal sector in section 1.4 and locate home-based work within this context.

Various push and pull factors, such as unemployment and underemployment, technological change, innovation in organizational strategies to minimize transaction and labour costs or to circumvent labour legislation are responsible for informal sector expansion in general and home-based work in particular.[3] Also, employers are able to keep overheads and costs of production low and evade taxes. The trends in Pakistan indicate that formal sector employment is actually decreasing with less than 7 per cent labour unionized, according to the Human Rights Commission of Pakistan Report (1999), and less than 3 per cent according to estimates, of the unionized labour force reported in the *Labour Gazette of Pakistan*. Thus, contract labour and home-based work are taking precedence over formal employment. In section 1.5, we review the literature on home-based work in Pakistan that documents working conditions for women and children home-based workers.

1.2   CONCEPTUAL ISSUES

One framework, posited by economists, for examining household work decisions, including sub-contracted work by women and children has given rise to household utility maximization production models.[4] These models require some assumptions about the nature of the utility function households are likely to maximize. Given that, consumption and leisure are generally the main arguments of the function, which is maximized subject to a budget constraint mainly determined by hours of work and the wage rate.

The most straightforward assumption is that the household head (usually male) is benevolent and that his decisions to maximize household welfare lead to both his individual and collective household welfare. Critics have long argued that this is an over-simplification and that households encompass competing interests and that the interests of women and children at times conflict with those of the household head and other males who control household resources.[5] This may endanger the well being of women and children.

No attempt has been made in this study to frame the analysis in the straight-jacket of neo-classical household production model for explaining why and how much different members of the household work. We assume instead, based on a large number of empirical studies, that acute poverty drives children to work.[6] However, two other assumptions are implicitly embedded in this overarching assumption. First, on average, it is poverty and need, and not the maximizations of welfare of a household tyrant, that drives children to work.[7] Second, if this is correct, there must be some threshold level of income beyond which households pull their children out of home-based work and invest in their human capital. Thus, we also test this second assumption, although the nature of the purposive sample we are constrained to work with allows only for suggestive findings.[8]

We assume that poverty drives children to work, an assumption consistent with both the neoclassical model as well as alternative (Sen's) models. We do not differentiate among and explicitly test alternative household models that explain the determinants of child labour. If poverty, rather than perversity, is driving children to work, how should society view this and what would be an optimum intervention to enhance the welfare of women and children. One view is that since child work comes at the expense of schooling, it adversely affects the individual and society (by reducing the overall stock of human capital and social productivity), and therefore, a ban on child work would make society better off. Also, a large-scale withdrawal of child labour would raise the adult wage, which would more than compensate for the loss in child income. This would also improve schooling as the increased household income enables children to be put in school.

We are not persuaded by the above arguments. First, given the excess supply of labour, we doubt that there would be any impact on wages.[9] Second, even if our contentions were not empirically valid, the implementation mechanism simply is not there to achieve a ban on child labour. Finally, child labour now has to be viewed in a global context since globalization pits one poor country into intense competition with another. Thus, such a ban would have to be universally enforced. From the point of view of child welfare, it may be easier to approach the issue with a set of policies that eradicate work hazards, encourage schooling along with work and focus on raising household income of the poor.[10] In the next section, we review the macro-economic situation that pushes women and children into home-based work.

1.3   THE MACRO-CONTEXT

Pakistan's agreements with the IMF demonstrate the kind of policies it has to 'own' as the price of seeking loans.[11] We indicate in this sub-section that these policies and their inherent contradictions worsen the income and unemployment situation and drive more people into home-based work.

On 4 November 2000, the Government of Pakistan sent a letter addressed to the Managing Director of the IMF signed by Pakistan's Minister of Finance and the Governor of the State Bank. A Memorandum of Economic and Financial Policies 2000/01 was enclosed. This reviewed the economic developments during 1999/2000 and described Pakistan's macroeconomic and structural policy programme for 2000/01. The last line of the letter stated 'however, [Pakistan] stands ready to take any additional measures appropriate [for the programme] and will consult the Fund in accordance with the policies of the Fund on such consultations.'[12] Again, paragraph 66 of section VII of the standby agreement says, 'The government

believes that the above described policies are adequate to achieve
the objectives of the program and, the government stands ready to
take any additional steps that may be necessary —.'

The letter and Memorandum are available on the IMF web site
and the Government stated that it also will post the Memorandum
on its web site.[13] This transparency, which is the result of efforts of
international civil society that fears the worst about such
agreements, is welcome. The fear is well founded as will be briefly
indicated below. Meanwhile, the letter and memo indicate that
sovereignty was signed away. This outcome is, no doubt, because
Pakistan had been in a desperate financial state and without the
IMF green light, there would be no loans forthcoming from any
source.

Out of the 41 conditions Pakistan signed off on for the standby
agreement, a dozen were actions to be taken prior to the loan
disbursements. This represents a qualitative change in such
agreements, possibly to stop errant countries from taking the money
and reneging. These prior actions include the usual prescriptions. A
devaluation of the rupee by 12 per cent, an increase in the interest
rate of 3 per cent (which banks balked at) and trade liberalization
requiring a reduction of the maximum tariff from 35 to 30 per cent
by 1 July 2001 (ahead of the WTO schedule). These policy measures
can have positive or negative effects depending on when and in
what manner they are taken, and our economic managers need to
be the best judges of that.[14] The plethora of performance criteria
(18), indicative targets (3) and benchmarks (10), and the stringent
reporting requirements based on these, however, leave no space for
maneuver for local economic managers.

Perhaps the most unfortunate prior action is 'adequate
implementation of an orderly process to resolve the commercial
dispute with HUBCO and action to address the dispute with
KAPCO.'[15] Nations need to honor their contracts, but why should
this have anything to do with the IMF? It is unfortunate to see the
IMF so overtly backing the interests of foreign companies.

The last prior action is a sweeping cross-conditionality that says
'—implementation of sufficient reform measures in the structural
areas that are in the World Bank's domain to allow the World Bank
to provide assurance of financial support.' This covered everything
that was not already covered. In fact, reading the fine print of
proposed structural measures shows that many are very sensible.
However, many of the IMF prescriptions are also self-contradictory
and ensure failure. For example, devaluation, GST, higher utility
prices all lead to inflationary shocks. Reducing tariffs could
adversely impact domestic industry and also directly reduce tax

revenues. In an economic slowdown, meeting stringent deficit targets exacerbates the slowdown, generates poverty, and makes meeting the deficit targets more difficult. It is not difficult to find many such examples, and Pakistan also provides an example.

In Pakistan, many seem to believe that the government now needs the IMF to save it from its own incompetence. An alternative view is that the IMF's overbearing intrusiveness is unjustified and that it is tragic for the Pakistani government to lose control of the nature, timing and quantum of economic reform. As mentioned earlier, a worsening macro situation, induced ironically by structural adjustment, leads to higher unemployment rates and declining incomes which push households into survival strategies that include taking on home-based work. Since the onset of the intensive bout of structural adjustment in Pakistan in 1988-89, economic and social indicators have worsened. We focus here on reviewing the main elements of the macro-economy that have an important bearing on household income and welfare, starting with the unemployment rate.

The aggregate unemployment rate between 1987-88, as the base period, and 1999-00, the latest year for which unemployment rates are available, increased by 4.7 per cent i.e. from 3.1 per cent to 7.8 per cent.[16] Note the weight of agriculture in the labour force (48.4 per cent) pulls down the unemployment rate, which would otherwise be much higher. This aggregate trend is also reflected in the statistics by major industry divisions reported in Table 1.1.

In all but one of the seven major industry divisions cited in Table 1.1 above, unemployment has been increasing continuously since 1987-88 and at least doubled or tripled relative to the base period. The double-digit unemployment rates in 1999-2000 for mining and manufacturing (13 per cent), construction (17 per cent), transport, storage and communications (12 per cent) and community and social services (12 per cent) are particularly notable. The total unemployment rate was almost 8 per cent in 1999-2000, and overall, the open unemployment rates are high by any standard. The Federal Bureau of Statistics has changed the format for calculating unemployment rates by occupational groups to a more sensible one, but unfortunately this means that a comparison over time is more restricted.[17] However, it is safe to infer that the unemployment rates across these groups, as reflected in the aggregate statistics and those of the major industrial divisions, increased over time.

Except for the very top cadre of officers, managers and legislators and in agriculture, unemployment in all other categories in 1996-97 was above 8 per cent with a high of 13.6 per cent for manufacturing sector workers and 12 per cent for professionals. Between 1996-97 and 1999-2000, the unemployment rate across all categories

Table 1.1
Unemployment rates by major industry division over time

Major Industry Divisions	1987-88	1992-93	1996-97	1999-00
Agriculture, forestry, hunting and fishing	1.0	1.7	3.1	3.6
Manufacturing and mining	4.5	9.0	11.1	12.7
Electricity, gas and water	7.8	3.8	9.1	8.7
Construction	9.9	7.2	7.8	17.0
Wholesale & retail trade	3.1	2.8	4.1	7.2
Transport, storage and communication	7.8	7.9	8.4	11.8
Community, social & personal services	4.5	9.9	10.4	11.7
Others (financing, insurance, real estate and business services and activities not adequately defined)	6.9	10.3	5.4	13.7
Total	3.1	4.7	6.1	7.8

Source: Calculated from Government of Pakistan, *Home-based work Force Surveys*, 1987-88 (1989, p. 151, 232), 1990-91, (1992, p. xix) 1992-93 (1994, p. 28, pp. 215, 420), 1996-97 (1997, p. 26, pp. 116,189) and 1999-00, (2001, p. 18, pp. 142, 215).

Note, scholars have generally viewed the LFS unemployment rates to be understated.

Table 1.2
Unemployment rate by major occupation groups, 1996-97

Major Occupation Groups	Unemployment Rate (1996-97)	Unemployment Rate (1999-00)
Legislators, senior officials and managers	3.2	5.6
Professionals	12.1	9.3
Technicians and associate professionals	7.1	14.5
Clerks	9.1	12.9
Service workers, and shop market sales workers	10.1	21.1
Skilled agriculture and fishery workers	1.6	2.7
Crafts and related trades workers	8.8	13.4
Plant and machine operators and assemblers	13.6	13.8
Elementary (unskilled) occupations	8.2	7.8

Source: Calculated from Government of Pakistan, *Home-based work Force Survey*, 1996-97 (1997, pp. 111, 215) and 1999-00 (2001, pp. 137, 245).

increased except for professionals (about a 3 per cent decline) and it stayed roughly the same for elementary unskilled occupations. The alarming increases are the doubling of the unemployment rate for technicians to 14.5 per cent and of service workers to 21.1 per cent. Also notable is the increase in the unemployment rate for crafts and related trade workers to 13.4 per cent.

The *Labour Force Surveys* also provide data on the underemployed who are defined as individuals ten years and above who worked less than 35 hours a week involuntarily, but were seeking and available for more work. The underemployed, as a percentage of the total labour force, increased from 10.66 per cent in 1987-88 to 12 per cent in 1996-97.[18]

Unemployment and real wage rates are the two key macro variables in determining household welfare. Table 1.3 below reports the range of nominal wage rates deflated by the food price index for the lowest and highest paid skilled and unskilled workers across the major cities in the country.

Table 1.3

Nominal daily wage of skilled and unskilled workers deflated by the food price index (1980 - 81 = 100)

Year	Unskilled workers (labourer)		Skilled workers (mason)	
	Peshawar (lowest)	Karachi (highest)	Peshawar (lowest)	Karachi (highest)
1988 - 89	18.5	30.6	44.8	67.0
1989 - 90	20.0	30.1	48.0	63.8
1990 - 91	18.3	27.9	48.9	59.6
1991 - 92	21.0	26.2	40.1	58.2
1992 - 93	20.0	26.1	40.4	60.2
1993 - 94	17.6	25.8	40.0	56.9
1994 - 95	17.8	23.3	40.0	51.4
1995 - 96	17.2	27.0	35.8	57.4
1996 - 97	16.6	31.6	35.6	55.6
1997 - 98	16.6	34.6	38.7	54.2
1998 - 99	16.6	33.2	41.4	51.8
1999 - 00	16.5	35.5	41.2	58.9
Period change (%) (1988 - 89/1999 - 00)	(-10.8)	(+16.0)	(-8.0)	(-12.1)

Source: Government of Pakistan, *Economic Survey, various issues.*
Note: Peshawar and Karachi were selected as the two major cities with the lowest and highest daily wages in the base period.

Except for unskilled labour in Karachi, wages in the other three categories declined between 8 and 12 per cent. With unemployment rates rising and real wages declining, it is a fair bet that household incomes would be falling and the poverty rate rising. Table 1.4 below reports household incomes for five quintiles.

Table 1.4
Changes in household monthly real income

Income Groups	Household monthly income in real terms		
	1987 - 88	1992 - 93	1996 - 97
I	634.5	416.6	484.6
II	1084.2	966.5	1052.7
III	1744.1	1583.2	1568.9
IV	2742.2	2416.1	2279.3
V	5250.6	5110.4	4295.8

Source: Calculated from Government of Pakistan, *Household Income and Expenditure Survey, 1987-88* (1990, p. 183), *Household Integrated Economic Survey 1992-93* (1993, p. 254) and *Household Integrated Economic Survey 1996-97* (1999, p. 20).

Notes: The consumer price index drawn from Government of Pakistan, *Economic Survey 1999-00*, Statistical Appendix (2000, p. 73) was used to deflate 1992-93 and 1996-97 nominal values to a 1987-88 base. The quintiles across the three years respectively represent 8.9, 36.7, 20.5, 23.4, 10.5 per cent, 9.5, 31.9, 23.1, 22.1, 13.4 per cent, and 9.1, 26.2, 22.1, 18.0, 24.7 per cent of the population.

Prior to a discussion of the main findings in Table 1.4 above, the reader is cautioned that the numbers are a very crude reflection of a change in household percentages by income category over time because the quintiles are not stable over time. This is the case because, although we have used the Federal Bureau of Statistics (FBS) classification of income group over time, we are not confident that the FBS has adequately accounted for inflation in classifying different households between the low, middle and high-income categories. Thus, while in most cases there is an equivalence of household percentages across the income categories, there are increasing percentages of households in the high-income category over time with a dramatic increase for 1996-97. This results from the FBS's use of a very modest definition of what constitutes high income.

We also assume an equal number of earners per household. Findings reported in Banuri et al. (1997, Table 4.8, p.72) suggest that this assumption is only partially borne out, since the mean earners for rich and poor households are 2.1 and 1.2 respectively. Thus, households can be bumped up into a higher category merely because they have more earners. Clearly, per capita household classification, when possible, is preferable.

Keeping in mind the above caveats, it is nonetheless significant to note that all income quintiles suffered a loss in household income between the base period and 1996-97. The largest loss is evident for the lowest income group whose household income in 1996-97 depreciated by about a quarter of its 1987-88 value. Another way of verifying that a loss in household welfare did indeed occur for the poorest is by calculating income ratios and poverty lines. Table 1.5 below reports these.

Table 1.5

Inequality and absolute poverty in Pakistan

	Income share	Overall		Rural		Urban	
		Gini	Poverty	Gini	Poverty	Gini	Poverty
1987-88	5.5	.37	26.4	.31	29.9	.38	22.7
1990-91	8.7	.43	23.3	.41	26.2	.44	18.0
1992–93	7.8	.41	20.3	.37	22.5	.42	16.8
1993–94	7.3	.40	20.8	.40	24.4	.35	15.2
1995-96	7.0	.40	31.0	.40	32.0	.38	27.0

Sources: HDC, (1999, p. 137, 141) for 1987-88 to 1993-94 and SPDC (2000, pp. 25 – 30) for 1995-96.

Inequality in Pakistan is high, though it appears to have been somewhat contained after a sharp rise over the first bout of structural adjustment between 1987-88 and 1990-91. Thus, the income share ratio, which measures the ratio of income of the top to bottom quintile, jumped over three points and subsequently declined gradually. The same story is evident from the gini coefficients.[19] However, our main concern is with absolute rather than relative poverty. In this regard, the most dramatic finding is the sharp jump in the percentage of people who are below the poverty line in both urban (from 15.2 to 27.0 per cent) and rural areas (from 24.4 to 32 per cent) between 1993-94 and 1995-96 respectively. If this trend has continued, as is likely, it implies an increase in poor desperate households who are looking for sub-contract work to supplement their meager income.[20]

The more desperate the condition and the larger the numbers that the poor have to compete with, the more likely it is that the sub-contractors will take advantage of them. The literature review in section 1.5 provides some indication of the intensity of exploitation and the hazardous conditions in which women and children have been made to work. However, prior to that, the next section provides an overview of the informal sector, as officially defined in the statistics, within which home-based work is situated.

1.4   THE INFORMAL SECTOR IN PAKISTAN: OFFICIAL DIMENSION

The Federal Bureau of Statistics (FBS) of The Government of Pakistan. (1998a, p. 3) defines the informal sector based on the Resolution of the 15th International Conference of Labour Statisticians. Thus, the informal sector is viewed as comprising units, ' — such as household enterprises, engaged in the production of goods and services with the primary objective of generating employment and income [for] the persons concerned, not necessarily with the deliberate intention of evading payment of taxes or other legislative or administrative provisions.' Furthermore, 'the units typically operate at a low level of organization, on a small scale, and with labour relations mostly based on casual employment.' Other features include the ownership of assets by 'owners' rather than workers, expenditures that are indistinguishable from household expenditures and entities that are not party to contracts or incur liabilities.

The operational definition includes household enterprise, size and registration. Since the latter is not relevant for Pakistan, the first two are used to define the informal sector for Pakistan for statistical purposes as follows: All household enterprises owned and operated by own-account workers, irrespective of the size of the enterprise; Household enterprises owned and operated by employers with less than ten persons engaged, excluding agricultural or non-market production.

The definition and operational definitions above are interesting in that they seem to exclude the kind of home-based work investigated in this book.[21] First, it would be difficult to categorize the work we investigate as constituting 'units' or 'enterprises'. We study a 'putting-out' system whereby contractors supply material and have households do the processing. Second, as we point out in chapter 7, 'evading payment of taxes or other legislative or administrative provisions' is clearly cited as a reason for the existence of such work. However, the work is homebased and the labour casual, so perhaps it does partly fit into the informal or 'sub-informal sector.' In terms of the operational definitions, the first definition in the paragraph above would, in most cases, include the home-based work we investigate in that it is home based and size is not the issue. However, this would be true only if a very lose definition of enterprise as 'activity' is adopted. Even so, the equipment, such as in the case of carpet weaving, is generally not owned by the workers, as assumed even by the first operational definition.

Notwithstanding definitional difficulties, we document the size and other dimensions of the officially recognized informal sector, that the home-based work we explore is loosely a part of, in the tables that follow. To avoid cluttering up the tables, we have presented the results from the *Labour Force Survey 1999-2000* only, but indicate notable changes that have occurred between 1996-97 and 1999-2000.[22] Table 1.6 presents the broad dimensions by gender and region.[23]

Table 1.6

Proportion of non-agricultural workers (10 years and above) in the formal and informal sector by gender and region (1999-00)

(Percentages)

Sector	Rural		Urban	
	Female	Male	Female	Male
Formal	26.9	32.4	39.3	35.9
Informal	73.1	67.6	60.7	64.1
Total	100	100	100	100

Source: Drawn from Government of Pakistan, *Home-based work Force Survey 1999-00* (2001, p. 21).

Table 1.6 suggests that of all the females who work, about three-fourths in rural areas and just about three-fifths in the urban areas do so in the informal sector. For males, these proportions are about a third in the rural areas and about three-fifths in the urban areas. Between 1996-97 and 2000-2001, urban female informal sector workers, as a percentage of the total, increased from 55.3 per cent to 60.7 per cent and there was a corresponding drop in formal sector workers. A similar relative percentage increase in urban informal sector work was also evident for males. The higher proportion of males than females in the urban areas working in the informal sector suggests to us the exclusion of much activity that actually goes on in the informal sector. However, this becomes even more evident from Tables 1.7 and 1.8, in which the percentage distributions by gender rather than proportions are presented.[24]

Table 1.7

Percentage distributions of employed persons (10 years and above) engaged in the informal sector by occupation, gender and region (1999-00)

Occupation groups	Rural		Urban		Total
	Male	Female	Male	Female	
Legislators, senior officers and managers	4.36	0.19	6.31	0.13	10.99
Service and sales workers/shop-owners	2.12	0.02	2.40	0.04	4.58
Craft and related trade workers	6.18	0.65	7.52	0.70	15.05
Plant and machine operators and assemblers	1.72	0.02	1.53	0.01	3.28
Elementary/unskilled occupations	11.8	2.47	3.96	0.62	18.85
Other	33.36	8.14	4.74	1.01	47.25
Total	59.54	11.49	26.46	2.51	100

Source: Drawn from Government of Pakistan, *Labour Force Survey 1999-00* (2001, p. 137).

The most striking finding in Table 1.7 above is how few women allegedly work in the informal sector. In all, about 14 per cent in all occupations combined in both rural and urban areas are indicated as working in the informal sector. This appears unbelievable because, in the homebased sectors we explored, 92 per cent of all adult workers are women, and even among children, most were girls. Other than that, there appears to be a notable increase, in percentage distribution terms, in male and female informal sector work in the rural, relative to the urban, informal sector between 1996-97 and 2000-2001.

In Table 1.8 below, the same numbers are re-allocated by employment sectors. As expected, the bulk of those working in the informal sector are either self-employed or employees and at most about two per cent are employers among urban males.

Table 1.8
Percentage distribution of employed persons (10 years and above)
by employment status, gender and region (1999-00)

Employment status	Rural		Urban		Total
	Female	Male	Female	Male	
Employer	0.01	0.16	0.04	2.26	1.82
Self-employed	2.62	43.02	1.62	32.26	47.11
Unpaid family helpers	9.42	16.66	1.14	8.83	11.09
Employee	4.13	23.99	5.87	47.98	39.98
Total	16.18	83.83	8.67	91.33	-

Source: Drawn from Government of Pakistan, *Labour Force Survey 1999-00*
(2001, pp. 147-149).

Most of the literature on the informal sector in Pakistan is dated
and also the scholars' perception of informal is often constrained by
the official definition given above. Thus, there is an 'enterprise' or
'unit' orientation as is clear from the literature review in Kemal
and Mahmood (1993, pp. 5-15). It is, therefore, not surprising that
these authors conclude that unskilled females form a negligible
proportion of the workforce in the informal sector (pp. 96-102).
Similarly, the leading piece by Viqar Ahmed (1993, pp. 3-4), in
another volume edited by Ghayur (1993), is influenced by an
enterprise orientation due to data constraints, but the limitations
of such a definition is acknowledged. Hussein et. al.'s (1991) more
promising sectoral approach is premised around defining what
constitutes formal and informal in various sectors like finance,
housing, manufacturing, education, health, housing and transport
and then identifying the informal activities by sector. Nigar Ahmad
(1993, pp. 63-83) is notable among other scholars like Mumtaz and
Shaheed (n.d.) for bringing home-based piece rate women workers
into the ambit of the informal sector. However, she concedes that,
given the ephemeral nature of such work, it is understandable that
the FBS is not documenting it (pp. 68-69).

To sum up, while the effort by the FBS to document the informal
sector is a welcome first step, much progress is needed both with
the operational definition and measurement to include home-based
work in the informal sector. This would have to be done using a
household and not an enterprise approach and so the FBS would
need to use the *Household Income and Expenditure Survey* rather
than the *Labour Force Survey* to document the household component
of the informal sector. The literature review in the next section
focuses on this undocumented component of the informal sector.

1.5 LITERATURE REVIEW: HOME-BASED WORK IN PAKISTAN

No attempt has been made here to present a comprehensive review of literature. Of the recent cross-country literature reviewed, Basu (1999), Chen et. al. (1999), and Binder and Scrogin (1999) are particularly noteworthy. Our focus is on the recent research on home-based work in Pakistan in terms of the conceptual framework outlined above. Unfortunately, there is a dearth of this, which provides ample justification for this book for confirming some of the findings and for extending the empirical work.

Ahmad, Qaisrani and Tahir (n.d.) present a useful analysis of the secondary data to get a handle on the size of the informal sector. Citing a World Bank study, they estimate that about 750 thousand women are engaged in sub-contracted home-based work in the urban sectors. Awan and Khan (1992, p. 3) estimate that there are about 1.2 million children, less than 15 years of age, working in the carpet weaving industry alone, the bulk of them working at home.

Awan and Khan (1992), SCF (1997), Ahmad, Qaisrani and Tahir (1998) and Khattak and Sayeed (2000) are among the reports that have addressed the issue of home-based work in a systematic manner in Pakistan. Based on a small, rural, purposive sample, Awan and Khan covered 5 districts, 10 villages, 19 households and 175 children for their study. They date the growth of home-based carpet weaving in the Punjab to the early 1980s. The usual practice was for a *thekedar* (contractor) to install one or two looms in the household, based on a loan, and the household paid off the loan with their labour. Indebtedness, for this reason, or because loans for house-building or marriages had been taken, gave the *thekadar* leverage, which he exploited by finding excuses to pay less than the contracted rates. Earnings were higher in situations when the households provided their own material. Men contracted the loans and received payment. On some occasions, men use this to support a drug habit or as a substitute to working themselves.

The children worked long hours (9-10) with a one-hour break and one day off. They often claimed to be too tired to play. Over half the children reported having received finger tip injuries with the sharp knives, particularly during start up. Up to a third reported getting backaches from sitting long hours and many reported ankle pains. The researchers observed severe musco-skeletal disorders and stunting. In addition, wool dust caused allergic reactions, anthrax and lung disorders. About 70 per cent reported beatings either by family members or the contractor. The home work-environment was typically cramped, poorly lit and poorly ventilated.

Over half had attended school and left due to low income of the household, although a majority expressed a desire to return to school. About three-fourths thought school going children were superior to them and expressed a sense of envy when seeing them going to school dressed in their uniforms. The parents, however, thought of school as a waste of time and money, but also did not see carpet weaving as an appropriate future occupation for their children.

SCF (1997, p. 16) focused on the sub-contracting of football stitching and interviewed 326 households in Sialkot district engaged in football stitching. They point out that sub-contracting to households resulted partly due to variation in the size and number of orders received by the large manufacturers. It is more economical for them to sub-contract rather than maintain excess capacity. In addition, the simplification of the production process also enabled such sub-contracting to be done. Social security legislation of the 1970s was a further inducement towards sub-contracting. Finally, worsening economic conditions, reviewed in the previous section, also generated the push towards home-based work.

An interesting finding of the study is that despite various incentives, like free transport, free meals and segregated rooms, used to induce women to go to stitching centres, they preferred to work out of their homes.[25] Women represented only two per cent of the workforce in the stitching centres, although they represented 58 per cent of the total workforce engaged in stitching. The greater intensity of work and ease of supervision, monitoring and quality control were the obvious incentives for the employers' preference to draw workers into home-based work. However, the greater flexibility of being able to intersperse domestic work with paid work, as well as cultural resistance to greater female mobility, kept women at home.

Primary school attendance among children of a control group of non-stitching households was much higher at 48 per cent relative to 20 per cent for stitching households, though surprisingly, secondary school enrollments were higher among stitching households.[26] Children reported tiredness, headaches, eyestrain, finger strain, calloused hands and back and knee pains. However, since the children were able to intersperse domestic chores and play between working bouts, these stitching related maladies were contained. In fact, home-based work was preferred for this reason to stitching centres where work was more prolonged and beatings were meted out for mistakes.

Only 4 per cent of the males were found to be unemployed while the others worked hard to contribute to household income working at several activities. Even so, most reported that they were unable to make ends meet. Most of the households were indebted, about a third to the contractors. A consistent theme throughout the studies reviewed here and even earlier studies concede that poverty is the main reason why children were not in schools and working at home.[27] In the control group of more prosperous households, it was rare to find children engaged in stitching. Contractors dealt with the males for all household payments. About a quarter of the children reported getting some spending money and their contribution to household income amounted to 23 per cent of the total.

Ahmad, Qaisrani and Tahir. (n.d, p. 18) based their study on a purposive sample of 821 women (240 from Faisalabad, 175 from Sialkot, 216 from Lahore and 190 from Multan) doing home-based sub-contracted work on a range of activities including garments and football stitching. They reported extreme poverty among the households who did such work in deplorable living conditions. In fact, the living and working space was the same and it was noted to be cramped and unhygienic. Premature aging among women was noted to be one indicator of both poverty and hard work. Illiteracy among the women was high and the mean education rate was low for those who did get an education. The family sizes were uniformly large with several earners in the family. Children joined in the home-based work as soon as they were judged capable of doing so. In some areas, making the daughter-in-law do home-based work was considered a social embarrassment, but she was expected instead to shoulder the burden of domestic chores.

It appears that home-based work had been going on for a long time, with poverty as the main driving force. However, the recent macro-trends in the economy that have affected men's employment seem to have made the need for it more acute (see section 1.3). The wages were low and the hours long (11-14 hours working day) and unemployed men were often dependent on their women, who resented that the men did not seem to try hard enough to find work.

Male and community pressure to stay at home and the convenience of being able to combine domestic chores and child-care with remunerative work were the main stated reasons for working at home. Other reasons included not having to worry about appropriate clothes, commute time, fear of harassment, illiteracy and the lack of skills. The women were engaged in multiple activities over the course of the year due to the seasonal nature of the work.

They made it a point never to refuse work and if they took on more than they could deliver, they invited relatives and friends to help finish it on time. The idea was to establish credibility with the contractors.

Maintaining good relations with the contractor was critical for the continued flow of work. Sometimes, they were only able to work two to three times a week. Despite being very solicitous of their deadlines and the contractors, they found the contractor tardy on payments and delayed them from two to three months until after the work was completed. Repeated reminders produced rejoinders that other households will be given work if the nagging continues. Also, the contractors reacted by finding fault in the work and imposing fines. While both the workers and contractors kept accounts, if the workers lost their records, there were cases in which the contractor took advantage of the subsequent uncertainty created.

Excess demand for work provided contractors with leverage to exploit workers and there were situations when they even reduced the rates. Women stitching footballs had more leverage because the footballs were worth a lot more than the payment due. This sector was the exception regarding prompt payment.

Women complained of many work related health side-effects. Watering eyes, muscle pains, exhaustion, aching back, chest and shoulders, cracking hands, discoloration of skin, finger deformity, leg pains, swelling knees, frequent coughing and asthma were among the problems cited. As women grew older, they had to slow down or abandon the harder work.

Khattak and Sayeed (2000), reviewing female work in the garment, plastics and textiles sector, based on an interview of 161 women workers (60 in Karachi, 61 in Lahore and 40 in Peshawar), confirmed many of the findings cited by Ahmad, Qaisrani and Tahir. Their study was, however, not exclusively confined to home-based work.[28] The first chapter (pp. 6-14) provided a useful account of the factors that pulled women towards sub-contracting or pushed them into it. The push factors were associated with structural adjustment that induced an increase in costs of production and generated pressures for cost saving, including via sub-contracting to the informal sector. The cost pressures included an increase in utility prices, higher interest rates via financial sector reform, higher costs via exchange rate liberalization and the subsequent devaluation and higher prices via deregulation. These cost pressures generated unemployment pressures and to this was added the unemployment from the increased competition induced by tariff cutting and public sector downsizing. The 1990s also represented a period of a continued slowdown in manufacturing sector growth and decline in real wages of workers.

As earlier indicated, Khattak and Sayeed reinforce findings reported by Ahmad, Qaisrani and Tahir. The average family size of sub-contracted workers at about 8 persons (with three earners per family) was large. Family indebtedness was high and the work hours long at low rates. The main motivation for the work was to supplement family income that has been eroded by inflation or a job loss of the household males. The manufactures/contractors were happy to circumvent labour legislation on minimum wages and working conditions and deal with women who had limited ability to bargain and retaliate.

Another interesting chapter in this study pertained to women's empowerment issues (pp. 41-60). The authors note that the employment contributed little to women's empowerment and the home-based work fit into the existing pattern of female subordination. Thus, female work did not change gender relations, and while about half managed to get help with domestic chores, these remained in the female domain.

Women generally preferred home-based work due to the implicit pressure (a form of self-censorship) of family members and neighbours. In addition, harassment faced in the workplace or while taking public transportation was forbidding even though the remuneration was better. For most women working outside the home, the thought of staying behind to attend a meeting that would be part of joining some collective such as a Community Based Organization (CBO) or union was completely alien. However, poverty was slowly changing social attitudes in that many men accepted the necessity of women joining the workforce.

One important source of protection for women and children is improvement in economic conditions and increased economic opportunities, which strengthen their bargaining power. However, this is neither a necessary or sufficient condition and there are examples of sub-contracting under terrible conditions even in economies that are booming and have a high per capita income. Thus, the protection of legislation is very important. It is inevitable that implementation, particular in a poor country like Pakistan, will lag behind legal protection. However, the legal framework is a starting point, and given that, it is possible for civil society activists to assist in providing the necessary protection as has begun to happen in the case of bonded labour. The next chapter examines the progress Pakistan has made in this legal context.

SUMMARY AND CONCLUSION

We started by reviewing the conceptual framework of the neo-classical household model and use it only as a very broad framework within which to review the findings relating to sub-contracted home-based work in Pakistan. Two main findings emerge from the empirical literature across the board. First, that poverty drives women and children into home-based work. Second, that much of this work is hazardous to both women and children. Some facets of globalization, like structural adjustment, are also associated with a macro situation that will continue to increase the numbers of women and children engaged in sub-contracted home-based work.

A review of the macro-economic conditions, starting with the intensive period of structural adjustment in 1988-89, shows high and increasing unemployment and sharply declining real wages. Thus, it is no surprise that real household incomes have continued to decline and poverty rates have risen. In view of the worsening macroeconomic scenario and its obvious micro consequences, home-based work needs urgent policy attention.

Home-Based Work is a very neglected part of the neglected informal sector. Based on the first and most recent survey by the Federal Bureau of Statistics, we chart the dimensions of the informal sector. We indicate that the official definition, adopted from the ILO, is very 'enterprise' or 'unit' oriented and that scholars have been influenced by this definition, with some exceptions, in their research on the informal sector. Such analysis underestimates the involvement of women and children in this sector. Thus, the Federal Bureau of Statistics will need to redress this bias by having the *Household Income and Expenditure Survey* document the extent of home-based work from a household perspective, since the *Labour Force Survey* has an enterprise orientation.

Since the late 1980s, scholars have acknowledged the existence of home-based work as an important component of the informal sector. The findings with regards to the conditions of work and the extent of exploitation are frightening. We later address these issues again based on our own empirical findings. Here, we merely state that a solution cannot be piecemeal and would need to address the 'causes', including poverty and the poor quality of state services, rather than merely the 'effects'. Policy solutions would also need to address the legal framework that we turn to in the next chapter.

NOTES

1. Our research is focused on hazardous home-based work which again is a sub-set of all home-based work.
2. For details see Bullock (1994), which has an insightful synopsis on the subject.
3. Refer to Khattak and Sayeed (2000, pp. 5-7).
4. Basu (1999) has presented an extensive analytical review of this literature. For a much more in-depth conceptualization of women's home-based work and empowerment issues refer to Chapter 8 of this book.
5. Sen (1990) proposes a cooperative conflict framework for analyzing household decision-making.
6. We also subject this assumption to an empirical test in chapter 6 and 7.
7. We do not, however, rule out the abuse of power by self-interested household heads.
8. See section 6.6 for findings.
9. Unemployment rates are cited in the next section of this chapter.
10. These issues will be revisited in the following chapters of this book.
11. Based on Khan (2002).
12. This clause is once again included in the more recently signed three-year poverty reduction and growth facility (PRGF).
13. This site address is hhtp://www/imf.org.
14. Refer to Khan (1999) for details on specific structural adjustment policies like interest rate liberalization and an analysis of their impact.
15. HUBCO stands for Hub Power company and KAPCO for Kot Adu Power Company.
16. Unemployment is defined in the *Labour Force Survey* as follows: 'The unemployed comprise all persons ten years and above who during the reference period were 'without work' i.e. were not in paid employment or self-employment, 'currently available for work' i.e. were available for paid employment or self-employment in the reference period and 'seeking work' i.e. had taken specific steps in a specified recent period to seek paid employment or self-employment. Unemployment rates therefore only compute open unemployment rates as per the above definition. While the rates computed probably give a reasonable measure of the trend in this statistic over time, this measure of unemployment ignores other measures of unemployment more important for the informal sector such as sub or disguised unemployment. All population above ten currently active (working more than one hour per week) is included in the labour force except the elderly, students, homemakers, infirm, disabled and those living on rents, charity or 'immoral pursuits'. Data on the under-employed are separately reported in the surveys and these have been reported on in the text.
17. The new classification is more refined and will also enable the researcher to track the lower and higher paid occupational categories over time. This has not been possible so far.
18. Government of Pakistan, *Labour Force Survey 1996-97*, p. 24, and *Labour Force Survey 1987-88*, p. 161. Equivalent numbers are not available for 1999-2000, but underemployed defined as those who worked less than 15 hours involuntarily was 8.9 per cent, [*Home-based work Force Survey* 1999-2000 (2001, p. 27)].
19. Gini coefficients vary from zero (complete equality) to one (complete inequality) and a ratio of .40 is considered to be quite high as a reflection of inequality.
20. A more recent report of the Government of Pakistan (2001, p. 9) utilized the Pakistan Integrated Household Survey data for 1998-99 to show that rural poverty increased in 1998-99 to 36.3 per cent but that urban poverty declined to 22.4 per cent. However, the data for 1998-99 is based on a better but different data

collection field methodology, involving the use of female enumerators, compared to earlier data.

21. Shaheed and Mumtaz (n.d.) referred to piece-rate home-based workers as 'the invisible workers' for this reason.

22. The Labour Force Survey defined the informal sector for the first time in the 1995-96 volume.

23. Khan (1993), reports data on the informal sector for 1987-88 by assuming that all 'self-employed' and 'unpaid family helpers' reported in the *Labour Force Survey1987-88* constitute the informal sector. This is clearly a misplaced assumption, since the Labour Force Survey 1996-97 is the first and only one with explicit coverage of the informal sector and it separately reports the two categories of workers cited above for both sectors.

24. Clearly a very literate definition of informal is being used as indicated by the inclusion of legislators, senior officers and managers in the informal sector.

25. Saeed (1998, p. 9) reported that the stitching centres offer much higher rates.

26. The explanation given was that perhaps earnings from stitching enabled children to go to secondary school.

27. UNICEF/GOP (1990, p. 8) rightly points out that while it may be true that poverty induces children to work, it is also true that child labour perpetuates poverty by keeping children out of school. However, SCF (1997, p. 25) pointed out that abusive, incompetent and under-qualified teachers were one of the main reasons why children stayed away from school. Like studies reviewed in more detail in the text, Hameed (1994, p.19) also finds poverty to be positively correlated with child labour.

28. This study was part of a broader cross-country set funded by The Asia Foundation. Other studies in this set are by Boonmathya et. al. (1999) for Thailand, Jayaweera et. al. (1999) for Sri Lanka, Joseph et. al. (1999) for the Philippines and Unni and SEWA (1999) for India.

References

Ahmed, N., S. Qaisrani and M. Tahir, n.d., 'Social Protection for Women Workers in the Informal Home-Based Sector in the Leather and Textile Industries,' Aurat Foundation, Lahore.

Ahmed, N., 1993, 'Women Home Based Piece Rate Workers: A Study,' in ed. S. Ghayur, 'The Informal Sector in Pakistan: Problems and Policies,' The Informal Sector Study No. 3, Friedrich Ebert Shiftung, Islamabad.

Ahmed, V., 1993, 'The Informal Sector: Needs and Options,' in ed. S. Ghayur, 'The Informal Sector in Pakistan: Problems and Policies,' The Informal Sector Study No. 3, Friedrich Ebert Shiftung, Islamabad.

Awan, S. A. and A. Khan, 1992, 'Child Home-based work in the Carpet Weaving Industry in the Punjab,' UNICEF, Lahore.

Banuri, T., S. R. Khan and M. Mahmood, 1997, eds. *Just Development: Protecting the Vulnerable and Promoting Growth* (Karachi: Oxford University Press).

Basu, K., 1999, 'Child Labour: Cause, Consequence and Cure, with Remarks on International Labour Standards,' *Journal of Economic Literature*, Vol. 36, No. 3.

Binder, M. and D. Scrogin, 1999, 'Labour Force Participation and Household Work of Urban School Children in Mexico: Characteristics and Consequences', *Economic Development and Cultural Change*, Vol. 48, No. 1.

Boonmathya, R., Y. Praparpun and R. Leechanavanichpan, 1999, draft report on 'The Situation of Women Subcontracted Workers in the Garment Industry in Bangkok Thailand', mimeo.

Bullock, S., 1994, *Women and Work* (London and New Jersey: Zed Books Ltd).

Chen, M, J. Sebstad and L. O'Connell, 1999, 'Counting the Invisible Workforce: The Case of Home Based Workers', *World Development*, Vol. 27, No. 3.

Ed. Ghayur, S., 1993, 'The Informal Sector in Pakistan: Problems and Policies,' The Informal Sector Study No. 3, Friedrich Ebert Shiftung, Islamabad.

Government of Pakistan, *Economic Surveys*, Economic Advisors Wing, Finance Division, Islamabad, several years.

Government of Pakistan, 1988, *Household Income and Expenditure Survey 1987-88*, Federal Bureau of Statistics, Statistics Division, Islamabad.

Government of Pakistan, 1993, *Household Integrated Economic Survey 1992-93*, Federal Bureau of Statistics, Statistics Division, Islamabad.

Government of Pakistan, 1998, *Household Integrated Economic Survey 1996-97*, Federal Bureau of Statistics, Statistics Division, Islamabad.

Government of Pakistan, 1998a, *Labour Force Survey 1996-97 and 1999-2000*, Federal Bureau of Statistics, Statistics Division, Islamabad, also other years.

Government of Pakistan, 2001, 'Poverty in the 1990s' Draft, Federal Bureau of Statistics, Islamabad.

Hameed, S., 1994, 'A Micro Analysis of Child Home-based work: Some Determinants of Labour and its Conditions,' *The Pakistan Development Review*, Vol. 33, No. 4.

Herman, B., 1993, 'A Note on do we Need a Survey of Surveys,' in ed. S. Ghayur, 'The Informal Sector in Pakistan: Problems and Policies,' The Informal Sector Study No. 3, Friedrich Ebert Shiftung, Islamabad.

HDC (Human Development Center), 1999, *A Profile of Poverty* (Karachi: Oxford).

Hussein, M. et. al., 1991, 'Pakiatan: Informal Sector Study,' Submitted to USAID/ Pakistan, Development Research and Management Services (Pvt.) Limited, Islamabad.

Jayaweera, S., T. Sanmugam and C. Rodrigo, 1999, draft report on 'Women in Subcontracting Industries – Sri Lanka', Colombo, mimeo.

Kemal, A. R. and Z. Mahmood, 1993, 'Labour Absorption in the Informal Sector and Economic Growth in Pakistan,' Friedrich Ebert Shiftung, Islamabad.

Khattak, S. G. and A. Sayeed, 2000, 'Subcontracted Women Workers in the World Economy: The Case of Pakistan', SDPI Monograph series # 15, Islamabad.

Khan, Shaheen, 1993, 'An Assessment of the Changes in the Employment Situation of Pakistani Women in the Informal Sector,' in ed. S. Ghayur, 'The Informal Sector in Pakistan: Problems and Policies,' The Informal Sector Study No. 3, Friedrich Ebert Shiftung, Islamabad.

Khan, S. R., 2002, 'IMF Conditions Stunt Growth,' *Economic and Political Weekly*, Vol. 37, NOs. 44 & 45.

Khan, S. R., 1999, *Do IMF and World Bank Policies Work?* (London: Macmillan).

Joseph, L. Y., R. P. Ofreneo and L. Gula, 1999, draft report on 'Subcontracted Women Workers in the Context of the Global Economy: Philippine', mimeo.

Sathar, Z. A. and S. Kazi, 1990, 'Women, Work and Reproduction in Karachi,' *International Family Planning Perspectives*, Vol. 16, No. 2.

Sayeed, A. and K. Ali, 2000, 'Labour Market Policies and Institutions: A Framework for Social Dialogue', Pakistan Institute of Labour Education and Research (PILER) Research Report No. 3, Karachi.

Sen, A. K., 1990, 'Gender and Cooperative Conflicts,' in ed. Irene Tinker, *Persistent Inequalities* (New York: Oxford University Press).

SCF (Save the Children Fund), 1997, 'Stitching Footballs, Voices of Children,' Islamabad, mimeo.

Saeed, A. S., 1998, 'Women Stitching Centers: Exploring Avenues,' Sialkot Implementing Team, Sialkot Child Labour Project.

SPDC (Social Policy and Development Center), 2000, *Social Development in Pakistan, Annual Review 2000, Towards Poverty Reduction* (Karachi: Oxford University Press).

Shaheed, F. and K. Mumtaz, n.d., 'Invisible Workers: Piecework Labour Among Women in Lahore,' Women's Division, Government of Pakistan.

UNICEF/Government of Pakistan, 1990, 'Discover the Working Child,' National Commission for Child Welfare and Development, Islamabad.

Unni, J. and SEWA (Self Employed Women's Association), 1999, draft report on 'Subcontracted Women Workers in the Global Economy: Case of Garment Industry in India', mimeo.

Chapter Two
THE LEGAL CONTEXT

2.1 INTRODUCTION

Labour laws in Pakistan, forming a part of industrial law with its origins in the industrial revolution, have developed in conjunction with conceptions of social justice, democracy and citizens' rights. They have also been promoted by the labour movement world-wide. In the Pakistani context, three major issues emerge in relation to labour legislation: first, the bulk of labour laws are inherited from Pakistan's colonial past with some modifications. This means that many of them are unable to address the numerous labour issues arising from changing patterns in relations of production. Second, these laws have an inbuilt bias in that their assumed subject is a man rather than a woman or a child. This bias springs from the conception of man as the main bread earner who does productive work in the public sphere. This is not to imply that protective legislation is completely absent for women and children but to assert that the main body of law assumes its subject to be male, and therefore, it caters to a social construction of the world that reinforces the sexual division of labour. Third, and related to the above two, is the complete absence of labour laws that apply to the home as a workplace.

Keeping in mind the issues outlined above, how can one safe guard women and children? One important source of protection for women and children is the improvement in economic conditions and increased economic opportunities that strengthen their bargaining power. However, this is neither a necessary nor a sufficient condition and there are examples of sub-contracting under terrible conditions even in economies that are booming and have a high per capita income. Thus, legal protection is very important. This chapter reviews the progress Pakistan has made in this legal context by reviewing the various sources of possible legal protection for workers in general and home-based workers in particular.

2.2   LEGAL PROTECTION AND HOME-BASED WORK

This section reviews legal protection emanating from three sources: international treaties and conventions, national legislation and government policy statements. We conclude that the lack of legal protection for home-based work is related to multiple factors but that civil society pressure needs to be built and sustained to move political representatives and international institutions to provide protection for the weaker sections of the population.

A major contributory factor to the expansion of the informal sector, and specifically, home-based work in Pakistan, is the lack of legal protection. Tracing the history of Pakistan's labour policies and pointing out their flaws, Sayeed and Ali (2000) assert that the government's labour policies and laws favour industrialists and investors. They maintain that the steadfast refusal by different governments to take any measures, even on paper, despite the worsening of conditions due to the IMF imposed policies of liberalization and privatization, results from their indifference to the vulnerable. As earlier indicated, women and children constitute the bulk of this labour because they are under increasing pressure to supplement the dwindling value of household incomes. As such, they are not only invisible due to their place of work but also rank nowhere on the labour policy priority list.

Although no direct legislation exists to protect home-based workers, international conventions as well as the Constitution of Pakistan and certain other laws, interpreted broadly, can be applied toward such protection. The existence of these documents, however, does not ensure enforcement. Nevertheless, we examine below the relevant international conventions and national acts that may help protect the legal rights of children and women workers.

2.2.1   HOME WORK CONVENTION, 1996

Pakistan became a member of the International Labour Organization (ILO) soon after its independence and has since ratified more than 30 ILO conventions. However, it has not ratified the Home Work Convention [ILO (1996)]. This convention begins by stating that it is cognizant that a number of laws concerning the working conditions of labourers also apply to home-based workers referred to as home-workers. Article 1 of the convention defines home work as 'work carried out by a person, to be referred to as a home-worker, in his or her home or in other premises of his or her choice, other than the workplace of the employer for remuneration;

which results in a product or service as specified by the employer, irrespective of who provides the equipment, materials or other inputs used, unless this person has the degree of autonomy and of economic independence necessary to be considered an independent worker under national laws, regulations or court decisions...'.

Article 4 stresses the promotion of equality of treatment between home workers and other wage earners including the right to establish or join organizations of their own choosing. It also provides for safety and health at work, e.g., protection in the field of occupational safety and health, maternity protection and declares that certain types of work and substances may be prohibited in homework for reasons of safety and health. It also addresses the issue of wages and social security for home workers. Most significantly, it sets a minimum age for admission to employment or work from home, thereby prohibiting child labour in the context of home-based work and sub-contracted work.

Furthermore, Article 9 of the convention also stresses the need for effective enforcement mechanisms and recommends both a system of inspection and penalties and sets out that the convention will not affect more favourable provisions applicable to home workers under other international labour conventions.

2.2.2 WORST FORMS OF CHILD LABOUR CONVENTION, 1999

This convention adds to the existing body of laws for the prohibition and elimination of the worst forms of child labour including minimum age for admission to employment (1973), forced labour convention (1930), the convention on the rights of the child (1989), and the convention on the abolition of slavery, the slave trade, and institutions and practices similar to slavery (1956). According to this convention, ratified by Pakistan in July 2001, the term child shall apply to all persons under the age of 18. A majority of the articles cover some of the subjects mentioned above as well as child prostitution and the use of children for drug trafficking. However, article 3 (d) prohibits work that 'by its nature or the circumstances in which it is carried out, is likely to harm the health, safety or morals of children.' The convention further elaborates that the types of work that are considered harmful shall be determined by national laws or regulations and should take into consideration relevant international standards. It also makes it incumbent upon the signatories to consult with employers' and workers' organizations to establish appropriate mechanisms to monitor the implementations of the provisions giving effect to the convention, and to provide the

necessary and appropriate direct assistance for the removal of
children from the worst forms of child labour and for their
rehabilitation and social integration. Furthermore, the signatories
should provide access to free basic educations, and where possible,
appropriate vocational training. The convention also specifies to
take account of the special situation of girls.

2.2.3 EQUAL REMUNERATION CONVENTION, 1951

Pakistan became a signatory to this convention in July 2001. This
convention elaborates that the term remuneration includes the
ordinary basic or minimum wage or salary and any other
emoluments payable directly or indirectly in cash or in kind and
attempts to ensure that equal remuneration for work of equal value
should be determined without discrimination based on sex. This
means that job appraisals will be necessary. These appraisals are to
be carried out by the authorities responsible for determining the
rates of remuneration, and workers' and employers' organizations
must be consulted for the purpose of giving effect to the provisions
of this convention. Although the determination of equal value is
highly problematic, this convention is a step forward for women
who get paid less for the same work compared to men. Furthermore,
this convention can be used effectively to argue for increased
remuneration for home-based women workers.

2.2.4 MAINTENANCE OF SOCIAL SECURITY RIGHTS CONVENTION, 1982

This convention [ILO (1985)] is broad ranging in that it encompasses
refugees, stateless persons and migrant labour besides regular
workers. It sets out the branches of social security to which a worker
is entitled. These include the following: medical care; sickness
benefit; maternity benefit; invalidity benefit; old-age benefit;
survivors' benefit; employment benefit with regard to occupational
injuries and diseases; unemployment benefit and family benefit. It
applies to all general and special social security schemes, both
contributory and non-contributory and encompasses regular
employees, frontier workers as well as seasonal workers, self-
employed persons and home workers, and members of their families.
The latter are included due to the Home Workers Convention. The
Convention also lays down in great detail the manner in which
more than one member state may divide responsibility toward the

social security benefits of a refugee or frontier worker or their
survivors.

1.2.3 LABOUR STATISTICS CONVENTION, 1985

According to Article 1 of this convention [ILO (1985)] 'each member
which ratifies this convention undertakes that it will regularly
collect, compile and publish basic labour statistics, which shall be
progressively expanded in accordance with its resources to cover
the following subjects: (a) economically active population,
employment, where relevant unemployment, and where possible
visible underemployment; (b) structure and distribution of the
economically active population, for detailed analysis and to serve as
benchmark data; (c) average earnings and hours of work (hours
actually worked or hours paid for, and where appropriate, time
rates of wages and normal hours of work (d) wage structure and
distribution; (e) labour cost; (f) consumer price indices; (g) household
expenditure, or where appropriate, family expenditure and where
possible, household income, or where appropriate family income; (h)
occupational injuries and, as far as possible, occupational diseases;
and (i) industrial disputes. The convention sets out the details
regarding the collection of these basic statistics and the need for
national level data collection.

2.2.4 THE CONSTITUTION OF PAKISTAN, 1973

The Constitution of Pakistan [Government of Pakistan (1973)]
guarantees certain rights across the board. According to Article 3,
'The state shall ensure the elimination of all forms of exploitation
and the gradual fulfillment of the fundamental principle, from each
according to his ability to each according to his work'. According to
Article 38 (a), the state shall ' secure the well-being of the people,
irrespective of sex, caste, creed or race, by raising their standard of
living, by preventing the concentration of wealth and means of
production and distribution in the hands of a few to the detriment
of general interest and by ensuring equitable adjustment of rights
between employers and employees, and landlords and tenants'.
Furthermore, subsections (d) and (e) of the same article indicates
that the state shall '...provide for all persons employed in the service
of Pakistan or otherwise, social security by compulsory social
insurance or other means; provide basic necessities of life, such as
food, clothing, housing, education and medical relief, for all such

citizens, irrespective of sex, caste, creed or race, as are permanently or temporarily unable to earn their livelihood on account of infirmity, sickness or unemployment; reduce disparity in the income and earnings of individuals...'. Article 17 explicitly states, 'every citizen shall have the right to form associations or unions, subject to any reasonable restrictions imposed by law in the interest of sovereignty or integrity of Pakistan, public order or morality'.

Certain provisions of the constitution specifically protect the rights of women and children. Article 25, after stating that all citizens are equal and that there shall be no discrimination on the basis of sex, adds that the state may undertake protective provisions in favour of women and children, thereby recognizing, according to Ahmad, Qaisrani and Tahir (n.d., p. 42), the need for special provisions to provide protection to the more vulnerable groups of the population. Article 11(3) states that 'No child below the age of fourteen years shall be engaged in any factory or mine or any other hazardous employment'. According to Article 37(e), 'The state shall make provision for securing just and humane conditions of work, ensuring that children and women are not employed in vocations unsuited to their age or sex, and for maternity benefits for women in employment'.

2.2.5 NATIONAL LEGISLATION ON WOMEN'S AND CHILDREN'S EMPLOYMENT

While legislation exists that may also be applied to home-based workers, no specific laws have been enunciated for this group of workers. A majority of the laws have been inherited from the British colonial era, with some modifications added during the later part of the twentieth century. Although, there are a number of Acts that prohibit the employment of children (defined as someone who is below 14 years of age), a majority of these laws relate to formal sector industrial employment. Thus, the Mines Act, No 4 of 1923, as amended in 1973, the Merchant Shipping Act, 1923, the Factories Act, 1934, as amended in 1977, the Employment of Children Act, No 26 of 1938 and 1991, the Road Transport Workers Ordinance, No 28 of 1961, do not apply because these relate to factory employment.[1] A factory is defined as any premise employing ten or more workers thereby meaning that a factory or establishment employing less than ten persons may employ children.

The Factories Act, 1934, the Payment of Wages Act, 1936, and the Industrial Relations Ordinance, 1969, the Maternity Benefits Ordinance, 1958 could have had significance for home-based women workers but have been limited in scope due to the definition of

'worker' and 'work place' which render home-based workers outside
the purview of these laws. The same is true for Employees Old Age
Benefit Act, which provides for pension, and the Provincial
Employees Social Security Ordinance, which allows sickness
benefits, maternity benefits, educational facilities for children
require contributions from employers and registration of the workers
[Ahmad, Qaisrani and Tahir (n.d., p. 41)].[2]

Only the Children (Pledging and Labour) Act, No 2 of 1923 and
the Shops and Establishments Ordinance, No 8 of 1969 have some
relevance for home-based children and women workers. The
Children (Pledging and Labour) Act prohibits anyone to pledge the
labour of children below 15 years of age. The Act states that in case
of a dispute about the age of a child, a certificate from a recognized
medical authority must be obtained. It also specifies a range of
processes from which children below 14 are expressly prohibited.
Some of the relevant areas to the present study include bidi making,
carpet weaving, manufacture of matches, explosives and fireworks,
soap manufacture, and wood cleaning (Awan and Khan 1992, pp.
50-51). In a somewhat similar vein, the Employment of Children
Act (1991) prohibits the employment of children in certain industries
similar to the ones cited above. It also regulates their work
conditions, rest periods, weekly holidays, and health and safety.
However, this Act applies to children above 14 years of age who are
employed in factories, and not to those doing home-based work.
Additionally, Javed and Jillani (1997, p. 44) point out that child
labour is exempted from the law if the children are working for
families. According to Ahmad, Qaisrani and Tahir (n.d., p. 41), 'The
provisions of the Shops and Establishment Act, 1969, are general
enough to cover a wide variety of workers and establishments. A
similar law in force in India has been the one most frequently used
to obtain some legal cover for home-based workers. Although the
applicability of this statute to home-based workers has not been
tested in a court of law in Pakistan, the interpretation of the Indian
courts may well hold in this country. The social security cover under
this Act could then become operative'. The Bonded Labour System
(Abolition) Act of 1992 is often not applicable, as payment may not
be made well in advance to a family in lieu of the labour of its
women and children.

Although the current situation with regard to home-based
workers appears to be bleak, various policy statements and
recommendations emanating from government sources also indicate
that there is some awareness about the unfair work conditions and
remuneration of home workers. We discuss some of these statements
below.

2.2.6 Policy statements[3]

The shift toward home-based work is on the rise as women's and children's labour is relatively cheap and their organizational abilities are very limited. The latter impacts their bargaining abilities for better working conditions and fair remuneration. There is some degree of awareness in government circles about this trend and the need for protection. In 2002, the government announced the fifth labour policy after a gap of twenty years. The four labour policies preceding it had been announced in 1955, 1959, 1969 and 1972. Outlining the troubled history of industrial relations in the backdrop of deteriorating economic conditions and increasing pressures for competitive pricing due to globalization processes, the present policy points to changed perceptions about fostering trust and cooperation among employers, employees and government as a means of improving industrial relations and thereby the economy. Among its list of nine objectives and initiatives, it includes the 'progressive extension of labour laws and welfare measures to informal and unorganized sectors'; 'combating child and bonded labour'; and, 'elimination of gender discrimination to reinforce gender equality' (Government of Pakistan, Labour Policy 2002, pp 4-5). The policy also points out that, 'About two-thirds of the non-agriculture employed labour force in Pakistan is in the informal sector. A large number, especially women are engaged in home-based work. Currently, the labour in the informal as well as the home-based sector is not covered by any labour welfare legislation. The Labour Policy aims at gradual extension of coverage of labour welfare laws to the workers of the informal/home-based sector.' (ibid, p.19).However, the policy fails to mention the means or timeframe through which labour welfare laws will be extended to this unprotected segment of labour.

Aside from the labour policies formulated by the government, four tripartite labour conferences were held in 1977, 1980, 1988 and 2001, and two labour commissions were set up in 1978 and 1987 to address the issues of labour welfare and industrial relations. In addition, two task forces, one on social security and the other on labour were formed in 1993 (ibid, 12). All these conferences, commissions and task forces have made recommendations that have been ignored for the most part. For example, in 1994, the Task Force on Labour [Government of Pakistan (1994, pp. 14-25)] recommended the '...constitution of a special committee to study and identify the problems faced by working women and their needs [,] and to suggest ways and means to evolve certain minimum standards to protect women workers and prevent their exploitation'.

The tripartite labour conference discussed the equal wage convention and the possible mechanisms through which equal wage could be ensured. It also emphasized the basic right of association for all workers, including informal sector and agricultural workers and job security as well as social security for all. These principles were also reflected in the draft labour policy of 2001. However, the Labour Policy of 2002 ignores these principles and suggests no effective policy measures to put the gender related recommendations into effect. The Industrial Relations Ordnance (IRO) 2002 also denies workers the right of association and job security by stating that the federal government can take this right away. This effectively precludes the possibility of effective organizing around rights based issues, especially in the informal sector and for women. As it is, women are shy about articulating protest due to cultural and economic impediments. When they know that the state frowns upon such activity, they require more persuasion and strength to protest against such conditions.

Aside from the Ministry of Labour, other ministries of the government have also made recommendations for the protection of women workers. The Pakistan National Report for the Fourth World Conference on Women in Beijing [Ministry of Women's Development, Government of Pakistan (1995, pp. 54-55)] cites the Pakistan Integrated Household Survey (PIHS) of 1990-1991 which indicates that, '...the overwhelming majority of women workers, more than three-fourths of the economically active women in urban areas, are employed in the informal sector. Nearly four-fifths of women in this category work at home as subcontracted labour working on a piece-rate basis, as unpaid family helpers, or as self-employed workers. It is precisely these women who are likely to get excluded from official labour force statistics'. It further states (p 55), 'The majority of home-based workers are engaged in petty manufacturing, and produce a variety of goods involving intensive labour inputs. These women are confined to working at home, due mainly to cultural restrictions to outside work, which is associated with a loss of social status. The lack of job options, the dispersed nature of work, and their pressing need for income limits their bargaining power, making them the lowest paid group, even within the unregulated informal sector'. This book also points out that aside from culturally biased attitudes toward women's employment, manufacturers circumvent labour regulations on wages and working conditions to maintain flexibility in the size of their workforce and to keep costs low.

The Report of the Commission of Inquiry for Women, [Government of Pakistan (1997)] contains a detailed critique of the different loopholes contained in the various laws applicable to women workers and gives recommendations for anti-discrimination laws, affirmative action as well as the scope and wording of laws. This Report (p. 47), states that, 'The exclusion of some sectors of the economy from the ambit of the labour laws is likely to leave women unprotected in certain industries where their participation might be disproportionately high. On an analogous note, because the informal sector of the economy, by its very nature, goes unmeasured, the substantial contributions of women to the economy are both unrecorded, and often made under conditions unprotected by law'.

Such policy statements, emanating from important national committees and ministries, point to knowledge and understanding, not ignorance. However, the apathy with regard to the lack of action remains the main hurdle toward achieving any semblance of justice. A combination of recognition and apathy applies to the case of children also. However, the state and its institutions display a more supportive and open attitude towards child rights as they consider children to be the future of the nation. Therefore, the inertia in policy remains more blatantly paradoxical, especially in the face of international pressures.

The main instrument for child rights at the international level is the United Nations Convention on the Rights of the Child (CRC), 1990 and the 1999 ILO Convention on worst forms of child labour or Convention 182. These conventions have been preceded by a number of other international instruments, starting with the League of Nations Committee on Child Welfare in 1919 and followed by a number of international initiatives, including the Geneva Declaration on the Rights of the Child, 1923, endorsed by the League of Nations in 1924. In 1959, the UN adopted an expanded version of the same document as the Declaration of the Rights of the Child. Other initiatives include the declaration of 1979 as the Year of the Child and the CRC.

The 2002 Labour Policy (p. 18) clearly states that, 'Targets and activities set out in the National Policies and Action Plans to Combat Child Labour (May 2000) and for Abolition of Bonded Labour (2001) need to be actively implemented.' In 2001 when the Government of Pakistan ratified ILO Convention 182 [on Worst Forms of Child Labour], it requested ILO-IPEC's (International Programme on the Elimination of Child Labour) technical assistance in the form of Time Bound Programme (TBP) to help it fulfill its international commitments. This programme will first help generate information on worst forms of child labour and then develop a comprehensive TBP to take immediate measures to eliminate the worst forms of child labour within a 5 to 10 years time frame.

Pakistan, as one of the first signatories of the CRC, submitted its national report to the CRC and recognized that the state needs to take more responsibility in a number of areas related to the rights of the child. This was a deviation from the norm whereby Pakistan is generally reluctant to accede to international human rights treaties for fear of scrutiny by the international community [Ali and Jamil (1994, 20-21)]. Article 32 of the CRC states that 'States parties recognize the right of the child to be protected from economic exploitation and from performing any work that is likely to be hazardous or to interfere with the child's education, or be harmful to the child's health, or physical mental, spiritual, moral or social development'. Although there is some degree of protection for child workers (discussed above), yet, as Ali and Jamil (1994, pp. 119-20) point out, '...these laws do not cover all working children in Pakistan. For instance, firstly, children working in the informal sector, in domestic service, in the fields and other such areas are excluded. Secondly, there is no uniform age for defining a child, which results in immense confusion for all concerned. Most important is the fact that the penalties provided under the existing Pakistan laws regarding child labour are so insignificant that they fail to make an impact'.

Article 31 of the CRC addresses the right of the child to rest and leisure and to engage in play and recreational activities appropriate to the age of the child. According to Ali and Jamil (1994, p. 117), no Pakistani laws address such rights. The Constitution only addresses it in the context of workers, but children are not addressed at all. A government report entitled, 'Government of Pakistan Response to Queries Raised by the Committee on the Rights of the Child' authored by the National Commission for Child Welfare and Development [Government of Pakistan, NCCWD, (1994, p. 29)] acknowledges the limitations of national laws with regard to child labour.[4] It states: 'These laws, however, fail to cover child labour employed in areas such as domestic labour and agriculture; seventy per cent of Pakistan's population lives in rural areas. There is also no minimum age where a child is carrying on an occupation 'with the help of the family or in a school established, assisted or recognized by Government'.

NCCWD (p.29) has proposed to all the relevant Ministries to improve upon these legislations and also to raise the minimum age from 14 to 16 years. [This age was later raised to 18 years when Pakistan ratified Convention 182 and accepted the obligation to enhance age limit to 18 years in respect of worst forms of child labour, for entry into the labour force (Government of Pakistan, Labour Policy 2002, p. 18 and 26)]. The NCCWD report (p.30), in response to a query seeking specific information on the way child labour in agriculture and in the informal sector is inspected, acknowledges that, 'Presently no law in Pakistan governs employment of children in [the] agricultural sector; and the informal sector which employs less than ten employees'. The discussion above underscores the need for policy reform, legislation and most important, its enforcement. While Pakistan's latest Labour Policy states that the elimination of child labour is a key objective, it has only initiated the preparatory phase of the time-bound programme (TBP) at present, while the actual time frame of the TBP is five to ten years. As discussed earlier on, at present there are no means or provisions to cover agricultural labour including children. Thus, these laws are limited in their scope and need to be pursued far more seriously than is being done at present.

A review of legislation indicates that there are no laws that directly address home workers. It is partly this absence that makes home-based work so attractive to producers/investors. Although there has been some degree of awareness about the lack of legal protection for children and women working in the informal sector for some years now, yet the government has failed to take any concrete measures toward this end. According to Sayeed and Ali (2000, p. 43), the government's labour policies have always been pro investors and industrialists, while labour has even been excluded from labour policy formulation as gleaned from a historical overview of labour policy. Examining labour-state and labour-capital relations in their political context, they are able to explain why governments in Pakistan have failed to deal with labour issues under the umbrella of an explicit labour policy. They assert that any new labour policy must necessarily be based upon an unconditional recognition of the fundamental rights of workers. Although the Musharraf government uttered labour friendly rhetoric, the formal announcement of a new labour policy has been disappointing at the very least.[5] Meanwhile, some labour federations in the country have been included in the policy making process. The bottlenecks in the new labour policy remain, as expected, employers' emphasis on safeguarding their interest, with regard to hiring and firing as well as other social clauses. The government's commitment to a worker-friendly labour policy as well as a child-friendly labour policy remains to be tested.

CONCLUSION

The issue of legal protection is one of political will, which can only be induced by internal and external pressure. Unless the state, and international institutions, especially the lending agencies, display the political will to protect the marginalized, the existence of formal legal protection on paper will not make a difference. This is not to imply that the complete absence of laws is the same as their presence, but to point out that the existence of laws without enforcement can make laws meaningless.

It is inevitable that implementation, particularly in a poor country like Pakistan, will lag behind legal protection. However, the legal framework is a starting point, and given that, it is possible for civil society activists to assist in providing the necessary protection as has begun to happen in the case of bonded labour.

NOTES

1. The list of laws relating to child labour has been taken from a UNIICEF report by Awan and Khan (1992).
2. For a detailed critique of these laws, see Chapter 5 of the Book on the Commission of Inquiry for Women, Government of Pakistan (1997).
3. This subsection is partially based on Khattak and Sayeed (2000, pp. 41-43).
4. The Ministry of Health and Social Welfare, Government of Pakistan, set up this Committee in 1980 following the International Year of the Child.
5. For example, President Musharaf made a labour friendly speech at the fourth tripartite labour conference in Islamabad in July 2001, and the Minister and the Secretary, Labour regularly addressed workers concerns and showed a high level of awareness of the problems labour faced because of globalization and an increasingly large informal economy. The Minister's speeches emphasized the abolition of child labour as well as workers rights to collective bargaining and the right of association. However, these speeches needed to be translated into concrete plans of action.

References

Ali, S. S. and B. Jamil, 1994, *The United Nations Convention on the Rights of the Child, Islamic Law and Pakistan Legislation: A Comparative Study* (Peshawar: Educational Computing Services and Publishers).

Government of Pakistan, Labour Policy 2002, Ministry of Labour, Manpower and Overseas Pakistanis, Islamabad.

Government of Pakistan, 1997, *Report of the Commission of Inquiry for Women*, Ministry of Women Development and Youth Affairs, Islamabad.

Government of Pakistan, 1995, *Pakistan National Report to the Fourth World Conference on Women*, Beijing, Ministry of Women Development and Youth Affairs, Islamabad.

Government of Pakistan, 1994, *Report of the Task Force on Labour*, Ministry of Labour, Manpower and Overseas Pakistanis, Islamabad.

Government of Pakistan, 1973, *The Constitution of Pakistan* (Lahore: Publishers Emporium).

Government of Pakistan, n.d., National Commission for Child Welfare and Development (NCCWD), 1994, Implementation of the Convention on the Rights of the Child. Government of Pakistan's response to Queries raised by the Committee on the Rights of the Child.

Human Rights Commission of Pakistan, 1999, *State of Human Rights in 1999* (Lahore: HRCP).

ILO, 1996, *Home Work Convention,* http://ilolex.ilo.ch: 1567/scripts/convde.pl?query= C177&query0+177.

ILO, 1985, *Labour Statistics Convention*, http://ilolex.ilo.ch:1567/scripts/ convde.pl?query=C160&query0+160.

ILO, 1982, *Maintenance of Social Security Rights Convention,* http://ilolex.ilo.ch:1567/scripts/convde.pl?query=C157&query0+157.

Javed, S. and Z. Jillani, 1997, *Child Labour in Islamabad* (Islamabad: Society for the Protection of the Rights of the Child and Friedrich Naumann Stiftung Foundation).

Sayeed, A. and K. Ali, 2000, 'Labour Market Policies and Institutions: A Framework for Social Dialogue', Pakistan Institute of Labour Education and Research (PILER) Research Report No. 3, Karachi.

Chapter Three
DATA COLLECTION AND SETTING

3.1 INTRODUCTION

In this chapter we describe how we collected the qualitative and quantitative data for the analysis. We start with a brief review of the debate on research methods, next we describe our survey design and follow that with a description of instruments used for the qualitative and quantitative data collection. Finally, the urban setting, Karachi city, in which the home-based work was located, is reviewed and the specific home-based work activities surveyed are profiled.

3.2 RESEARCH METHODS

Up to a decade ago, the most common method of social science data collection was a survey based on a probability sample. The survey design was, and still is, quite complex to ensure equal probability of selection to ensure that the findings can be generalized to a specified universe. The data so collected lends itself to quantitative empirical analysis the output of which is often precise correlations using bivariate or multivariate statistical analysis. When driven by theory, it is possible to use such data to specify policy recommendations for government or business. For example, it is possible to estimate precisely how much demand for a particular product responded to a change in the price of that product. Not all data analysis is, however, driven by theory that is so highly formalized. Thus, the data are also used via repeat analysis to establish empirical regularities, i.e. patterns in the data repeated across time or space, which become part of social knowledge.

Appendix 3.1. Location of home-based, sector activities in Karachi

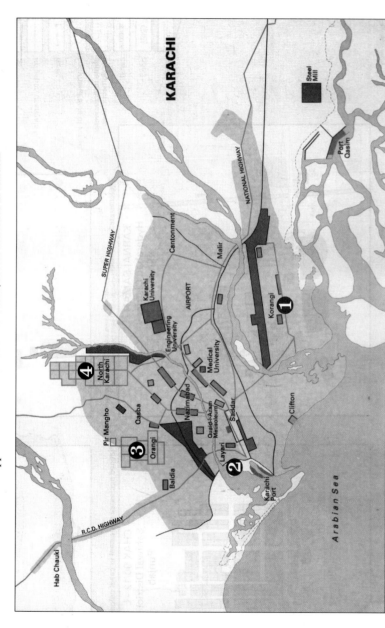

1. Korangi, Incense stick making. 2. Machar Coloney (Mohammadi Coloney), Prawn shelling.
3. Orangi, Unit 12C, Carpet weaving.4. Godhra, Sack stitching.

Source: OUP,UK

Appendix 3.3. Pictorial Description of Sector Activities

Incense-stick (*Agarbatti*) making

Prawn shelling.

Carpet weaving

Sack (*Bori*) stitching

While the advantages identified above of quantitative survey analysis are formidable, there are several drawbacks. For the sensitive researcher, this method of generating social knowledge is extractive and the researchers concern is with publishing findings based on the data collected.[1] The quality of the data is also viewed as being poor since the expert is away from the field and likely to be using an unmotivated field-team with whom s/he has not personally bonded. There is a more severe limitation when a structured questionnaire is utilized since the close-ended questions assume that the expert knows what is important and that is often not the case. On a more mundane level, such data collection is enormously expensive and generally under-utilized.

In view of this, alternative research methods, which focused on qualitative information collection, have become more popular since they are cheaper and more sensitive. Some of these are quasi-anthropological such as RRA/PRA (Rapid Rural Appraisal/ Participatory Rural Appraisal) and these have also been critiqued for promising more than they can reasonably deliver.[2] Notwithstanding the critique, the emphasis on local knowledge for local use and the use of knowledge for social change are laudable goals.

In general, different tools are best utilized for different purposes. There is no research method that would meet all purposes. However, the controversy has been valuable in sensitizing social scientists regarding the limitations of the information they collect, particularly if great care is not exercised in the process. The controversy has also been valuable in making researchers sensitive to using more than one kind of data and that is the approach we used by using both semi-structured and structured questions and other instruments such as observation-based field journals for field reports, case studies and focus group discussions. The details are reported below in section 3.3.

3.3   SURVEY DESIGN

We picked Karachi, Pakistan's largest industrial city by far, because the greatest amount of home-based work is going on over there. Also, SDPI's close links with PILER (Pakistan Institute of Labour Education Research), which is based in Karachi, was expected to and indeed facilitated the fieldwork. Even so, it was extremely challenging to find sectors that satisfied the first of the following three criteria identified for sector selection prior to the fieldwork:

1. That the home-based work be hazardous, where hazard is defined mainly in terms of health risks;
2. That women and children be present as home-based workers;
3. That at least one of the sectors be engaged in an international value chain in that the products are exported (see chapter 4).

The field team, based on discussions with PILER project leaders, did the sector identification sequentially. We originally planned to study 400 households that were to be distributed across several sectors. Based on the pre-test, it was decided that 300 households would be selected where home-based work was going on, and another 100, where home-based work was not done, would be selected as a control group from the same neighborhood. In the actual fieldwork, 303 home-based work households and 94 households for the control group were selected. A distribution of households across the four sectors selected (shrimp cleaning, carpet weaving, bag stitching and incense stick making) and the locality they are situated in are provided in Table 3.1 below.

Table 3.1
Distribution of sample across home-based workers
and the control group

Activity/ Locality	Home-based work	Non-home-based work	Total
Incense stick making/Korangi	77	22	99
Carpet weaving/Orangi	77	22	99
Sack stitching/Godhra	75	25	100
Prawn shelling/Machar Colony	74	25	99
Total	303	94	397

Source: SDPI survey.

The purposive sampling used for the data collection was based on a paired snowball method. Initially, four teams visited four households and references were sought from those households regarding who engaged in home-based work. The obvious reason for doing this was that it was difficult to trace the home-based workers. Once the fieldwork started, information was procured about other households in close proximity also doing home-based work, and of those not doing home-based work, to be part of the control group. The proximity was important to ensure similar socio-economic conditions across the home-based work and control sub-samples. In general, one would also expect the control households to be from the same ethnic group. We selected households in the control group where no child labour of any kind was in practice to understand why that was the case.

Each of the four field teams, comprised of one male and one female member, had training up to the masters' level in various social science disciplines. A female doctor also accompanied the teams due to the strong focus of the study on health issues (selection criteria 1). Thus the doctor was entrusted with gathering the health and nutrition information. The field team supervisor was entrusted with the task of oversight, trouble-shooting and identifying and interviewing the relevant people all across the value chain.

3.4 INSTRUMENTS[3]

3.4.1 Field journal and reports

We utilized several instruments to facilitate data collection and analysis. First, each member of the field team maintained a journal. As earlier indicted, there were four male-female teams and a doctor. Each team took notes in the journal every day based on their observations and was assigned a task of writing a field report at the end of the fieldwork. Aside from introductory and concluding remarks, they were provided with the following format within which to report their observations:

- Extent of exploitation visible in the contractor/worker relationship[4]
- Impact of home-based work on health of women and children
- Impact of home-based work on overall well-being
- Impact of home-based work on women's empowerment
- Other issues

The specific tips for fieldwork provided to the field teams, based on pre-tests, can be made available on request. We anticipated there would be repetition in the field-reports, but we felt it was nonetheless important to have independent reporting from each team to avoid a loss of insights. We also anticipated that there might be conflicting views, which would require subsequent discussion and clarification. Based on interaction with field-teams and the training, we anticipated valuable qualitative insights forthcoming from these reports. This was the case and these edited reports, along with the case studies and focus group discussion reports, were the primary data sources for chapters 5 and 7. The reports, edited for language, are included in Annexure 2 at the end of the book.

3.4.2 FOCUS GROUP DISCUSSIONS

Focus Group Discussions (FGD) were our second source of qualitative information. These were held with women and children in each sector and FGD reports were based on these. Once again, a great deal of care was exercised in training the field-team during the pre-tests and in providing instructions that can be made available on request.

The method adopted in conducting these FGDs was as follows: for the women's FGD, the three women in the field team used to sit with the women from the locality in a room in the locality. One person asked the questions and others took notes and intervened if clarifications or explanations were needed. Since one or two assertive people can dominate discussions, all participants were individually addressed. In the case of contradictory opinions, the field-team probed deeper to see if a consensus could evolve.

The three men handled the four child FGDs. Since the team spent more than a week in a locality for fieldwork, they established contact with working children through key informants. They also invited some of the children who were not engaged in home-based work for their perspective.

A total of eight FGDs were conducted. Two FGDs were held in each sector, one for women and one for children. There were approximately 10-12 participants from the household respondents in each discussion. The main topics discussed in children's FGDs were schooling, relationship with the sub-contractor and the impact of home-based work on health. The children also talked about their views regarding work, whether they liked working, whether they had enough time for rest and recreation and whether they liked to go to school. The women's FGDs focused on children's education, health, violence in the community, perceptions about the sub contractor and the type of work performed, ethnic issues, reasons for engaging in home-based work and the impact of home-based work on health.

3.4.3 INTERVIEWS AND CASE STUDIES

Case studies were developed based on in-depth interviews of two key informants identified by the field team for each sector. A total of eight case studies were conducted: five in the carpet weaving sector and three in the sack stitching sector of which seven were about women and one about men. Households were selected for more in-depth case studies if they were either much worse off or much better off than the average i.e. there was some interesting distinguishing factor. The information collected for the case studies included general demographic information, relationship between spouses and household members, environment in the community, health status and relationship with sub-contractors. The case studies, edited for language, are reported in Annexure 3.

3.4.4 SEMI-STRUCTURED QUESTIONNAIRES

Finally, we utilized nine semi-structured questionnaires covering the same key themes. There were two each for women, children and households (for workers and control group households), and, in addition, we included health/nutrition, contractor and employer questionnaires (see Annexure 4 for questionnaires).

Thus, in order to collect detailed information from each respondent (women, children, household, owner/*seth*), nine different types of questionnaires were designed. The respondent questionnaires included one for home-based work households and another for control group (CG) households. The latter consisted of the same questionnaire, excluding the section on work-related questions. The questionnaires filled by the interviewing team consisted of two sets of questions regarding working and living conditions (to be filled by interviewer) and health conditions (to be filled by the doctor).

The questionnaires directed to women consisted of seven sections including general information, education, level of empowerment, work related questions, non-economic activities (housekeeping activities/household chores), home-based work organisation, and nutrition. The information from work related questions allowed us to understand and quantify the extent of exploitation of home-based workers in the value chain. The structure of the questionnaire included two additional sections on women's empowerment and nutrition. The latter consisted of questions aimed at understanding the power of decision-making in the household on aspects such as female mobility,[5] household financial management,[6] children's education, marriage, and household expenditures. In the section about nutrition,[7] women were required to select from a list of types of food divided into meals per day. The aim was to learn about women's dietary habits and nutrition levels. Finally, a health section was incorporated into the women's work section.[8]

The questionnaire directed to children consisted of seven sections including schooling, work-related questions, time organisation, household chores, earnings, social/family, and nutrition. The section on nutrition was the same as the section used in the women's questionnaire. The section on time organisation included questions regarding consequences of faulty work including options referring to abuses by contractors and family members.[9]

A third questionnaire was designed for household respondents. This questionnaire was divided into seven sections and included information of household activity, and detailed questions about living conditions, ownership status, number of households, income generated from home-based work, level of expenditure, and indebtedness.

The fourth questionnaire consisted of information filled in by the interviewer on working and living environment of workers.[10] The fifth questionnaire included three questions specifically for *seth/* owners[11] regarding reasons to recruit home-based workers, and information about the value chain. A sixth questionnaire was filled in by the doctor and was aimed at collecting detailed information about the health status of children and women. As earlier indicated, the household, women and child questionnaires were also administered to the control group, without the work section, making for a total of nine.

3.5   CONTEXT: KARACHI CITY

Karachi is a multi-ethnic city with a population estimated at over 12 million.[12] It is estimated that there are 54 per cent Urdu-speaking/Mohajirs, fourteen per cent Punjabis, nine per cent Pathans, six per cent Sindhis, four per cent Balochi and twelve per cent belong to other ethnicities including Bengalis/Biharis and Burmese [Parveen and Ali (1996, p. 140)]. Known also as mini-Pakistan, Karachi continues to serve as the political hub for both the left and the extreme religious factions. As the industrial centre of Pakistan, it is important not only because it has the highest concentration of labour, but also because it has contributed to the evolution of the labour movement in Pakistan. Given the complex social and political backdrop of Karachi, it best represents the issues that Pakistan's labour faces today.

According to Hasan (1997, p.195), 75 per cent of Karachi's population works in the informal sector, while various estimates suggest that over thirty five per cent of this population either works at home, or its neighborhoods. The trend whereby an increasing number of persons are working in the informal sector, aside from being driven by the national and international macro-economic policy environment, might have been exacerbated by the violence that has gripped Karachi since the mid-1980s. According to media reports, an average of 630 violent deaths (95 per cent male) per year were recorded in the city during the ten-year period starting 1990 (Hisam, 2000, p.23).

The violence in Karachi has multiple reasons. Initially, Karachi suffered from ethnic violence, which was politically motivated by the state and this was subsequently followed by state-sponsored terrorism. This, in turn, was followed by plain criminalization, which is now changing into predominantly sectarian violence. Over the years, violence has been more or less restricted to the low-income areas of Karachi. These areas are, understandably, concentrated around Karachi's industrial estates and around the port/harbor. These localities have been populated through ethnic and communal bonds, which are encouraged by state policy due to a variety of reasons, both good and bad.[13] Many of Karachi's illegal migrants have also settled in these areas. According to Hasan (1999, p.41) Karachi's illegal immigrants and refugees include Bangladeshis, Sri Lankans, Burmese, Filipinos, Iranians, and Afghans. Barring the latter two, a majority of the others work in the garment and fishing industries while some, along with the Afghans, work as domestic servants. People in these areas thus suffer from a number of problems, including poverty, ethnic tensions, discrimination, and at times intimidation at the hands of the police while political parties of all ilk try to gain influence for the vote.

Since a majority of these localities also have a concentration of home-based work, it was natural for the present study to concentrate on these communities in Karachi. The areas where the survey was carried out have been the hub of violence and curfews. Korangi and Orangi have suffered the worst forms of politically motivated ethnic violence including religious/sectarian violence. In fact, the first incidence of violence erupted in and around Orangi on 15 April 1985 when the locality was cut off from the rest of Karachi for three days and there were ethnically motivated killings. Violence continues to haunt these communities to date, affecting them in a very direct and damaging manner so that aside from physical destruction, the psychological scars of violence persist.

3.6   HOME-BASED WORK PROCESS DESCRIPTIONS[14]

This section provides a description of process and working conditions in the four sectors based on observations of the field team.

3.6.1 INCENSE STICK MAKING (*AGARBATTI*)

In a dark and barely lit room, women and children of the family sit toiling in the sweltering heat. There is barely enough breathing space, since more often than not, it is the only room in the house. Thick *agarbatti* dust carpets the floor. A huge bundle of sticks lies on one side and a large bowl filled with thick black tar like paste (which includes the saw-dust and toxic chemicals) sits in the middle of the floor. One can feel oneself being congested by the heaviness that hangs in the air due to the heat, dust and humidity. On one dirty piece of cloth is piled the sawdust, while an infant lies crying next to it, since the mother prefers keeping him close as she works hard to meet the target set by the contractor.

The woman making the *agarbatti* sits crouched on the floor with her hands covered in the black paste up to her knuckles. She takes a stick, puts the paste on it with her hands, and then rolls the *agarbatti* in the pink dust until it clings tightly to the paste. She then puts it on one side to let it dry. She repeats the same process, sitting in the same tiring position for hours at a stretch.

3.6.2 PRAWN SHELLING

In one small corner of the courtyard sit the women and young girls of the house with prawns scattered all around them. They sit crouched in a pool of freezing and muddy water. The ice filled water gets splashed around while they take prawns out from overflowing bowls. The ice is meant to ensure the prawns do not rot. They take the prawns out of the basket, one at a time, they put them in a tub of water, take them out, shell them and then again put them in water in another tub to preserve them. The whole house has a sickening stink, for an outsider, as the day's work goes on. Scales and shells of prawn cover their hands and cause skin irritation from constant scratching. The cold water also freezes the hands.

3.6.3 CARPET WEAVING

A *khuddee* (loom) for carpet weaving is placed in one corner of the courtyard, and it takes up most of the space there. Sitting behind it are the women and children of the household. They sit upright, with their backs stiff, and their hands move with amazing speed on the taut strings and threads of the *khuddee*. With great concentration, they weave the thread around the strings, giving life to a pattern built-in by the contractor, and then, with a sharp sickle like instrument, they push it down. The women's finger joints are hard and swollen, betraying years of hard work that they have been doing at the *khuddee*. Their eyes are vacant, and their expressions completely empty as they speak from behind the *khuddee*, still weaving and not stopping for a second.

3.6.4 *BORI* (SACK) STITCHING

Sitting in a relaxed manner, the *bori* stitching women get together and indulge in friendly conversation as they stitch for the day. They laugh and joke as they measure and stitch the *boris*. Their work is tedious and tiring. However, they try to make it less onerous by getting together and doing it jointly. This work hence has the elements of a social gathering.

They scratch their hands often, since the fibers from the *bori* causes irritation and often they let out a cough and complain of flu due to fiber inhalation. Their rooms, however, are brightly lit and airy and they work in an organized manner. They pile up the *boris* in neat stacks as they work so that the house does not get messy. Often, the men join them to stitch a *bori* or two, and if nothing else, then just to share the day's happenings with them.

SUMMARY

In view of controversy surrounding the use of large structured data sets and the analysis based on poor data, and given the nature of the population being surveyed, we opted for a small high quality survey. We also utilized several different instruments including journals and observation-based field reports, in-depth interviews and case studies, focus group discussions and semi-structured questionnaires. Thus, we gathered extensive and intensive qualitative and quantitative data that yielded rich information on the identified study themes. We also provided some details of the rich and complex urban setting in which the home-based work is located and a descriptive profile of the activities we surveyed. Many more details follow in the next three chapters.

NOTES

1. Chambers (1997) is best known for a critique of conventional social science research methods. In his view, the extractive nature of the research means that the researcher is not accountable to those being studied and gives nothing back. If the research contributes to policy change that enhances the well being of the poor, something may indirectly be given back and this is, in fact, the premise of such policy research.

2. Again, Chambers (1997) is a good source as a practitioner who popularized the alternatives. Not all anthropologists are as enamored with these alternative research methods and some feel that they are even misleading. For example, it may be much too difficult to identify the complex dynamics of village or urban communities in short visits, notwithstanding the numerous tools a PRA practitioner is armed with. For a comprehensive critique, see Bastian and Bastian (1996), particularly the chapters by Mosse and Stirrat.

3. Some of the descriptions of our instruments are drawn from the UNICEF summary of our original report.

4. Exploitation is used here in a loose sense including verbal and physical abuse, delayed payments and poor rates rather than in the Marxian sense of the extraction of surplus value. Of course, exploitation in the Marxian sense is also likely to accompany exploitation based on unequal power as defined above.

5. W4 'Do you get outside the house on your own when you need to? And W5: 'If yes, do you need permission from your brother, parents, husband?'.

6. Examples of questions include W6: ' Who keeps the earning from home-based work?' and the optional answers of ' husband/guardian and others'. Question W7: 'Do you save money through a *bachat* (rotational saving) committee system?', ' W10 'How much income do you keep for yourself'.

7. Examples of questions are W78: ' How much milk do you consume?' and the optional answers of: never, only one cup/glass, two cups/glass, more than three cups/glass, and W38: 'What did you have yesterday for breakfast'?, with the optional answers of 'roti', (unleavened bread) *paratha* (unleavened fried bread), tea, milk, left over, others'.

8. W76, Do you complain of Home-Based Work related health problems?', optional answers consisted of a list of ailments including eye infection, ear infection, cough and asthma.

9. Question C22 and C23: 'Has it ever happened that you did not perform your work well?', 'If yes, what were the consequences?' and the optional answers were ' none, scolded by family, scolded by contractor, beaten by family, beaten by contractor, not allowed to play, not allowed to go to school, others'.

10. The questions included: 'Nature of the house' and ' Evaluate the workspace in the home for each of the following categories: space, light, dust, smell, temperature, noise'.

11. Questions included were S1: 'What are the main reasons for recruiting house based workers?', the optional answers were: 'Possibility to recruit from a much larger area, possibility to hire workers in accordance with variations in demand, minimization of the risk of unionization, no labour problems, can pay labour less to beat the competition, no problems with government regulations as in the formal

sector, freedom to vary the volume of the production, greater opportunity to vary the nature of the work, reduction of costs since most costs are born by household, greater flexibility in responding to the fluctuations and irregularity of the market, other'.

12. According to the 1998 census data, Karachi's population was 9,802,134 persons. However, Sindh's political parties contest this figure as being understated. There is broader consensus that Karachi's population is over 12 million; refer to Hasan (1999, p. 40).

13. The 1947 partition of India led to a vast influx of refugees from India that settled in the heart of the city and later on shifted to some of the new settlements and colonies that were constructed for them at the government's behest. Pathan migrant workers came in the 1950s and 1960s under Ayub Khan's policy of bringing in these workers to work in the industries of Karachi. They were also given the transport business as part of state patronage. In the 1960s, Punjabi migrant workers also found their way into Karachi. Balochi migrant workers had also been present in Karachi due to its proximity with their province. Sindhis, who were in a majority in the past, became a minority in their own provincial capital. Karachi's ethnic mix thus represents inter- as well as intra-provincial politics in Pakistan

14. Process description by Ayesha Khurshid.

References

Eds. Bastian, S. and N. Bastian, 1996, Assessing participation: a debate from South Asia (Delhi: Konark).

Chambers, R., 1997, *Whose reality counts?: putting the last first* (London: Intermediate Technology Publications).

Hasan, A., 1999, *Understanding Karachi. Planning and Reform for the Future.* (Karachi: City Press).

Hasan, A., 1997, 'The Growth of a Metropolis' in eds. Hamida Khuhro and Anwer Mooraj, *Karachi. Megacity of Our Times.* (Karachi: Oxford University Press).

Hisam, Z., 2000, 'Karachi 2000: Life at the Fringe' in *The News International*, May 21, 2000.

Parveen, F. and K. Ali, 1996, 'Research in Action: Organizing women factory workers in Pakistan,' in Amrita Chhachhi and Renee Pittin (editors), *Confronting State, Capital and Patriarchy*, Macmillan Press Ltd. and St. Martin's Press, Inc in association with the Institute of Social Studies (ISS).

Chapter Four

EXPLOITATION OF HOME-BASED WORKERS IN THE VALUE CHAIN CONTEXT

4.1 INTRODUCTION

As mentioned in Chapter 1, outsourcing or home-based sub-contracting, is a way of denying workers reasonable working conditions and fundamental rights. Reasonable working conditions should include the right to a safe and healthy work environment and fundamental rights should include freedom of association to vie for better remuneration and working conditions (see chapter 2).

The working conditions observed during the fieldwork by the field teams, as described in Chapters 5 and 6, were the equivalent of sweatshops. The term 'sweatshop' was first used in the nineteenth century to describe an exploitative sub-contracting system. Sub-contractors extracted high profit margins by the high differential between what they earned from delivering on a contract and what they paid to the workers. Thus, workers were viewed as having been 'sweated' for their labour, because they were paid a meager amount for extensive working hours under unsanitary conditions.

Unfortunately, sweatshops are not relics of the past, but are still present even in advanced countries. The data in Box 4.1 indicates that 90 per cent of garment workplaces in New York City are still sweatshops. The majority of sweatshop workers are illegal immigrants into the United States. Although this system is in vogue in industries where expensive tools and equipment are not yet required, it is also present in the hi-tech Silicone Valley. Here, such practices go by the name of home assembly. An article titled 'Long Nights and Low Wages' carried by Mercury News, describes the plight of a Vietnamese family that worked collectively to fix transistors on printed circuit boards.[2] Quyen Tong's wife and seven children lent him a helping hand, and they get one penny per one transistor loaded to the board.

Box 4.1

- In 1994, the General Accounting Office (GAO) of the USA reported that about 4,500 of the 5,000 garment shops in New York City were sweatshops
- 400 of the total 500 garment shops in Miami were sweatshops
- According to the US Department of Labour, over 50 per cent of the 22,000 garment factories in the USA, located in major cities like California, New York, Dallas, Miami, and Atlanta, violate minimum wage and overtime laws

Source: UNITE, Research Department, cited in NOW-NYC Fact Sheet on Discrimination and Affirmative Action, hhpt://nownyc.org/ factsheets/fssweatshops.htm.[3]

Thus, while workers are denied reasonable working conditions and their fundamental rights even in developed countries, the exploitative conditions of home-based work in Pakistan and other developing countries requires urgent and well thought-out attention. There are many facets to this exploitation, which are described in Chapters 5-7. In this chapter, we adopt a narrow definition in order to quantify it. Value chains here can be defined as links between stages of exchange relations between the home-based workers and the final consumers. Ideally, the quantification should be done in terms of surplus accruing across different tiers of the value chain. However, since all the cost data were not available, we used revenue as a fairly indicative substitute. Hence, exploitation is defined as the share of remuneration of home-based workers as a percentage of revenue accruing across the other tiers of the value, commodity, or production chain.[4] In the sections that follow, we first describe our analytical approach, and next we identify the nature of the production chains by sector and present details of activities by sectors and actors.[5] In the last section, there is a quantification of the distribution of revenue across the chain in the four sectors.[6]

4.2   ANALYTICAL APPROACH

Much has been written in the last decade on various kinds of value chains. Raikes et. al. (2000) trace the origin of value chain analysis to Wallerstein's (1974) World Systems Theory. They point out that prominent among the recent contributors to this (a historical) analytical approach is Gereffi, who has written extensively on global commodity chains (GCC).[7] Gerriffi (2000, p. 11-12) defines a global commodity chain to include a whole range of related activities involved in the design, production and marketing of a product.

A distinction is made between a producer driven and a buyer chain. In producer driven chains, large multi-national companies (like Toyota or IBM) engage in core production and marketing and coordinate the producer network.

In buyer driven chain, large retailers or marketers (like Sears or Nike) play the central role in setting up decentralized production networks in a number of exporting countries. These companies retain the high value research, design, finance, sales and marketing activities. As Gereffi puts it, the central aspects of GCC analyses are the international dimension, the power dynamics and governance (where control lies), the use of networks as a strategic asset and the efficient flow of information.

Raikes et. al. (2000, p. 15) contrast the GCC approach to the Filière approach used by French scholars writing about a chain of activities from producer to final consumer. However, this analysis lackes an international dimension and the focus has been on quantifying the distribution of value added or profit across commodity chains in the former French colonies.

The term 'value chain' analysis has now gained currency in the literature. Even Gerrefi (2000) has adopted the term global value chain. Kaplinski and Morris (2002) have produced an exhaustive handbook for value chain research. Among other interesting issues discussed in it is whether value chains constitute a heuristic device or an analytical tool? In any case, substituting 'value' for 'commodity' makes sense because central to the analysis is the production and distribution of value across the chain. Since our concern is also essentially with the production and distribution of value across a chain, we have utilized the value chain approach in a very broad sense.

The commonality between our research and value chain analysis is that we are concerned with a chain and that the chain often has an international dimension. However, our concern is largely with the power dimension in the chain originating in the home-based work sector. What we found particularly interesting is that monopsony power comes into play in each rung of the production chains we consider, and we view this to be a very typical situation for work of this kind. Thus, the home-based worker operates in a monopsony market relative to the sub-contractor.[8] The same is true for the sub-contractor relative to the factory or wholesaler and the wholesaler relative to the international dealers (refer to the value chain mapping in section 5). Thus, it is not surprising that the mapping of revenue distribution in Table 4.2 indicates larger percentages of revenue higher up in the production chain. Thus, it would not be inaccurate to refer to these value chains as monopsony chains.

4.3   THE PRODUCTION CHAINS BY SECTOR

All the four sectors involved different actors between production and final consumption, local or foreign, as shown below. The value chains across these sectors differed slightly, and the details of different tiers involved in production to final consumption in all the four sectors are illustrated. As evident from Figure 1 below, the chain is more complicated when export is involved.

In all these sectors, the sub-contractor is the pivot. Except for the carpet-weaving sector, the production dynamics in all the other sectors were simple and straightforward. The sub-contractor distributed material collected from the factory, contacted the home-based workers, got the work done and returned the product back to the factory and/or exporter. In the carpet-weaving sector, the sub-contractor also added value to the product.

As shown below, the chains included home-based workers, sub-contractors, wholesalers, retailers and the final consumers. Carpet weaving, incense stick making, and prawn shelling also included exports, and so additional tiers were involved in these sectors before the good finally reached the foreign consumers.

Figure 4.1

Incense stick making   **Carpet weaving**

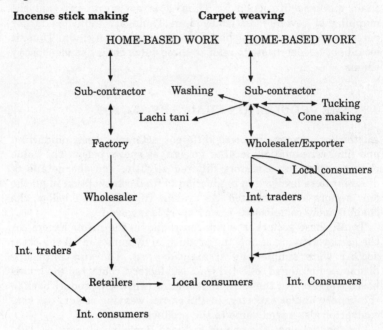

Sack stitching   **Prawn peeling**

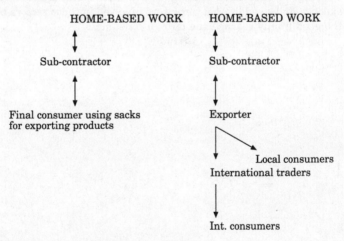

Note: Double arrow suggests a two-way link.

The detail of activity by sector and actors is provided below in Table 4.1.

Table 4.1

Details of activities by sectors and actors

Activities by actors	Activities by sector			
	Incense sticks making	Carpet weaving	Sack stitching	Prawn shelling
HOME-BASED WORK	Mixing of saw dust with color	Weaving	Stitching	Shelling
	Making paste			
	Making agarbatti			
	Drying			
	Making bundles			
Sub-contractors	Supplying inputs	As in incense sticks	As in incense sticks	As in incense sticks
	Sorting	Cone making	Sorting	
	Organizing activity (Networking with retailers and workers)	Lachi tani		
	Providing inputs	Kanni kichai		
	Providing credit	Tucking		
	Collecting output	Washing		
	Sorting/quality control			
	Delivering output			

Source: SDPI survey.
Notes: Activities marked to sub-contractor in the carpet-weaving sector are done by artisans whose services are hired by the sub-contractors.

All the sectors were characterized by poor working conditions that included repetitive and hazardous work, long hours, and low wages. The average monthly per capita income from incense stick making was the lowest (Rs. 115) and it was the highest in prawn shelling (Rs. 503). It was Rs. 169 in carpet weaving and Rs. 203 in sack stitching.[9] Children worked an average 3.7 hours during the day and 1.6 hours in the evening whereas women worked on average of 4.8 hours during the day and 2.1 hours in the evening. Women and girls mainly did the home-based work in three out of four sectors. The communities involved in the home-based work were illegal immigrants from Myanmar and Bangladesh.

We interviewed two sub-contractors and two wholesalers/exporters in each sector respectively.[10] All sub-contractors were unaware of labour laws. Household interviews revealed that no health and safety equipment (like glares or air masks) was provided by the sub-contractors and in 88 per cent of the cases, the contract was in oral form. In 88 per cent of the cases, women in the household were contacted by sub-contractors, children in 50 per cent of the cases and the head of the household in 38 per cent of the cases.[11] In sectors like incense stick making, workers viewed the provision of work as a favour extended to them by the sub-contractors. Thus, they did not even ask for any revision in wages due to a fear of loss of work. Faulty work resulted in fines or the severing of relations with the sub-contractors. Exploitation in a narrow economic sense is quantified in the next section.

4.4   REVENUE DISTRIBUTION ACROSS THE PRODUCTION CHAIN

Exploitation is quantified in this section as the share of remuneration of the home-based workers as a percentage of the revenue accruing to other tiers in the value chain. The distribution of revenue across the chain, and hence the intensity of exploitation, as defined above, of home-based workers for the four sectors is computed and reported in Table 4.2 below. We also collected information from New York City on the retail price of a pack of incense stick containing 20 sticks, of a square ft. of a hand-knotted woolen carpet and of one kg. shrimps.

The actors further up the chain from the home-based workers assume a risk and play a crucial coordination function in bringing together supply and demand as detailed in Table 4.2. In a market where there were many competing agents all across the chain, there would be a competitive allocation of revenue across the chain. Since it is clear that there is massively unequal power and excess labour supply at the lower end of the chain, the earnings of the home-based workers do not even assure subsistence above the poverty line for men of the working households. The numbers in Table 4.2 are discussed below in the sector context.

4.4.1 INCENSE STICK MAKING

Value was added by the home-based workers and by the brand name firm, Metro Milan.[12] The sub-contractor collected material from the factory and distributed it among several home-based workers. After collecting the *agarbatis* (incense sticks) from the

Table 4.2

Daily earnings of home-based workers as a percentage of sub-contractors earnings and as a percentage of what consumers pay

1	2	3	4	5	6	7	8	9	10
Sectors	Units produced (average)	Unit rates (average)	Daily earnings of home-based work (2x3)	Daily earnings of sub-contractor on units produced by home-based work per day	4 as % of 5	Domestic Consumer's payment for units produced by home-based work per day	4 as % of 7	US Consumer's payment for units produced by home-based work per day US$	4 as % of 9 after converting 4 into US$
Incense stick	4000 sticks	5.5 per 1000 sticks	22	26	84.6	4000	0.6	200	0.2
Carpet weaving	25 rounds	1.5 per 1 round	37.5	135	27.8	206	18.2	31.9	2.0
Sack stitching	174 sacks	32 per 100 sacks	55.7	61	91.3	na	na	na	na
Prawn shelling	11 kg	10 per kg prawns	110	3,245	3.4	4345	2.5	164.8	1.1

Source: SDPI survey.

household, the sub-contractor counted and sorted them, separated the defective units and informed the company whose representative collected it from him. According to the sub-contractor, he had to bear the loss in case of any defective sticks, but workers mentioned that they had to bear the cost.

Normally, the sub-contractors contacted women in the household. This is possible in a highly orthodox Muslim community practicing *purdah* (veil) because, in most cases, these sub-contractors were from the same community and had kinship relations with the home-based workers. In case a woman in the household was inaccessible, a male in the household or a child was contacted.

There were some big sub-contactors who purchased their own material, got the work done by the home-based workers and sold the product directly to the company, retailers or other small brand names active in this sector. A sub-contractor earned Rs. 9000 to 12,000 per month on average. At the factory, various perfumes were added to *agarbattis,* which were packaged in packs of various sizes for retail sale or export.

A household got Rs. 5 for making one thousand *agarbattis* and made three to four thousand agarbattis collectively in a day. A sub-contractor got Rs. 6 per one thousand agarbattis, leaving Rs. 1 per one thousand as his share. Retailers sold one pack of agarbatti containing six sticks at Rs. 6 or Rs. 6,000 per one thousand agarbattis. A home-based worker got 0.6 per cent of what a consumer paid for one thousand agarbattis and 84.6 per cent of what was earned by a sub-contractor. The share of home-based workers was lower as a percentage of what an average American consumer pays for the same number of incense sticks. According to price data collected from New York City, the share of home-based workers amounted to 0.2 per cent of what the consumer paid in the USA.

4.4.2 CARPET WEAVING

Sub-contractors worked as agents for exporters/wholesalers and ensured a regular flow of work. They collected materials from the exporters/wholesalers, although, in some cases, they used their own material.[13] Women and children wove carpets in their houses. There were also *karkhanas* (work places) where children worked to pay off loans taken by the parents from the sub-contractors. This bonded work took place in *karkhanas* that were poorly lit and ventilated. The working conditions in the houses were equally poor. Houses were small and the *khaddis* (weaving frames) were placed in one corner of the already congested house. Household members took turns to work on the *khaddi* and completed *pheras* (rounds, standard units for measuring a day's work). The wage rate per *phera* varied from Rs. 1.5 to Rs. 3 and a household completed 30 to 40 *pheras* per day collectively.

The sub-contractor bought wool from the wholesaler and hired workers to make cones out of the wool for use by the home-based workers. A *karegar* (artisan) set up the *lachi* and *tani* (main horizontal and vertical chords that embody the design) along which workers wove the carpet. The carpet was collected from the household after completion, and was given to another worker to cut the extra strings, a process called *kanni kichai*. Other processes before handing over to the wholesaler/exporter were washing and tucking. During tucking, extra threads were cut and then the carpet went to another artisan who washed it using some chemicals that gave shine to the carpet. The details of all the processes with costs for a piece of five by eight carpet are as follows:

	PK. Rs.
Thread 7 lbs @ R. 115/lbs	805
Cone	14
Lachi	125
Tani	150
Labour (home-based work wage)[14]	3500
Kanni kichai (cutting)	40
Washing	600
Transportation	200
Total cost	5434

The price at which the sub-contractor sold this carpet to a wholesaler/exporter was Rs. 7,200 @ Rs. 180 per sq. ft. The wholesaler sold this carpet in the local market at a price ranging from Rs. 9,000 to Rs. 11,000.[15] The most important factors that determined the price of a hand-knotted carpet were the number of knots per sq. ft., complexity of design and the quality of wool. A carpet with an intricate design, more knots per sq. ft. and made with high quality wool fetched a higher price. The major markets were the USA, Europe, and Japan and exporters displayed their products on the web. According to the wholesalers, there was a limited domestic market for carpets, except for a few expatriate Pakistanis.

A home-based worker earned Rs. 1.5 per round and a sub-contractor sold at Rs. 210 per sq. ft. Thus, a home-based worker earned about 27.8 per cent of what a sub-contractor earned. A five by eight carpet sold at Rs. 11,000 in the domestic market and so a home base worker earned only 18.2 per cent of what the final consumer paid for one sq. ft. of carpet. The price of a five by eight carpet in the USA ranged from US$ 1,700 to 2,000 and based on these prices, the share of an average carpet was only 2.0 per cent of what the consumer in the USA paid.

4.4.3 SACK STITCHING

The demand for sacks is derived from the demand for onions and potatoes in foreign markets. Not many tiers are involved in the chain between home-based workers and the final consumers. Sub-contractors purchased material on behalf of exporters and provided the same to home-based workers. Workers were paid Rs. 30–33 per hundred bags stitched and a household stitched about 300 to 400 sacks a day collectively. The sub-contractor was paid Rs. 35 per hundred bags, a difference of Rs. 2 to Rs. 5. Thus, the share of the worker per bag was 91.3 per cent of what the sub-contractor got for it.

There were 40 to 50 households working with one sub-contractor, so the earning of the sub-contractor ranged from Rs. 7,200 to 12,000 per month. The exporters collected the sacks through their agents and the sub-contractor was given transportation cost if he had to deliver the stitched sacks.

4.4.4 PRAWN SHELLING

The sub-contractors bought prawn from the fishery via auction at the price of Rs. 60 to Rs. 80 per 1 kg. of raw prawn. Sub-contractors had to pay Rs. 7 per kg. tax, Rs. 2 per kg. commission and Rs. 200 to the workers for the day. Raw prawn was brought to a *wara* (a work place) and 50 to 70 workers, mostly women and children, worked at the *wara*. Some households took prawns to their houses for shelling for greater flexibility. Home-based workers were given Rs. 10 per *gala* (1 basket containing 4 to 5 kg. raw prawn). Agents of the sub-contractors issued tokens to workers and one token was the equivalent of Rs. 10. Usually, payments were made after a fortnight, once the exporters cleared their bills[16]. One *gala* of raw prawn yielded one to one and a half kg. of shelled prawn. After the prawns were shelled, workers sorted the prawns according to size because the rates varied positively with size. One kg. of mix-shelled prawns fetched Rs. 195, whereas, a *gala* containing prawns of five to eight inches long sold at Rs. 700 per kg. The exporters provided sub-contractors with a credit advance.

The details of the processing cost for 2,640 kg. of raw prawns are as follows:

	PK. Rs.
Raw prawn @ Rs. 60/kg.	158,400
Dalali (commission) @ Rs. 2/kg.	5,280
Tax	18,480
Mazdoori (wage for workers in fishery)	200
Transportation	800
Wage of agents at *wara*	900
Amount paid to workers	6,600
Total cost	190,660

At the average price of the whole lot of Rs. 295, a day's work yielded Rs. 4,040 to the sub-contractor.[17] But, as the work was not regular, the income of all the players involved in this work from sub-contractor to home-based worker was also not regular. The maximum catch of prawn was in the months of October through March, and subsequently, the volume of the catch decreased. In some months, work was available for more than ten days, and in slack months, it dropped down to once a week.

The main markets for prawns were in Europe, the United States and Japan. Small sized prawns were exported to Europe, whereas big prawns were in demand in the United States and Japan. The bulk of the catch was exported and a very small amount of small sized prawn was sold in the local market. The exporters in Karachi (Sindh province) sold to big international seafood companies and were of the view that it was becoming difficult to compete with exporters from Balochistan province. They thought that Balochi exporters were better off because they got a subsidy from the government and had an additional advantage of cheaper labour.[18]

As mentioned earlier, a home-based worker got Rs. 10 for one *gala* and one *gala* yielded roughly 1 kg. shelled prawns. Since there are differential rates for various sizes of prawns, if we take an average price of 1 kg. shelled prawn at Rs. 295, a home-based worker's share was approximately 3.4 per cent of what a sub-contractor earned and 2.5 per cent of what a consumer paid in the domestic market. One kg. shelled prawns fetched US$ 14.98 which means the share of a home-based worker to what a consumer paid for the same amount in the USA was 1.5 per cent.

CONCLUSION

The sub-contract system denies workers their basic rights of association and collective bargaining and entrepreneurs get rid of their corporate responsibilities such as fair wage rates, healthy work environment and the social welfare of the workers. This situation is not specific to Pakistan, and there is evidence of the presence of sweatshops elsewhere in the world. In all the four sectors we studied, workers got low wages, worked for long hours, did repetitive and hazardous work and were not provided with any safety equipment to guard them against health risks.

The distribution of the revenue across the value chain is in a very loose sense being used to gauge exploitation. The share of home-based workers relative to the revenue of the sub-contractors, contractors and final distributors is extremely low ranging from 0.6 of retail revenue per unit in incense stick making to 18.2 per cent in carpet weaving at the domestic level. At the international level, the amount the home-based workers got as a percentage of what consumers in the USA paid ranges from 0.2 per cent for incense stick making to 2.0 for carpet weaving.

In such a situation, we propose three ways for improving the well being of home-based workers that should be facilitated by the state. First, workers in this sector need to be recognized as citizens and registered as workers. Second, basic protections need to be provided to ameliorate the hazards. Third, civil society should be encouraged to organize workers in this sector to enable them to collectively win better rates. Since power is unequal in the market equation, redress is necessary. Our analysis shows that there are ample margins at the higher ends of the value chain so that even doubling the amount paid to the home-based workers would have a completely insignificant impact on final retail prices.

NOTES

1. This and parts of the last chapter draw on work submitted to *World Development*.
2. www.mercurycenter.com/svtech/news/special/piecework/d1_family.htm.
3. Union of Needle Trades, Industrial and Textile Employees (UNITE) was formed by the merger of two of the nation's oldest unions, the International Ladies' Garment Workers' Union (ILGWU) and the Amalgamated Clothing and Textile Workers Union (ACTWU).

4. Value chains here can be defined as links between stages of exchange relations between the home-based workers and the final consumers. Ideally, the quantification should be done in terms of surplus accruing across different tiers of the value chain. However, since all the cost data were not available, we used revenue as a fairly indicative substitute. Value chain analysis is discussed in more detail in section 4.2.

5. Unfortunately, despite extensive search, contextual background information for the sectors other then carpets was not available because they are economically insignificant. Contextual information on the carpet sector is reported as Appendix 2.1.

6. For more details regarding process and health impacts, refer to Chapter 5 and 6.

7. The pioneering work is Gerrefi (1994).

8. The supply curve of the home-based workers, in all the sectors considered, is highly but not infinitely elastic.

9. The exchange rate of one rupee (Rs.) for the dollar in early 2001, the time of the fieldwork, was Rs. 62.15 for $ 1.

10. The incense stick sector was the exception for which there was only one interview because managers were not available, and the other staff members were very reluctant to furnish any information.

11. The total exceeds 100 per cent due to the multiple response option on questions.

12. Mangers of this Pakistani company were extremely unforthcoming in providing information

13. Refer to TRDP/RDC/SCF (1999) for an account of home-based carpet weaving in Tharparker, Sindh. This study points out that parents may use the intermediation of a master artisan to get a loan from a contracter and have the child work for the artisan initially as an apprentice for no pay and later for modest remuneration. Thus, the master artisan may act as an intermediary between the parents and the contractor to facilitate the loan and undertake to deliver the carpets on time by utilizing the child labour of the household taking the loan.

14. It takes a household three months to complete a 5 x 8 carpet.

15. Rates are based on information gathered from visits to various display centres in Karachi during the survey.

16. We heard of cases in which the contractor disappeared prior to the cashing of the coupons.

17. The average is cited as Rs. 295 since out of total prawns on the day of visit at this *wara*, 89 per cent were of small and medium size. Rates for small and medium size prawns were Rs. 195 and Rs. 395 respectively.

18. Licenses to multinational companies for deep-sea fishing have reduced the catch enormously. According to the Secretary General, Pakistan Fisher Folk Forum, fish landing at the fishery was 24,837 metric tons in Oct.-Dec. 1999 and it increased to 32,550 metric tons in the corresponding period in the year 2000, an increase of 7,713 metric tones. This was possible because the government had cancelled licenses for the multinationals upon protests from the fishermen. The government has again started issuing these licenses, and the situation has started worsening. Although, these companies are not supposed to fish in the radius of 35 nautical miles from any harbor, this last condition is violated in collusion with government officials. Deep-sea fishing by foreign trawlers results in overharvesting and a wastage of the immense by-catch (up to three-fourths of the total catch). The dumping of small dead fish into the sea also represents an environmental problem and in economic hardships for the local fisher folk.

19. http://www.finance.gov.pk/summary/main.htm

20. An exhibition of hand-knotted carpets organized jointly by Pakistan Carpet Manufacturers and Exporters Association (PCMEA) and Export Promotion Bureau

(EPB) represents an effort to boost exports. Two proposed carpet-training centres in Karachi and Lahore and provision of loans from SMEDA (Small and Medium Sized Enterprise Development Authority) are some other steps in this regard.
21. For details see Chapter 5 and 6.
22. For more details, see http://www.anti-slavery.org/global/india/
23. For more details, see 'By the Sweat and Toil of Children: Consumer labels and Children', US Department of Labour, Bureau of International Labour Affairs, 1997.

References

Gereffi, G., 1994, 'The organization of buyer driven global commodity chains: how U. S. retailers shape overseas production networks,' in eds. G. Gereffi and M. Korzeniewicz, *Commodity Chains and Global Capitalism* (Westport, Connecticut: Praeger Publishers).

Gereffi, G., 2000, 'Beyond the Producer-Driven/Buyer – Driven Dichotomy: An Expanded Typology of Global Value Chains, With Special Reference to the Internet,' Duke University, draft.

Gereffi, G., 2000a, 'The Transformation of the North American Apparel Industry: Is NAFTA a Curse or a Blessing,' CEPAL ECLAC, desarrola productivo series 84, Santiago, Chile.

Government of Pakistan, 2001, Pakistan's Economic Performance during July-Jan./Feb. 2000-01, Finance Division, Economic Advisor's Wing, Islamabad.

Kaplinsky, R. and M. Morris, 2002, 'A Handbook for Value Chain Research,' Prepared for the IDRC, draft.

Raikes, P., M. F. Jensen and S. Ponte, 2000, 'Global Commodity Chain Analysis and the French Filière Approach: Comparison and Critique,' *Economy and Society*, Vol. 29, No. 3.

TRDP/RDC/SCF (Tardeep Rural Development Foundation/Raasta Development Copnsultants/Save the Children Fund, 1999, 'Blooming Colors Wilting Children: Children Working in the Carpet Industry in Thar, Islamkot, Sindh, Pakistan.

US Department of Labour, 1997, 'By the Sweat and Toil of Children,' Bureau of International Labour Affairs, http://www.dol.gov/dol/ilab/public/media/reports/iclp/sweat4/toc.htm

Wallerstein, I., 1974, The Modern World System (New York: Academic Press).

APPENDIX 4.1
HAND KNOTTED CARPETS: INTERNATIONAL AND NATIONAL CONTEXT

The major share of the world's produce of hand-knotted carpets had been taken by Iran. After the Iranian revolution in 1979, the USA imposed sanctions on imports from Iran and this created an opportunity that was seized by India, Nepal and Pakistan. Appendix Table 4.1 below gives the shares of the ten top suppliers of carpets from 1989 to 1996 to the US market.

Appendix Table 4.1
US Hand-knotted carpet imports, 1989-96, (million U.S. dollars)

Country	1989	1990	1991	1992	1993	1994	1995	1996
India	126.9	121.5	129.6	154.5	150.0	154.4	155.4	146.9
China	87.2	76.8	80.6	102.1	86.6	70.3	94.7	83.0
Pakistan	58.6	54.9	62.7	60.4	45.3	47.9	52.3	52.9
Turkey	16.5	18.6	24.2	30.4	23.1	29.1	25.6	21.4
Nepal	2.4	3.2	2.5	2.9	3.7	5.1	7.8	9.5
Romania	3.5	1.6	1.2	0.7	0.5	2.0	3.0	2.9
Egypt	0.3	0.3	0.7	0.8	0.8	1.1	2.0	2.8
Germany	0.6	1.0	1.1	1.0	1.0	0.7	1.0	1.3
France	0.6	0.3	0.2	0.4	0.3	0.6	0.6	0.6
UK	0.8	0.7	0.4	0.2	0.4	0.5	0.5	0.5
Total Imports	311.8	292.9	312.1	361.3	319.2	320.3	351.0	329.6

Source: Official statistics of the US Department of Commerce, cited in US department of Labour, 'Hand-Knotted Carpets' (1997, p. 2).

Appendix Table 4.1 indicates that in 1996, India, China and Pakistan together accounted for 81 per cent of total US imports. Carpet exports from Pakistan during July-Feb. 2000-01 were US$ 177.47 million. This represented a growth of 8.9 per cent over the corresponding period in 1999-00.[19] In 2000-2001, Pakistan exported carpets worth US$ 263 million and for 2001-2002, a target of $300 million was set and measures promised to achieve it.[20]

Carpet manufacturers employ children to weave carpets in almost all the major exporting countries of hand-knotted carpets such as India, Nepal and Pakistan. The actual extent of the child labour prevalent in the carpet-weaving sector is still unknown. During the survey for this study, we visited households where children were helping their parents in doing home-based work. In the carpet-weaving sector, we even found debt bondage of children. Parents took loans from the sub-contractors and children worked out these loans. There were also instances of children being beaten by sub-contractors.[21]

Pakistan's exports dropped in 1995 after the murder of Iqbal Masih, a child carpet weaver of Pakistan.[22] There are various efforts currently underway to tackle the problem of child labour in the carpet-weaving sector. Consumer labels such as Rugmark, Kaleen, STEP, Care & Fair International and Ten thousand Villages have been developed to ensure consumers that the production of carpets carrying these labels are child labour free.[23]

Chapter Five
SOCIAL EXPLOITATION: QUALITATIVE FINDINGS

5.1 INTRODUCTION

This chapter relies on three main sources. First, detailed field reports based on the observations of the field-team members (Annexure 2). Second, the documentation on focus group discussions (FGD) conducted by the field team on the main themes of the study, including women's empowerment, economic well being, exploitation and the hazardous impact on health due to home-based work (Annexure 3).[1] Third, detailed case studies for each home-based work sector that elaborate on the general sector accounts in section 2 (Annexure 1).

Apart from the themes identified above, this chapter contains a description of the nature of home-based work, the socio-economic conditions of households doing the work and the cultural norms of the communities they are a part of. While this chapter relies essentially on the above qualitative sources, these are complemented and substantiated by quantitative data analysis and the relevant tables are included in Appendix 1.[2] The next chapter exclusively focuses on a more detailed and general statistical analysis, with a particular focus on gender and on contrasting home-based workers on the above themes with a control group of households sampled from the same neighbourhood.

5.2 SECTORS

5.2.1 INCENSE STICK MAKING, ORANGI

The majority of workers in this sector were Burmese who came to Pakistan in the late 1960s and early 1970s due to the hostile treatment of Muslims in Burma. Some of them had residential plots leased to them by the government. Others lived in huts and paid *bhatta* (forced rent) to toughs of a local political party, the Muhajir Qaumi Movement (MQM).[3] Bengalis were the other community engaged in this work.

The locality was highly polluted and in poor condition with regard to urban infrastructure. The Burmese community was very conservative and strictly enforced *purdah* for women (segregation of the sexes and women were veiled in public places). Girls were prohibited from going outside the house after 'puberty', which is roughly at twelve years of age.[4] However, there was no intra-community *purdah*.

The majority of the children went to m*adrasah* (religious schools) because they could not afford regular school or because schools were inaccessible.[5] Some of these *madrasahs* provided both religious and regular education, while others provided religious education only. Preference was given to enrolling boys if a choice was necessary. Children reported being tired after the home-based work and unable to complete the homework, hence invoking the ire of the teachers.[6] Between work and other activities, children got little time to play.[7] Most would have preferred to to school, and some were even conscious that their work supported their schooling.

Although women earned a living for their households, their contribution was not appreciated or acknowledged. The home-based work that they engage in appeared to bring about little notable change in their living conditions. In fact, they were worse off because they had to engage in paid work besides doing the regular household chores and being responsible for childcare. Women, like men, often indulged in habits like chewing *pan* (a mix including tobacco enclosed in betel leaves) or smoking tobacco.

In many of the cases, men were not gainfully employed.[8] They were unemployed partly because of their illegal status that restricted mobility. Police harassed them and solicited bribes on a monthly basis. The field team observed many men of this community sitting outside the houses or at the teashops. Piece-rates were very low and a household was paid Rs. 5 to Rs. 5.5 to make one thousand incense sticks tied together in tight bundles. A family could jointly put together about four bundles a day. Children worked about six hours per day on home-based work and chores; not counting the time spent getting the raw material from the contractor.[9] Payments were often late, and fines were imposed for faulty work.

People were of the view that the presence of sub-contractors was welcome, because other work options were very limited. They did not complain much about the contractors profiting at their expense or their bad behaviour because, as relatives, the typical worker-employee relationship did not exist between them. They also believed that the contractors were not much better off than them, although section 4.5.1. indicated that contractors earned much more than them. These two reasons partly accounted for the lack of collective action for an increase in wages. Other reasons included lack of organizing skills, indebtedness to the contractors, the lack of citizenship, and the fear of loss of work.

While most felt that the home-based work was paying a pittance and not contributing significantly in a monetary sense, and also adversely impacting the quality of their life and that of their children, they saw this as keeping them from starvation. However, more than anything else, women attributed their exploitation to their lot as women.

The pressure to do this work came from the husbands, and many women appreciated husbands who did not impose such work on their families. They accepted the superior position of males as religiously mandated and hence did not complain. Since they had internalized these norms, they were unwilling to try to get work outside the house and believed home-based work to be meant for them and not for men. The earnings from the home-based work did not contribute to a sense of empowerment, and they saw the work as part of their lives, just as it was the case for their mothers and grandmothers. Hence, they did not question the fact that, within the religious framework imposed on them by their husbands, being the breadwinner was the husband's responsibility whether or not they were employed.

The number of children per household was high and one reason was likely to be early marriage.[10] Polygamy was another likely reason of the high number of children per household. Women again accepted this as a religious right of men, although many scholars point to various conditions under which the practice is sanctioned.[11] Finally, family planning was viewed by most of the inhabitants of Orangi to be against Islam.

The process of making incense sticks (*agarbattis*) was hazardous on several counts. Saw dust, mixed with various colors and toxic chemicals, was used to make a paste. The paste resulted in discoloring and injury to the skin. Also, workers inhaled the dust and toxins that caused irritation in the upper respiratory track that eventually developed into asthma in chronic cases. Women and children often complained of headaches, cough, flu, cuts on the hand, and exhaustion. Sitting for two-hour bouts caused the children's feet to hurt, and the field team observed nosebleeds possibly from the heat of the boiling incense stick mixture. On top of the pain, faulty work produced beating from the family and/or the contractor and also a fine. Children, mostly girls, also received a beating from the mothers if they resisted working due to the ailments that they suffered as a consequence. Long hours at work for women resulted in body, muscular, joint, back and shoulder pains possibly from the heat of the boiling mixture.[12]

Generally, they were unable to afford a doctor or buy medicine and relied on local remedies (*desi totkas*). Interestingly, there was a government institute called the Ojha Institute of Chest Diseases located in the area. The field-team visited this institute twice, and on both occasions, they were not able to meet the doctors.

5.2.2 CARPET WEAVING (KORANGI TOWN)

Korangi is much more remote than Orangi. Although the communities making the carpets were ethnically the same, not being part of the city meant that they had less access to city facilities and were less urbanized.[13] The population doing this work in this locality was mainly Burmese, though they claimed to be Bengalis. Bengalis seemed to have a higher status among the illegal immigrant community than Burmese, and they were pestered less for bribes by the police than the Burmese.[14] Illegal immigrants still continued to come to Pakistan, and this community was among the relative new-comers. Men worked as fishermen on an irregular basis.

Jihadi (religious militants) factions were very influential in this community as were members of the *Haqeeqi* faction of the MQM political party. They had *madrasahs* (religious schools) in this locality and also enlisted people for *Jihad*.[15] The majority of children went to these *madrasahs* or regular schools, mostly in the evenings. Many woke up early in the morning to do home-based work, or to go to *madrasahs* if they were going to regular school. Homework was done late at night after all other work and chores were completed. Some complained that they suffered physical abuse from their teachers because home-based work interfered with their homework. Children across the board expressed the desire to go to a regular school fulltime, if their contribution to family income by doing home-based work was not considered essential. Women realized this work was not good for their children, but felt they had little choice in the matter due to the poverty the household confronted.

Women were generally confined to their houses and most of them had not even seen any city centre in Karachi. Between home-based work, childcare and chores, all their time was taken up and there was no time left for socializing or entertainment. Most of the money they made was used up for household expenditures, and none was left over as savings or for spending in other ways.[16] When a curfew was imposed in the area due to ethnic conflict, work temporarily dried up and they confronted great hardship, and at times, had nothing to feed the family.

Women in Korangi were in a much worse condition than women in Orangi. Many women had not stepped out of their houses in years. They were much less responsive in discussing their problems. Most of them were even reluctant to come for the focus group discussion. Men in this locality were much more conservative and treated women like a commodity. Women complained of physical beatings by husbands and indicated that they were forced to weave carpets. They seemed to have little decision-making power regarding household issues.[17] They were not allowed to go to the schools or go outside to work. These women were made to believe that this behaviour was in accordance with Islam and any disobedience would mean disobeying Allah. It appeared that there was little socialization even among the women and they hardly met neighbours. Women also said that they did not get any time free for themselves, and had to work really hard to earn a living. Only those women looked more confident whose husbands were supportive of them.

Home-Based Work in this locality followed the traditional pattern of bonded labour. Adult males took the loan, and their children worked these off by foregoing a part of their daily wages. Often, the loans keep compounding, and so indebtedness keeps increasing.[18] There were reports that the contractors even molested the women in exchange for softening the terms of repayment. Children generally took about twenty-one weeks to learn the skill, and many of them did so at a factory.[19] Some later worked at home, though many continued to work in factories (*karkhanas*) in extremely poor conditions.

These *karkhanas* were poorly lit and ventilated. Once all the children got there in the morning, they were locked inside and not allowed to go out without the permission of the supervisors. This was done out of fear of the officials of the labour department. They were also afraid of NGO people, who according to them made films and published reports in the international press, and this in turn affected the volume of work coming to the country and the community. While children got fined in the factories for faulty work, most said they were not beaten. The children worked a nine-hour day (8:00 am to 5:00 pm) with a one-hour lunch break.

Work conditions in the houses were also not very good. The houses were small and congested. Poor work conditions aggravated health risks. Workers reported diseases common to this occupation, and both children and women were affected. According to the West Pakistan Law of Hazardous Occupations, 1963, handling 'wool, hair, bristle, hides and skins' is covered under the hazardous occupations category. Prolonged exposure to wool fibers causes bronchitis and other respiratory diseases and leucorrhoea for women.[20] Respondents reported these diseases along with posture related body aches, pains in the back, chest, joints, limbs, watering eyes and skin cracks, infections, allergies and exhaustion. Children were particularly susceptible to knife cut injuries on their hands and fingertips when cutting the wool thread. Treatment was often not sought because they felt unable to afford the doctor's fee.

Since this community was located on the outskirts of the city, the provision of basic public utilities was very poor. There was no proper arrangement of solid waste disposal and garbage dumps were found sporadically. Exposed and live wires, resulting from illegal electricity connections, created a potential risk of major disaster in this locality. There was no hospital near the locality, so people had to go to hospitals located elsewhere in the city.

Remuneration rates were based on 'rounds' (*phairas*) completed by the households on the frame. The rates varied from Rs. 1 to Rs. 3 per round and payments were made in installments. Most households completed around 40 to 50 rounds per day.[21] While rates were low, this source of income was key to household survival since, as fisher folk, the men often did not have regular jobs.

5.2.3 SACK (*BORI*) STITCHING, GODHRA

Godhra was different from all the other localities visited. In other localities, there was a concentration of one trade whereas, in Godhra, people were engaged in numerous activities. These people migrated from a village named Godhra in Indian Gujarat and they are viewed as coming from a tradition of very enterprising people. Women and children stitched sacks in the season for the export of onions and potatoes to the UAE.

Most of the children were attending both a school and a *madarasah*. They collected the materials from the contractor and started stitching after returning from school. The women joined them once the household chores were completed. The children were allowed to take breaks between work, and they worked over a seven to eight hour period. Some complained that the sack stitching interfered in their schoolwork.

Work decreased in the off-season, and people switched to other activities including garment stitching, sorting of waste towel cloth and ribbon making. Remuneration in the other activities was even lower than in sack stitching, which is why it was taken on even though it was hazardous work. It took about two to three minutes to stitch a sack, and the rate was Rs. 30 to Rs. 33 per one hundred sacks. Households stitched about 300 to 400 sacks per day.

It takes a lot of strength to pull the chord while stitching and it can be damaging for children's muscles. The dust caused throat irritation and work caused irritation, itching and infections on the hands. Sneezing, cough, runny noses, flu, breathing problems, neck and chest pains and watery eyes were common among the children. Women complained about breathing problems, cough and flu. Other ailments included leucorrhoea for women, watering and weakening eyes and pain in the chest, joints, back and limbs. However, many women had made sack stitching into a social activity by getting together and doing it collectively.

Once again, women did not approve of this work for their children, but felt they were compelled by their poverty. Women saved money from home-based work and spent it on the education of their children, but without discriminating between sons and daughters, unlike in the other communities visited. This, however, was possible when the men also had a job. Consistent with this, women were not as oppressed as in the other communities, and in general, they were congenial and cheerful and were often assisted by men, who generally worked, in doing household chores. Women were also more mobile and enterprising and some even ran shops.[22]

The higher level of mobilization meant that the women had even compelled contractors to increase wages by collectively negotiating higher rates. Even so, the women felt that the contractors cheated them by giving less thread (*sutli*) and that the men doing *bori* work get better rates.[23] They also complained about delays in payment for work done. The women felt they could engage in collective action to improve their lot, but needed assistance with organizing themselves.

Sindhi, Punjabi and Baloch were other ethnic minorities living in this area. People, other than Gujaratis, complained of the bias of Gujarati contractors who were viewed as giving priority to Gujarati families while allocating work and in determining rates. Gujarati families were worried about competition from cheap Afghan labour and were of the view that work was shifting from this locality to the localities inhabited by Afghans. Ethnic violence, just prior to the fieldwork, also contributed to a decreased availability of work in this area, but matters were returning to normal at the time of the survey.

There were also some households of Sindhi and Balochi tribes in Godhra. Some Sindhi tribes had a tradition of having three or four wives. These women were living in the most horrible conditions, and were subjected to physical beatings almost daily. Such major differences resulting, in close proximity, from different cultural backgrounds are notable.

5.2.4 PRAWN SHELLING, MACHAR COLONY[24]

Machar Colony is also referred to as Muhammadi Colony and it is a big locality of about two hundred thousand people. The segment of the colony that we visited was inhabited by illegal Bengali immigrants who were living in extremely poor conditions. They were settled in a landfill area, and therefore, the status of this locality was also illegal. The Karachi Port Trust (KPT) was planning to evict these people, and it had made such efforts in the past but was not successful due to public resistance.

There were more than two hundred contractors engaged in the *jheenga* (prawn) business. They bought *jheenga* from the fishery and got it shelled by women and children and the top quality prawns were exported to the USA and Japan. The second quality was shelled by workers at Machar colony, and these fetched between Rs. 150 - Rs. 700 in the market.

The contractors had their own workplaces called *jheenga waras* where children between the ages of 4 and 13 assembled early in the morning before sunrise and started shelling *jheenga*. Between five to seven supervisors worked on behalf of the sub-contractor. The sub-contractor generally visited the *wara* once a day and the supervisor remained there throughout. Women worked in their homes and had virtually no time for socializing after work, childcare and chores. The children would go and get the work from the *waras*. The other members of the household, especially children, also helped them.

One *challi* (small basket), containing one *gala* (4 to 5 kgs.) of raw *jheenga*, fetched Rs. 10 when shelled. The shelling took between one to two hours, and children managed to shell about 3 to 4 *galas* per day and the household (adults and children) shelled 10 to 15 *galas* per day.[25] After shelling, the children took the *jheenga* to the *wara* and handed it over to the agents of the contractor. While the rates were very low, the women felt that the community was very divided and hence unable to engage in any collective action.

Work started early (4:00 am), because the contractor brought prawns from the fishery very early, and finished at about 11:00 am because there were no storage facilities and prawns are highly perishable. The baskets were weighed before handing them over to the children and weighed when they were delivered back after shelling and cleaning. If the weight of the basket with shelled prawns was less than expected (about half the earlier weight), or if there were faults in the shelling (broken tails), the children were often beaten by the contractors. The women felt helpless about this, and they noted that the contractors treated the men with more respect.

Workers were issued tokens with the name of the contractor written on it. One token was considered equivalent to one *gala*, and if the contractor was reliable, these tokens were used as currency with shopkeepers. The name of the contractor was written on the token because there were numerous contractors in the same neighbourhood and workers got *jheenga* from various contractors. This method avoided confusion in payment and it was viewed to be a convenient way of keeping accounts. One of the agents of the contractor maintained a register and recorded the work assigned to various households and *wara* workers. Generally, payment was received on return of the basket and the token. However, the tokens could be cashed after a fortnight, after the clearance of bills of the contractor by the exporters. People recounted incidents where they worked for a contractor for one month and were issued tokens, but the contractor fled without paying them.[26]

Working hours, particularly for children, were long. Since the prawns are very perishable, they have to be kept in ice-cold water. Women and children complained that the freezing water and the work resulted in colds, coughs, flu, breathing problems, limb swelling and nausea. Also, the sharp shell edges cut their hands and often resulted in skin cracks, infections, allergies and rashes and they suffered from pains in their back, legs, feet and fingers. There was no government hospital in the area, and the home-based workers did not view the few private clinics in the locality as affordable. Generally, stopping work for a few days improved the patient's health.

As mentioned earlier, the majority of the inhabitants were Bengalis and a number of women interviewed were brought here from Bangladesh and sold off into marriages.[27] Sindhi and Punjabi men bought such women, and in most cases, the women were treated badly by their husbands and 'owners,' who physically abused them and compelled them to work. Beyond that, the men of the community were also very conservative and oppressive, and also did not help with household work. Unfortunately, there was no other work available in this locality, and so the women engaged in shelling prawns to contribute to family income. Going elsewhere for work was out of the question. Men even discouraged socialization with other women. Some women mentioned that the community had been involved in this work for many years, and that their parents also did it.

While most of the children were not attending school because of poor access and the expense, they expressed the desire to attend if it were possible. They did, however, attend the *madrasah* and read the Qur'an, even though they did have to pay a fee for this. They managed to find some time during the day to play and were also given pocket money by the parents. Punjabi families living in the same neighbourhood, with roughly the same income, were sending their children to school. Their view was that the Bengali community's preference for the more expensive food items e.g. fish, meant less left over for the children's schooling.

Despite the fact that some Bengali women were bought by Punjabi males, several Bengali women expressed the view that Punjabi men made better husbands because they were more liberal about letting girls go to school and were much less restrictive regarding women's mobility. These views once again point to the importance of community and culture in determining social preferences.

Communities were also very traditional concerning the work they were willing to do. Thus, even though fishing was seasonal in nature, the Bengali men preferred to do nothing in the off-season rather than take on other casual work. Similarly, Punjabi men were found engaged in certain trades like masonry and carpentry.

SUMMARY

This research focused on four home-based work sectors i.e. carpet weaving, shrimp shelling, incense stick making and sack stitching. This summary draws on the information reported in the sector descriptions in the chapter as well as other information available from the field reports, focus group discussion reports and the case studies.

The urban localities these communities lived in were highly polluted and deprived of adequate social and physical infrastructure. In many cases, individuals did not seek any medical attention because of unaffordable or inaccessible health facilities. Often they relied on local remedies or expired medicines dispensed by quacks.

The Bengali and Burmese communities of Orangi, Korangi and Machar Colony were very conservative in their religious interpretation of Islam and highly oppressive toward women. Being immigrants, they felt insecure and became easy targets for many predators like the police, *jihadi* groups, political toughs of parties like the MQM and the contractors.

In turn, the men oppressed the women. They severely restricted women's mobility, and contrary to conservative cultural practices required them to work and often to be the sole breadwinner. Women were also responsible for all the household chores and childcare and hence had little time to themselves or for socializing. In any case, this was not an option for most of the women in the Bengali and Burmese communities who required women to be confined to their houses. Some of the women had been sold off into 'marriages' by pimps enticing them with better prospects away from their homes in Bangladesh. With no protection from kinship groups, they were completely at the mercy of their husbands who often had other wives. These women reported being beaten and forced into doing home-based work to run their kitchens.

Bonded labour was going on in the carpet-weaving sector. As in the other activities, excess labour supply or the lack of organizing ability or community solidarity prevented them from engaging in collective action for better terms. Contractors took full advantage of their economic power. They paid late, cheated by providing fewer materials, and verbally, and sometimes physically abused the women and children. As expected, they generally treated the men with more respect.

Empowerment for women seemed more a function of the cultural norms of the community than work and earnings. Thus, in similar circumstances, Gujrati women of the Godhra locality were more mobile, and sometimes even engaged in collective action to get better rates. Other enlightened practices included encouraging girls to study and men assisting the women with chores even though they generally held jobs.

The control group of households were often Punjabi or Urdu speaking. While they observed *purdah* also, the restraints on the women were not as rigid as those on the Bengali or Burmese women. They also attached a high premium on the children's education. Interestingly, education did make a difference to how men treated the women even in the Bengali community. It also appeared that an educated woman was capable of getting the respect of a contractor.

Finally, the Bengali and Burmese communities in particular expected little from the state, since they did not view themselves as citizens. A question about expectations from the state thus puzzled them and some responded that they wanted money. Others asked that reasonable social and physical infrastructure, particularly education, healthcare and sanitation, should be provided. The Gujrati community was more willing to engage in collective action for better terms, but stated that they lacked organizing skills for this purpose. More generally, collective action was impeded by home-based workers being non-nationals, the contractor being a relative, or by the fear of loss of work due to excess supply of labour.

Overall, the qualitative reports show that the working conditions for women and children were bad and that the work also entailed serious health hazards. Women and children suffered multiple ailments like respiratory diseases, pains in the muscles and joints, and serious skin irritations and allergies from home-based work. Women across the board stated that they would have preferred for their children to be going to school and not doing such work if they could afford school and survive without such work. Thus, while they realized that home-based work was resulting in serious danger to their health, the alternative was starvation. Similarly, children stated their desire for attending regular school, but repeated that family compulsions forced them into home-based work and often kept them out of school. These and related issues are explored again in the next chapter using quantitative data.

APPENDIX

Many of the questions allowed for multiple responses. In these cases, the analysis requires reporting results in terms of the percentage of responses by different response options. Thus, in the relevant tables, total responses (r) are reported rather than the sub-sample size (n).

Appendix Table 5.1

Mean hours spent by children on home-based work and other activities

Sector	HOME BASED WORK	Chores	Home work	Meals	Play	n
Incense stick making	4.10 (3.44)	2.62 (2.40)	0.94 (2.14)	1.48 (0.80)	1.09 (1.78)	77
Carpet weaving	4.73 (3.69)	1.74 (1.45)	0.79 (2.07)	1.31 (0.67)	1.32 (1.74)	77
Sack stitching	2.00 (2.51)	2.03 (1.75)	1.69 (2.76)	1.25 (0.79)	1.47 (2.11)	75
Prawn shelling	1.74 (2.15)	2.20 (1.96)	0.18 (0.82)	1.31 (0.89)	2.64 (2.69)	74
Total	3.17 (3.28)	2.15 (1.94)	0.90 (2.13)	1.34 (0.79)	1.62 (2.18)	303

Source: SDPI survey.
Note: Parentheses contain standard deviations.

Appendix Table 5.2

Percentage of male household heads not working by sector

Sector	Percentage
Incense stick making	42.4
Carpet weaving	20.3
Sack stitching	15.3
Prawn shelling	22.0
Total	26.1

Source: SDPI survey.

Appendix Table 5.3
Daily hours worked by women and children and mean household
daily income from home-based work

Sector	Mean hours worked (children)	Mean hours worked (women)	Mean household daily income (Rs.)
Incense stick making	5.82 (2.78)	7.64 (2.26)	25.60 (14.32)
Carpet weaving	6.49 (2.92)	6.92 (2.67)	38.55 (25.86)
Sack stitching	4.15 (2.20)	6.59 (2.49)	55.63 (33.43)
Prawn shelling	4.85 (2.50)	6.68 (3.10)	113.24 (82.96)
Total	5.34 (2.76)	6.95 (2.75)	57.73 (57.19)

Source: SDPI survey.
Note: Parentheses contain standard deviations.
Households are identified by their primary activity. Twelve
households were also engaged in a second activity and in those
cases the combined income is reported. Note that the mean hours
worked in Table 5.1. are based on responses about the child's
activities on the day prior to the survey. The time spent on home-
based work reported in this table is based on a carefully constructed
time profile. The different reporting formats explain the differences
in the numbers.

Appendix Table 5.4
Mean household size and number of children per household

Sector	Mean household size	Mean number of children per household
Incense stick making	7.82 (2.70)	4.55 (1.72)
Carpet weaving	6.78 (2.11)	4.42 (1.72)
Sack stitching	8.00 (1.99)	4.82 (1.45)
Prawn shelling	8.41 (2.61)	4.17 (1.91)
Total	7.79 (2.46)	4.46 (1.74)

Source: SDPI survey
Note: Parentheses contain standard deviations.

Appendix Table 5.5

Major ailments by sector for children

(Percentage responses)

Ailment	Sector			
	Incense stick making	Carpet weaving	Sack stitching	Prawn shelling
General (fever, colds etc.)	18.9	15.3	16.0	20.1
Cough	16.6	11.2	17.9	15.0
Skin problems	0.0	0.0	0.5	8.1
Back pains	14.2	9.5	15.1	5.6
Anemia	14.9	14.9	12.3	3.0
Pain in leg or some limb	6.9	17.4	9.5	7.3
Pain in joints	2.0	6.6	4.7	6.0
Pain in chest	1.3	2.1	4.7	0.4
Blisters	0.7	2.1	1.4	10.7
Skin cracking/discolorization	0.7	0.4	1.9	11.1
No. of Responses	302	242	212	234

Source: SDPI survey.
Note: Ailment reported if responses in any category for any sector amounted to five per cent or more.

Appendix Table 5.6

Major ailments by sector for women

(Percentage responses)

Ailment	Sector			
	Incense stick making	Carpet weaving	Sack stitching	Prawn shelling
General (fever, colds etc.)	11.5	10.0	9.1	12.3
Watering eyes	5.1	4.0	5.1	3.1
Difficult to see	3.2	4.0	4.7	2.0
Cough	12.0	7.7	9.9	7.8
Breathing problems	3.5	1.1	6.2	1.4
Back pains	14.1	12.6	16.8	11.9
Anemia	14.3	14.9	8.4	1.7
Pain in legs or some limbs	7.1	9.5	4.1	4.4
Pain in chest	3.9	4.3	5.1	2.0
General body pains	6.0	5.7	6.2	5.8
Blisters	0.5	1.4	0.4	8.5
Skin cracking/discolorization	0.0	1.1	0.4	8.9
Gynecological problems	4.4	5.7	6.2	9.2
No. of Responses	434	350	274	293

Source: SDPI survey.
Note: Ailment reported if responses in any category for any sector amounted to five per cent or more.

Appendix Table 5.7
Living conditions by sector

(Percentages)

Facility	Sector				
	Incense stick making	Carpet weaving	Sack stitching	Prawn shelling	Total
Pakka house	32.5	20.8	46.7	6.8	26.7
Have running water	72.7	10.4	68.0	1.4	38.3
Private flush	57.1	32.5	48.0	8.1	38.3
Have electricity	85.7	84.4	98.7	67.6	84.2
Own house	74.0	71.4	82.7	50.0	69.6
Own radio	13.0	6.5	12.0	5.4	9.2
Own TV	27.3	10.4	52.0	13.5	25.1
Own VCR	0.0	0.0	1.3	1.4	0.7
Own fridge	0.0	0.0	2.7	1.4	1.0
Own bicycle	1.3	2.6	16.0	0.4	5.3
Own motorcycle	0.0	0.0	1.3	0.0	0.3
n	77	77	75	74	303

Source: SDPI survey.
n: Sub-sample size.

Appendix Table 5.8
Women's say in decision making by sector

(Percentages)

Have say in decisions regarding	Sector				
	Incense stick making	Carpet weaving	Sack stitching	Prawn shelling	Total
Schooling	85.7	84.0	85.3	85.1	85.0
Marriage of daughters	85.7	83.8	85.3	85.1	85.0
Family matters	87.0	85.7	85.3	83.8	85.0
Household expenditure	88.3	85.7	84.0	82.4	85.1
n	77	77	75	74	303

Source: SDPI survey.
n: Sub-sample size.

Appendix Table 5.9
State of indebtedness by sector

Sector	Total stock of debt (Rs.)	Mean monthly household exp. (Rs.)	Ratio of debt stock to annual exp. (Rs.)
Incense stick making	9,431.82 (22,973.28)	4,103.13 (1683.58)	19.2
Carpet weaving	11,984.62 (14,283.67)	4,032.23 (1,523.99)	24.8
Sack stitching	22,587.76 (28,871.99)	5,113.29 (2,327.80)	36.8
Prawn shelling	19,188.14 (26,185.95)	4,370.34 (1551.56)	36.6
Total	15,511.62 (21,789.08)	4,400.41 (1,841.46)	-

Source: SDPI survey
Note: Parentheses contain standard deviations.

NOTES

1. Refer to Chapter 7 for a fuller discussion on a conceptualization of women's empowerment.
2. In a couple of instances, there are differences in the reports based on the qualitative sources and the quantitative data analysis. When this occurred, the differences are alluded to in the footnotes.
3. The term *Muhajir* literally means immigrants. The bulk of this community immigrated at the time of the partition of the subcontinent in 1947, though the immigration continued as families united and others moved. This community was a minority at the time of partition, but the most educated and advanced and shouldered the bulk of the administrative burden of the city, province and country via key positions in the civil service. As the other ethnic groups claimed their share of positions, the *muhajirs* felt sidelined and the spectacular rapid emergence of the MQM in the 1980s gave expression to this feeling of exclusion. Given their large numbers in Karachi, the party was immensely successful during the first elections fielding MQM candidates, but later split and the violent internecine fighting is one cause of Karachi's social instability.
4. Some households considered it inappropriate for girls to leave the house after the age of seven.
5. They were taught the *noorani quaida* (basic religious textbook) and Urdu textbooks.
6. The quantitative responses indicated that overall this was not a major issue (section 6.4).
7. Appendix Table 6.1 reports the distribution of children's time between play and other activities, by sector, based on an accounting of activities on the day prior to the field visit. On average, children played about one hour a day in the incense

stick sector, but up to 2.6 hours in the prawn-shelling sector in which work finished earlier.

8. Overall, about a quarter of the males household heads did not work. Appendix Table 5.2 reports the disaggregation by sector. About 42 per cent of the male household heads in the incense stick sector were not working, while this was the case for only 15 per cent of the males in the sack-stitching sector. This justifies our statement made in the conceptual framework in section 1.2 pertaining to home-based work that we do not rule out abuse of power by self-interested household heads.

9. Appendix Table 5.3 reports the average daily income and hours of work by sector.

10. Refer to Appendix Table 5.4 for the number of children and household size by sector. The variation between prawn-shelling households at 8.41 and carpet weaving households at 6.78 is considerable, though both were very high compared to the national average or the control group of households (refer to Notes, Chapter 6, No. 10). In view of the purposive sampling, it is not really possible to infer anything about the norms of different ethnic groups from this variation.

11. These include exceptional wartime conditions in which this practice was permitted e.g. the ability to treat all partners equally and the ability to support them well.

12. Appendix Tables 6.5 and 6.6 report the major ailments for the children and women by sector. Naturally, even though women and children were asked to report Home-Based Work related ailments, several that they cited were of a more general kind. However, in so far as Home-Based Work weakened workers, it reduced the immunity to other more common ailments and enhanced their negative impact.

13. The living conditions by sector or Home-Based Work activity is reported in Appendix Table 5.7. Judging from the facilities they had access to in their homes, the Gujrati sack stitching community was the least poor, followed by the Orangi (incense stick making), Korangi (carpet weaving) and finally the Machar (prawn shelling) community that was the poorest.

14. In view of East Bengal having been a part of Pakistan, Bengalis may be perceived as having a greater legitimacy in being in Pakistan.

15. Literally, this means 'to strive' though the popular interpretation is armed struggle. The field-team ran into some people who had fought against soldiers of the Soviet Union in Afghanistan. Getting in with *jihadi* groups could have been a means to establish a sense of identity and protection for the immigrants. However, given that they migrated from Burma due to religious persecution, they may have been predisposed towards extreme forms of religious practice.

16. For more details on this issue refer to section 6.5.

17. Refer to Appendix Table 5.8 with regard to women's decision making. This table indicates that women in this sector were slightly less 'empowered' on the indicated decision-making criteria than in the incense-stick making sector. The differences, however, are minor and overall all women have a lot of say in decisions pertaining to family matters, marriage, schooling and expenditure. Refer to Chapter 7 for an in-depth interpretation that clarifies why such decision making power does not amount to empowerment.

18. Appendix Table 5.9 reports the state of indebtedness by sector.

19. See Chap 6, Note 7 for mean training period by activity.

20. Leucorrhoea is a common gynecological ailment among poor women in Pakistan. Usually it is a result of malnutrition and an unhygienic environment. The symptoms are a white discharge, weakness and lethargy.

21. Alternatively, they could be paid by the piece. A carpet could take a whole family up to three months to complete and fetch an income of about Rs. 1,600.

22. Greater mobility was only relative. Even in this community, working outside the house by women was frowned upon and an important part of the reason why they opted for Home-Based Work. For more on female mobility refer to section 6.5.

23. Case study 2.6 in Annexure 2 indicates that the more educated women are capable of getting the respect of contractors.

24. *Machar* is also the word used in Urdu for the common mosquito.

25. See Table 5.1 for mean time distribution for children by sector, including that on home-based work.

26. Ethnic or kinship ties did not bind the contractor in this sector as in the cases of incense-stick making or sack stitching sectors.

27. Refer to the Annexure case studies 2.4 and 2.5.

Chapter Six
QUANTITATIVE DATA ANALYSIS: A GENDER FOCUS

6.1 INTRODUCTION

In this chapter we complement the findings reported in the last chapter that was based on qualitative information gathering. While we focused in the last chapter on the differences in the four sectors of home-based work that were the subject of study, here we investigate the issue of home-based work in a more generic sense with a focus on the conditions of women and children. In some cases, sector is used as a control variable in cross-tabulations and regression analysis to explore if there is a systematic difference. However, sector is not an important part of the story for this chapter.[1]

A few reminders and pointers to the reader regarding the nature of the data analysis are in order. First, given that the sample is purposive as explained in Chapter 3, the reader is reminded that the multivariate analysis and test statistics are only suggestive or indicative. Second, many of the questions allowed for multiple responses. Thus, in these cases, the analysis requires reporting results in terms of the percentage of responses by different response options. Thus, in the relevant tables, total responses (r) are reported rather than the sub-sample size (n).

As explained in Chapter 3, for every three home-based work households, we picked a household in the same neighbourhood where home-based work was not being done, and interviewed a woman and child from such households as in the case of the home based worker households. This sub-sample is the control group to compare with groups doing home-based work to evaluate information on health, schooling, work, and the quality of life in general. We also hired a doctor to accompany the field team to collect health information.

In the rest of this chapter, we explore some of the key aspects of home-based work identified above. These include conditions of work for children and women, the nature of the double burden of work, i.e. chores and child care, that women confront, the 'empowering' aspects of work, nutrition and the health impacts of home-based work for women and children, the impact of home-based work on child schooling, and finally, the expectations of the home-based workers from the state.

6.2   WHY HOME-BASED WORK?

As expected, most of the women are engaged in home-based work due to poverty. Inflation or poverty directly accounted for 40.4 per cent of the responses. However, the other responses were indirectly associated with poverty. Thus, another 31 per cent of the responses concerned supplementing family income and the rest pertained to paying off loans, or were associated with illness, death, disability or unemployment of some earning member of the household. About 9 per cent of the responses indicated that the women would have engaged in some other activity if another option were available. Only 1 per cent of the responses suggested that the women were doing this to earn spending money for themselves.

According to the women, most of the children were working at home (88 per cent of the responses) to supplement family income. Only 5 per cent of the responses suggested that the children were doing home-based work because the family preferred they stay at home. About 3 per cent of the responses suggested that the child might have found an alternative way to supplement family income if other options were available.

The mean age at which women in the sample began work was 20, and at the time of the survey, they had been working for an average of 12 years. Many (38 per cent responses) picked up the home-based work skills on their own, or were taught them by the family (20 per cent responses). Friends and neighbours accounted for another 38 per cent responses but the contractors only accounted for 4 per cent of the responses.

About a fourth (23 per cent) of the women started home-based work because they were approached by a contractor, and another fifth because they were approached by family or a neighbour. Approximately another fourth (23 per cent) simply picked it up because it was being done in the neighbourhood. Home-based work is predominantly a female activity. While there were an average of 1.41 adult women per household doing home-based work in our sample, only 0.11 men were engaged in it.[2] Alternatively, there was no adult male doing home-based work in 90 per cent of the households visited. Similarly, while an average of 1.40 girls per household were engaged in home-based work, there was an average of 0.51 boys per household engaged in it. Part of the reason for child labour was that over a quarter (26.1 per cent) of the male household heads did not work.

In 74 per cent of the 303 cases, women decided to work of their own volition and another 14.5 per cent responded that it was a joint decision. In only 11.5 per cent of the cases was this decision that of the husband's or the family's, without taking the woman's views into account. Eighty-four per cent of the women stated they preferred home-based work. However, 69 per cent of the respondents expressed this preference because of family pressure (51.4 per cent) or the pressure of relatives or neighbours (17.6 per cent). Of the 15.5 per cent who expressed a preference for factory work, more than half (56.5 per cent) did so because of better remuneration.[3] Over a third (36.9 per cent) expressed a preference for factory work because they found home-based work too hard (21.7 per cent), too hazardous (10.9 per cent) or too tedious (4.3 per cent).[4]

Most of the responses on the advantages of home-based work were actually disadvantages of alternatives. Only 3.4 per cent of the responses cited the lack of skills for outside work as a reason for doing home-based work and only a fifth of the responses cited the advantage of being able to watch over the kids. Thirty-eight per cent of the responses cited mobility problems or feeling unsafe going out as an advantage, and, once again, 37.1 per cent of the responses cited family or neighbourhood pressure against work outside the house.

6.3 WORK CONDITIONS

The bulk of the responses concerning the disadvantages of home-based work pertained to the negative health impacts (34.7 per cent) or fatigue (28.1 per cent). An untidy house was cited as a disadvantage by 13.9 per cent of the responses. Only 9.6 per cent of the responses cited less time for the family as a disadvantage. Perhaps the pressure of survival and the family at least being in the same premises accounts for the low response on this count. Child responses also indicated that the main disadvantages of home-based work were that it resulted in health problems (33.8) or was very tiring (30.9). It is significant that these responses dominated the 18.8 per cent who regretted having less time for play or for friends.

Women worked an average of 3.5 hours on home-based work alone. They worked on average a six-day week and two-thirds of them worked the whole year round. Of those who did not work the whole year around, 93 per cent said it was because work was not available the whole year around.[5] The mean daily household income derived from home-based work was Rs. 57.7.[6] This amounts to about one-third of the Rs. 172.1 earned by unskilled daily labour in November 1999 in Karachi.[7] However, it does not compare as unfavourably with the mean daily income of Rs. 84.8 earned by the non-home-based work earners in the household.

Children reported working an average of 3.7 hours during the day and 1.6 hours after sunset on home-based work.[8] They also worked a six-hour week and 58.4 per cent said they worked the whole year round. Of those who did not work the whole year, 87 per cent said this was because work was not available and 4 per cent said they did other work. Three-quarters of the children said that there were times when they did not perform the work well. The responses indicated that the consequences were: scolding by the family (28.9 per cent) or the contractor (19.7), a fine (14.4 per cent), a beating by the family (12.2) or a beating by the contractor (7.8).

For children, the average age of starting work was seven and a half years and they had been engaged in this work for an average of 3.6 years. Unlike the adults, most of the children (85.1 per cent) received training. The responses showed that the bulk of the training came from within the household (76.9 per cent), relatives/friends (5.6) or neighbours (7.5). Only 3.7 per cent of the responses indicated that the contractor provided any training. Again, unlike for adults, the average training period lasted 8.2 weeks. The high standard deviation of 19.3 weeks suggests that many children were viewed as trainees for a long time.[9] The frequency distribution showed that 84.4 per cent of the children received training for four weeks or less, but 6.6 per cent of the children were considered trainees for between 52 and 97 weeks.

In just over half the cases (51 per cent), piece rates had increased between two to three times over an average home-based work history of 12 years. Only 7 per cent of the women respondents recollected that piece rates had also been reduced, but few responded regarding why this was the case.[10] Almost three-fifths of the women kept a record of the work done in the household. Among those who did not, a quarter stated having had a difference of opinion with the contractor regarding the amount of work done. When this happened, in over half the cases, the contractor prevailed (53 per cent), in a quarter of the cases there was a compromise (26 per cent) and in one-tenth of the cases the women prevailed. Thus, the lack of power women had *vis a vis* the contractor is clear from these statistics.

In almost two-thirds of the cases (63 per cent), the contractor was late in paying for the work. In most cases (53 per cent), the delay was up to two weeks, and in another two-fifths of the cases, it was more than two weeks but less than a month. In five per cent of the cases, the delay was up to two months and in only two per cent of the cases greater than two months. However, a quarter of the respondents stated that there were occasions on which they were not paid at all.

About half the women did not work subject to a deadline. Of the remainder, 67 women (28 per cent), claimed that they were either fined or their rate was reduced, two-fifths said they had to forego payment and 29 per cent said that the activity was terminated by the contractor. If the work was judged to be faulty by the contractor, the product was rejected in a small number of cases (7 per cent). A quarter of the women said that the contractor asked for the product to be repaired, while 34 per cent said they were fined.

In all, 31 per cent of the women felt that the contractors made work difficult for them by engaging in malpractices. These included supplying poor quality material (19 per cent), miscounting, wrongly measuring or arbitrarily rejecting products. Women did not have much protection, since only 12 per cent of them had a written contract. Even so, 46 per cent of the women responded that they had a good working relationship with the contractor, 31 per cent felt it was indifferent and only 23 per cent thought it was bad.

We inquired about the causes for the bad working relationship and 37.2 per cent of the responses cited verbal (23.1) or physical (14.1) abuse. Too much work (10.9), poor pay (20.5), late payments (23.1), and malpractices (8.3) accounted for the other responses. Approximately the same percentage of children (18.9) viewed relations with the contractor to be bad. The stated responses included wanting too much work (12.6), poor pay (10.5 per cent), and late pay (11.6 per cent). However, it was disturbing to note that the main reasons cited for the bad relationship of the child with the contractor were verbal abuse (29.5 per cent) and physical abuse (28.5).

The doctor accompanying the field-team was asked to assess the nature of the work the children were engaged in from the perspective of the physical burden involved. According to this assessment, 15.3 per cent of the boys and 4.2 per cent of the girls were engaged in light to normal work respectively. However, 83.1 per cent of the boys and 94.3 per cent of the girls respectively were perceived as engaging in hard work. Only 1.7 per cent of the boys and 1.1 per cent of the girls respectively were engaged in extra hard work.

Women engaged in very little collective action to improve their work conditions, but there was considerable willingness to engage in it. Only 12.5 per cent of home-based workers (38) managed to negotiate a rate increase via collective action with other home-based workers. However, 53 per cent indicated a willingness to engage in such collective action. At the time of the survey, there were virtually no organizations capitalizing on this potential for collective action. Only two women indicated an association with an organization of any kind in a work related context.

Overall, women were not highly mobilized. Only five in all were associated with and participating in the activities of any welfare or other grassroots organization (none among the control group) and only ten (two among the control group) were accessing available services out of the 25 (seven in the control group) who knew of the presence of such organizations in their neighbourhood.

6.4 CONTRAST WITH THE CONTROL GROUP: CHILDCARE, HOUSEHOLD WORK AND DECISION-MAKING

Home-Based Work did not lighten the burden of child-care and chores that women had to do at home. A good way of investigating this was by comparing women doing home-based work with women in the control group. Prior to this comparison, a profile of the two groups of women and their households is provided to set the comparison in context. Table 6.1 below reports the marital status of the two groups.

Table 6.1

Marital status of women doing home-based work and women not doing home-based work

(Percentages)

Marital status	Women doing home-based work	Women not doing home-based work
Single	1.7	0.0
Married	84.2	92.6
Divorced	1.0	0.0
Separated	3.6	1.1
Widowed	9.6	6.4
n	303	94

Source: SDPI survey.
n: sub-sample size.

As might be expected, there were more widowed, separated, divorced and single women among those doing home-based work. While a quarter of the women in the home-based work group were the heads of the household, surprisingly, 22.3 per cent of the women also said this was the case for the control group. The mean age of the two groups of women was virtually identical at 32.3 years for the home-based work group and 32.5 years for the control group respectively. Three times more women in the control group were functionally educated (12.8 per cent) as compared to the home-based work group (4.3 per cent).

The two groups of households where women/children were doing home-based work and where such work was not being done differed in terms of their socio-economic background. Table 6.2 below provides a comparison in this regard.

Table 6.2
Socio-economic profile of households where women were doing home-based work and of households where women were not doing home-based work

Socio-economic profile	HHs where women were doing home-based work	HHs where women were not doing home-based work
Mean monthly expenditure (Rs.)	4,408.36 (1890.6)	4,575.02 (2,548.3)
Mean household size (nos.)	7.57 (2.35)	6.52 (2.47)
Mean monthly per capita expenditure (Rs.)	622.16 (287.57)	739.30 (388.10)
Living condition index@	6.78 (2.10)	9.14 (2.47)
n	303	94

Source: SDPI survey.
Notes: Parentheses contain standard deviations.
@ The living condition index ranges from a minimum possible of 1 for the poorest household to 18 for the most well off. Houses scored 0 for the worst living condition on various categories, 1 for a slightly better state, 2 for a lower middle class condition on a particular category and 3 for a mark of wealth. Only households possessing a VCR could have scored a 3 (two among home-based work households and three among the control group). Thus, the poorest household lived in a *kaccha* house, had access to community water supply, did not have access to running water or electricity and possessed no

durable assets like a radio, cassette player, fridge, TV, VCR or a source of transportation. For more details on this index, see Appendix 6.1.

n: sample size.

While the two groups were similar with regard to mean expenditure, the mean household size of the control group was significantly lower and this resulted in a significantly higher per-capita monthly expenditure.[11] SPDC (2001, p. 29) reported a mean monthly per capita expenditure cut off for defining poverty in urban Sindh to be Rs. 610 for 1996-97. Inflating this to 2001, and using the subsequent cut-off of Rs. 751.4, 76.9 per cent home-based work households and 64.9 per cent non-home-based work households were below the poverty line.[12] This compares very unfavourably with the 20 per cent households in income poverty in urban Sindh, calculated using 1996-97 data (p. 30). The relatively higher prosperity of the control group was reflected in the life-style as judged by household facilities and assets, which is significantly better for households not doing home-based work.[13] This is also reflected in a substantially greater investment in health as evident from Table 6.3 below and also from the results reported in the sections 6.6 and 6.7 that follow.

There were also other differences between the two groups in a substantive sense. Three-fourths of households doing home-based work had contracted a loan in the last six months compared to 45.7 per cent for those not doing home-based work. The mean accumulated debt of Rs. 15,511 was also higher compared to Rs. 13,946 for the control group, though not by much. The pattern of borrowing was quite similar, except that while 23 per cent responses for the home-based work category borrowed from the contractor, only 10.7 per cent of non-home-based work households borrowed from their employers. Fewer than five per cent of the loans in both cases were interest based and while 37.9 per cent of the households doing home-based work expected to pay off their debt based on this work, 84.6 per cent of the non-home-based work households expected to retire their debt from their savings.

We also utilized logit analysis to rigorously identify the predictors of home-based work and the results are reported in Appendix Table 6.2.1. The main predictors of households likely to take on home-based work were household size and living conditions (inverse association).[14] Part of the reason for the greater prosperity of the non-home-based work households was the slightly higher number of male earners per household (mean earners of 1.16 compared to 0.98).[15]

Table 6.3
Monthly expenditure patterns of households doing home-based
work and the control group

(Rs.)

Items	HHs doing home-based work		HHs not doing home-based work	
	Expenditures	% of total	Expenditures	% of total
Items of daily use	3294.52 (1643.59)	74.7	3056.88 (1867.20)	66.8
House rent	127.23 (283.79)	2.9	153.19 (347.87)	3.3
Health	341.82 (345.36)	7.8	462.51 (1037.31)	10.1
Schooling	110.15 (328.42)	2.5	117.83 (212.38)	2.6
Transportation	117.55 (216.05)	2.7	212.23 (395.70)	4.6
Gas	114.69 (132.11)	2.6	149.04 (265.06)	3.3
Electricity	116.11 (151.86)	2.6	176.44 (248.74)	3.9
Water	136.99 (238.96)	3.1	118.24 (168.62)	2.6
Other	49.32 (156.32)	1.1	129.04 (724.87)	2.8
Total	4,408.36 (1,838.63)	100	4575.41 (2543.30)	100
n	303		94	

Source: SDPI survey.
Notes: Parentheses contain standard deviations.

Only 28 per cent of the women not doing home-based work said
they would do it should the opportunity present itself. The rest had
no intention of taking on such work. The reason, according to a
quarter of the women respondents, was that they had enough
income. Twenty per cent cited various other disadvantages of home-
based work, another 10 per cent mentioned health reasons and 6
per cent mentioned that it was dangerous for children. Only one per
cent said that they prefer not to engage in it because they would
rather send their children to school.

Given the comparative profile of the two groups of women, we report below the household responsibilities they bear.

Table 6.4
Child-care and other household responsibilities of women doing home-based work and women not doing home-based work

(Percentages)

HH responsibilities	Women doing home-based work	Women not doing home-based work
Childcare	86.5	88.3
Shopping	25.4	29.8
Cleaning	74.3	80.9
Washing dishes	79.5	88.3
Washing clothes	82.5	87.2
Ironing clothes	8.6	36.2
Mending	2.6	9.6
Cooking	80.2	85.1
Caring for sick/elderly	14.5	18.1
Caring for HH members	60.1	47.9
House repairs	0.3	0
Household items repair	2.0	0
n	303	94

Source: SDPI survey.

As evident from Table 6.4, doing home-based work does not lighten women's childcare and other domestic work responsibilities by much. Across the board, there is a slightly higher responsibility for chores assumed by women not doing home-based work with a notable difference in mending and ironing responsibilities assumed by the control group of women. However, women doing home-based work assumed much more responsibility for caring for household members than was true for the control group.

A comparison of the time profile for the two groups of women is revealing of a better quality of life for women not doing home-based work. In general, women doing home-based work spend about sixteen hours a day awake. Based on activities the day prior to the survey, the average amount of time allocated to work and leisure is indicated in Table 6.5 below.

Table 6.5

Time profile of women doing home-based work and women not
doing home-based work

(Hours)

Time profile	Women doing home-based work	Women not doing home-based work
HOME-BASED WORK	3.49	-
HH chores	4.32	4.94
Leisure	1.49	2.11
n	303	94

Source: SDPI survey.

Note: These hours are based on activities on the day prior to the survey
and the reported time spent doing home-based work is much lower
than the 7 hours reported in Appendix Table 5.3 based on a carefully
constructed time profile.

Women doing home-based work spend an additional four hours a
day working and about as much time doing household chores. The
means leisure time for women not doing home-based work was 2.1
hours. This was mostly spent watching TV and visiting with
relatives, friends or neighbours.

Over three-fourths of the women doing home-based work
indicated that their domestic work burden was made lighter by
help from others. However, 87 per cent responded that daughters
picked up the burden of domestic work and 5 per cent responded
that sons did so. Only one per cent of the respondents said that
husbands pitched in. About a third of the women mentioned that
family members react negatively because home-based work meant
less time for chores. Angry responses of family members included
fighting (55.5) and verbal (28.3) and physical abuse (7.6). It is
distressing to note that 71.4 per cent of the women felt that home-
based work affects their child-care abilities. Of the 28.6 per cent
(72) who thought otherwise, 58 per cent said this was because they
had to work much harder and a fifth said this was because other
family members were pitching in. By contrast, 83.3 per cent of the
boys and 87.4 per cent of the girls doing home-based work felt that
the family had enough time to take care of them. The responses to
this question were 100 per cent and 98 per cent in the affirmative
for boys and girls respectively among the control group of children
not doing home-based work.

Once again, we utilized information collected for a control group
to assess if there was a systematic difference in women's autonomy
and control between women doing home-based work and those not
engaged in such work. Surprisingly, there seems to be less constraint

on the mobility of women not doing home-based work. While two-fifths of the women doing home-based work said they are free to go outside the house when they need to, half the women not doing home-based work said this was the case. However, of those who said yes, while 42 per cent of the women doing home-based work said they needed some male's permission to go out, 47 per cent of the women in the control group needed such permission.[16]

Once again, we were surprised to find that women doing home-based work did not have notably more say in household decision-making as indicated by Table 6.6 below.

Table 6.6
Participation in decision making by women doing home-based work and women not doing home-based work

(Percentages)

Participation in decisions regarding	Women doing home-based work	Women not doing home-based work
Schooling	84.5	84.0
Marriage	84.5	83.0
Expenditures	85.5	83.0
Other family issues	85.1	85.1
n	303	94

Source: SDPI survey

Autonomy can also be manifest in being able to control earned resources. Women retained 84.5 per cent of their earnings from home-based work. Some of them (9.5 per cent) managed to save and 12.5 per cent engaged in saving via a 'committee' system.[17] Only three women said they were retaining income for their daughter's dowry. About a fifth of the income (23 per cent) was retained for personal expenses and almost two-fifths of the responses suggested this was to support a personal habit including the chewing of tobacco or various local equivalents. The other significant categories on which there were high responses included food (11.5 per cent), health (13.2 per cent), children's education (7 per cent) and children's other needs (13 per cent).[18]

6.5. NUTRITION AND HEALTH

We contrasted the nutrition and health status of children and women engaged in home-based work with children and women in the control group. Table 6.7 below reports on the immunization history of children within the two groups.

Table 6.7

Immunization history by gender for children doing home-based work and children not doing home-based work

Vaccination status	Children doing home-based work		Children not doing home-based work	
	Boys	Girls	Boys	Girls
Not vaccinated	73.1	62.0	29.3	49.1
Partially vaccinated	3.8	5.6	17.1	11.3
Fully vaccinated	23.1	30.8	51.2	39.6
Vaccination status unknown	-	1.6	2.4	-
n	50	250	41	53

Source: SDPI survey

It is quite evident from Table 6.7 above that families not doing home-based work also invest much more in the human capital of their children. Perhaps this is due to the availability of more resource and higher literacy rates of adults in non-home-based work households. This was evident in schooling decisions also (see section 6.6). The doctor judged 80.8 per cent and 72.1 per cent respectively of the boys and girls to be anemic among the children doing home-based work and this was the case for 65.0 and 67.3 per cent respectively of the children in the control group.[19] Thus, both groups revealed a very high incidence of anemia, although girls fared better in this regard. Diet has much to do with anemia among children and we turn now to a review of food intake.[20]

Appendix Table 6.2.3 contrasts nutritional intake. Overall, the nutritional intake was poor, but consumption among children was better than among women.[21] Within the control group, consumption was better for girls for meat and legumes, while it was better for milk and fruits for boys. Among children doing home-based work, this pattern was similar. Overall, the nutritional intake of the control group was better than the home-based work group. Almost nine-tenths of the children, both boys and girls in both groups, responded that they got enough staple (rice or *roti*) to eat. Table 6.8 below provides some background information about the two groups of children.

Table 6.8

Age and physical characteristics by gender for children doing
home-based work and children not doing home-based work

Activities	Children doing home-based work		Children not doing home-based work	
	Boys	Girls	Boys	Girls
Age	10.08	10.84	8.62	9.57
	(2.36)	(2.24)	(2.77)	(2.88)
Height (cms.)	126.29	134.88	121.73	124.49
	(18.10)	(25.59)	(19.79)	(1.60)
Weight (kgs.)	24.54	28.32	22.04	24.69
	(7.22)	(9.20)	(7.13)	(10.53)
n	52	251	41	53

Source: SDPI survey.
Notes: Parentheses contain standard deviations.

Girls for both groups are a little older, taller and weigh more.
Also, children engaged in home-based work are older, taller and
weigh more than children in the control group.[22] Almost all children
doing home-based work (94.2 per cent boys and 97.6 per cent girls)
compared to three fifths of the boys and two thirds of the girls in
the control group claimed to have an ailment at the time of the
survey. Again, most of the children (88.0 boys and 85.0 per cent
girls) attributed the ailment to the home-based work they were
doing. We inquired about 25 possible maladies or ailments and
have reported the main responses (where response was five per cent
or more in any category) in Table 6.9 below.

In general, the gender differences are not large across the two
groups. Children not doing home-based work had a higher
percentage response on common maladies like fever and colds, but
they were not susceptible to work related ailments that children
doing home-based work were exposed to. These ailments include
pain in the back, limbs, joints, blisters, cracking skin and dis-
colorization. While only 8.5 per cent of the children in the control
group responded that they needed medical treatment but could not
afford it, this was the response of 42.7 per cent of the children
engaged in home-based work. Conversely, 72.9 per cent of the
children in the control group got medical treatment and were
released immediately, while this was the case for only 32.5 per cent
of the home-based work group of children. Finally, we inquired
about the frequency of illness in the past six months and the mean

number of times for home-based work was 5.2 times (almost once every month) while it was 3.8 times for the control group.[23] Only in about five per cent of the cases, for children engaged in home-based work, did the contractor assist with any treatment.

Table 6.9
Ailments by gender for children doing home-based work and
children not doing home-based work

(Percentage responses)

Ailments	Children doing home-based work		Children not doing home-based work	
	Boys	Girls	Boys	Girls
General (fever, cold etc.)	17.2	17.8	29.4	32.6
Cough	14.7	15.2	16.2	23.3
Back pain	10.4	11.4	2.9	1.2
Anemia	10.4	11.5	10.3	9.3
Pain in some limb	6.7	7.9	1.3	0.0
Pain in joint	7.4	7.9	2.6	0.0
Stomach/belly pain	1.8	2.5	7.4	2.3
Blisters	5.5	3.1	2.9	2.3
Skin problems	4.9	3.0	0.0	2.3
r	163	827	68	86

Source: SDPI survey.

The control group women revealed better food intake than that of women doing home-based work. While a fifth of the control group of women consume a cup of milk per day, only 7 per cent of the home-based work women did so. Both groups ate vegetables only a few times a week and fruit about once a week or less. While the median consumption of meat for the home-based work group was about once a week (46 per cent), a fifth of the women in the control group ate meat a few times a week or more.

Nine-tenths of the women reported having health problems as a result of home-based work, but 79 per cent of the women in the control group also reported having health problems. We also asked women about the kinds of maladies or afflictions they suffered from and the responses, significant in terms of percentages responding, are reported in Table 6.10 below.

Table 6.10

Ailments by gender of those doing home-based work and women
not doing home-based work

(Percentage responses)

Ailments	Women not doing home-based work	Women doing home-based work	Men doing home-based work
General (fever, cold etc.)	31.2	17.7	21.6
Ear infection	4.5	0.8	2.0
Cough	20.1	15.2	21.6
Asthma	0.6	0.9	5.9
Skin problems	0.6	2.0	9.8
Back pains	1.9	11.2	15.7
Pain in limbs	0.6	7.7	-
Pain in joints	1.3	4.6	3.9
Anemia	9.7	11.5	-
General body pains	4.5	2.4	-
Exhaustion	5.2	1.7	3.9
r	154	990	51

Source: SDPI survey.

Again, women not doing home-based work had higher percentage
responses on general ailments. They suffered from, as expected,
fewer pains in the back, limbs and joints. Surprisingly,
proportionately fewer women doing home-based work complained
about exhaustion. As in the case of the children, only 16.7 per cent
of the women in the control group responded that they could not
afford the needed treatment while this was the response for 53.9
per cent of the women doing home-based work. Conversely, 59.7 per
cent of the women in the control group got the needed treatment
and were released immediately, while this was the response for
only 26.3 per cent of the women doing home-based work. About one-
tenth of the men did home-based work (11.2 per cent) for an average
of two and a half hours per day. Two thirds of them complained of
health problems related to this work. There was a higher incidence
of reported back-pains, asthma and skin problems than for women.

Women in the control group reported getting ill an average of 4.8
times in the past six months at the time of the survey while women
engaged in home-based work reported getting ill 6.8 times during
the same period (on average more than once a month).[24] The
contractor assisted with the treatment in only 2.5 per cent of the
cases of home-based work related illnesses and provided health
related safety equipment in only 1.3 per cent of the cases.

As Table 6.11 below shows, both access to and expense of health care were problems and more so for the home-based work group relative to the control group.

Table 6.11
Percentage responding in the affirmative regarding easy access and affordability of health facilities

(Percentages)

Medical facility	Access		Affordability	
	Women not doing home-based work	Women doing home-based work	Women not doing home-based work	Women doing home-based work
Government dispensary	12.8	14.2	-	-
Private doctor	5.3	4.3	63.8	12.9
Hakeem (herbal doctor)	14.9	22.4	59.6	11.6
Homeopath	17.0	21.1	59.6	11.6
Government hospital	12.8	14.2	-	-
Private hospital	5.3	4.3	35.1	4.3
n	94	303	94	303

Source: SDPI survey.

As Table 6.11 above indicates, access was low for both groups. Consistent with earlier findings on treatment, the home-based work group indicated that medical treatment was much less affordable than did the control group. This difference reflects the ability of the control group households to invest more in human capital partly because of their smaller household size and higher per capita income.

6.6   CHILD SCHOOLING AND OTHER ACTIVITIES

Only a fifth (19.8) of the children doing home-based work were in school in contrast to more than double that percentage (42.6) among children not doing home-based work. Responses on why children were not in school from the two groups and their mothers are tabulated below.

Table 6.12

The main reasons why children doing home-based work and
children not doing home-based work were not in school

(Percentages responses)

Reasons for not being in school	Reasons of children doing home-based work	Reasons of children not doing home-based work	Reasons of mothers of children doing home-based work	Reasons of mothers of children not doing home-based work
School does not provide a better job	0.6	-	-	-
School too far	2.5	8.2	1.4	9.8
School too expensive	65.2	69.4	68.9	75.6
Prefer to stay at home	2.8	4.1	1.4	2.4
Family needs income from work/poverty	27.8	NA	19.4	NA
Parents think school is worthless	0.9	6.1	0.7	2.4
r	316	49	289	41

Source: SDPI survey.
r = number of responses.

Table 6.12 above only documents the main responses. The
surprising convergence is that, in both cases, expense appears to be
keeping children away from school. There is, perhaps not
surprisingly, remarkable consistency in this regard in the response
of the children and parents. Also, as earlier indicated, poverty, or
the need to supplement family income, was an issue as evident
from 28 per cent of the responses for children doing home-based
work. Women doing home-based work, as a group, understated the
importance of this factor and overstated the number of children in
school relative to the children's responses.[25] Only nine per cent of
the children doing home-based work thought that this work
interfered in any way in their schooling, mostly because they got
tired or work left little time for schooling. Of the 42 children who
dropped-out from school, the majority (57.1) did so because parents
did not have enough money for school.

Another way of exploring this issue was asking children what
their reasons for home-based work were. A tabulation of the
responses showed that only one per cent responses indicated

children working because they did not like school. Over four-fifths of the responses (82.7) pertained to the need to add to family income because of poverty, inflation, loans or the illness, disability or death of earning members in the family. This then confirms the earlier findings of why children engage in home-based work and are not in school.

Children were also asked what they would prefer to do if given a choice. Children not enrolled in school among those doing home-based work overwhelmingly indicated a desire to attend school (59.6 and 57.7 per cent responses among boys and girls respectively) and others indicated a preference for combining school with work or play (23.6 and 24.1 per cent responses among boys and girls respectively). Among the children in the control group, 81 per cent of the boy's responses and 85 per cent of the girl's responses expressed a desire to attend school for those children not enrolled in school.

We explored the determinants of schooling rigorously by using regression analysis. One reason for doing this was to see if household prosperity is a determinant of schooling and to see if there was an income threshold beyond which households start enrolling children. In fact, as the results reported in Appendix Table 6.2.2 show, there is a strong association of household prosperity and child schooling among home-based work households. The relationship is positive, significant and linear.[26] The living condition index and per capita household expenditure had a positive and significant association with enrollment, thus confirming the subjective responses of why children are not in school. By the same token, household indebtedness had a strong negative and significant association with the household enrollment ratio.

We explored time children spent in home-based work and other activities by gender and compared this to the time profile of the children in the control group, based on what they did a day prior to the survey, to get a sense of the quality of life of the children doing home-based work.

Table 6.13

Time allocation to home-based work and other activities by gender for children doing home-based work and children not doing home-based work

() [OK]

Activities	Children doing home-based work		Children not doing home-based work	
	Boys	Girls	Boys	Girls
HOME-BASED WORK	2.04 (2.42)	3.40 (3.39)	-	-
Chores	1.17 (1.48)	2.35 (1.96)	0.9 (1.48)	1.51 (1.60)
Play	2.67 (2.45)	1.40 (2.06)	3.44 (2.71)	2.64 (2.14)
School work	2.67 (2.45)	1.40 (2.06)	1.93 (2.75)	1.66 (2.43)
n	52	251	41	53

Source: SDPI survey.
Notes: Parentheses contain standard deviations.

For children doing home-based work, based on F-tests, it is quite clear that boys spend significantly less time doing home-based work and chores than girls and significantly more on play and school work. This gender pattern is also evident in the control group, although these children play more and spend less time doing chores. We explored the nature of chores further and report the results based on the responses below.

Other than shopping, girls were relied on much more heavily than boys for chores for both groups of children. A higher percentage of boys went shopping, since this activity required stepping out of the house, something discouraged among girls for cultural reasons. The surprise was the high reliance on boys for childcare, among children engaged in home-based work. As expected from earlier results, there was a much higher reliance on children for chores in the home-based work group compared to the control group.

Table 6.14
Time allocation to home-based work and other activities
by gender for children doing home-based work and
children not doing home-based work

(Percentage responses)

Chores	Children doing home-based work		Children not doing home-based work	
	Boys	Girls	Boys	Girls
Childcare	42.5	50.4	29.0	28.9
Shopping	80.0	21.7	87.1	10.5
Cleaning	24.4	85.7	16.1	94.7
Washing dishes	13.3	80.9	9.7	76.3
Washing clothes	2.2	52.2	-	26.3
Mending	-	1.3	-	-
Cooking	2.2	37.2	6.5	26.3
Pressing clothes	-	4.8	3.2	5.3
Caring for elderly and others	-	11.3	9.7	7.9
Repair/maintenance	-	0.8	-	-
None	13.5	8.4	24.4	22.6
n	52	251	41	53

Source: SDPI survey.

Children's play also revealed an interesting pattern also as
indicated below.

Table 6.15
Time allocation to play activities by gender for children doing
home-based work and children not doing home-based work

(Percentage responses)

Play activities	Children doing home-based work		Children not doing home-based work	
	Boys	Girls	Boys	Girls
Games	35.5	25.4	19.6	4.6
Watching TV	11.8	13.7	23.2	20.0
Friends	42.1	27.0	57.1	61.5
No time for play	3.9	15.9	1.8	4.6
N	52	251	41	53

Source: SDPI survey.

Children in the control group participated less in games (particularly
girls), watched more TV and spent more time with friends. Most
notable is that less than half of the responses for girls doing

home-based work, compared to the control group, indicated spending time with friends. Also, there were three times more responses suggesting that girls doing home-based work had no time at all for play.

6.7 GOVERNMENT ASSISTANCE

Both the qualitative and quantitative findings revealed little about the nature of assistance required and hence both responses are merged in this section. The qualitative findings indicate that at least the Bengali and Burmese communities expected little from the state, since they did not view themselves as citizens. A question about expectations from the state puzzled them, and some responded that they wanted money. Others asked that reasonable social and physical infrastructure, particularly education, healthcare and sanitation, should be provided.

The quantitative analysis indicated that of the third who responded to the question of what kind of assistance they would like from the government, or some other organization, technical training (31.5), credit (27.2) and framing better policies (28.3) accounted for the bulk of responses. However, the low response rate on this question indicates the pessimism women felt about the likelihood of anything concrete being done for them or their children.

SUMMARY OF FINDINGS

As could be expected, poverty and related factors are the main motivation for engaging in home-based work for women and children. This is mostly work taken on by women and girls. In over a quarter of the cases (26 per cent) in which the head of the household was a male, he was not doing any work and relying on the earnings of home-based work of the women and children. Women could have opted for work outside the house that could be less hazardous. However, almost two-fifths reported there were mobility problems in doing this and another two-fifths reported that family or neighbourhood pressures keep them at home.

Both women and children identified the negative health impacts or fatigue as the main disadvantage of home-based work. Children worked an average of about five hours on home-based work and on average started when they were seven and a half years old. The doctor accompanying the field team assessed the work done by 83 per cent of the boys and 94 per cent of the girls to be 'hard.' Children paid a price for mistakes and in about a tenth of the cases were beaten by the contractor.

Almost three-quarters of the women felt that home-based work affected their ability to engage in childcare. After spending seven hours doing home-based work, they spent another four on household chores. Only one per cent of the women responded that men assisted in anyway in lessening their work burden, and in fact, a third of the women reported that family members reacted negatively or harshly because home-based work meant less time for household chores. As expected, 87 per cent responded that daughters came to their assistance and 5 per cent responded that sons did so.

Judging by comparisons with the control group, the earnings from home-based work did not lead to any empowerment of the women when judged in terms of mobility, greater say in household decision making or independence in expending earned income. Control group households were relatively better off, and women and children in the control group enjoyed a better quality of life in terms of both leisure time and health. Any positive change in the lives of women doing home-based work appears remote as gender roles are reproduced among children e.g. girls do more domestic work than boys. Similarly, women's condition of work and bargaining and organizing ability are weak, so that women's chances of empowering themselves are low.

Children in the control group had a better immunization record, diet and suffered much less from anemia and other traditional ailments. Almost all the children in the home-based work group complained of some work related ailment. Pain in the back, joints, blisters and skin problems occurred with the greatest frequency. These children also had much less access to health care than children in the control group. The incidence of pain in the back, limbs and joints was much higher for women doing home-based work compared to the control group. Also, the incidence of illness, averaging more than once a month, was much higher. They also found health care to be much less accessible and affordable than did women in the control group.

School enrollment among the non-home-based work household eligible children at 42.6 per cent was over twice that of the home-based work group (19.8 per cent). Interestingly, between two-thirds and three-fourths of both groups of children and women mentioned school expense as the main reason why children were not in school. Only 28 per cent of the children and a fifth of the mothers mentioned home-based work as the reason why children were not in school. Further, less than a tenth of the children doing home-based work thought that it interfered in schooling because the work made them too tired.

The desire for schooling was also very high in both groups. About two-thirds of those working and not going to school said they would prefer to go to school and another quarter said they would like to combine attending school with work or play. Similarly, over four-fifths of the children in the control group not enrolled expressed a desire to attend school. Children not engaged in home-based work had a better quality of life otherwise in terms of more time spent at play and less time spent at work or chores.

The contractors generally paid late for the work done and in some cases did not pay at all. They had assisted only one per cent of the women and under five per cent of the children in the treatment of ailments that resulted from the home-based work. Despite this, only a quarter of the women felt their relationship with the contractor was not good. There was virtually no organization working with women to assist them to better their pay and working conditions. Over half the women indicated a willingness to be part of some kind of collective action to improve their working conditions if provided some kind of leadership and assistance.

Overall, women and children doing home-based work suffered greatly from the health hazards of home-based work, had less leisure time and spent as much or more time on household chores. Thus, one can say without reservation that their quality of life was much worse anyway, and so making the work more palatable and the remuneration fairer are important policy issues.

NOTES

1. The main reason is that there is little variation across sectors as evident from the appendix tables in Chapter 3. However, even if there is variation, in most cases it is not interesting (policy is not sector specific). The sector story is of interest with regards to work hazards and production chains and this has been captured in Chapters 4 and 5.

2. On average, there was one (0.98) non-home-based work earner in a household in which home-based work was being done. The mean earning members in the non-home-based work households were 1.16.

3. Note, this 15.5 per cent would appear to be different from the 9 per cent who had responded that they would take up other work if it was available. However, the context in which the responses are solicited are somewhat different. In one case, the women were asked to respond on whether or not they would actually take up some other activity if it were available. In the other case, they are merely asked to state a preference. Thus, expressing a preference for factory work does not mean they would actually take it up if it were available.

4. In most cases, women's stated preference for factory work is an abstract preference since they generally do not have first-hand experience of factory work.

5. Only 8 per cent of the children (24) shifted to other work during the year, and of these, ten did domestic work and seven engaged in another home-based work activity.

6. This was generally from one activity. There were only twelve households in our sample engaged in two activities. In only one of the 303 households was any home-based work related expense incurred. For mean daily income and working hours by sector, refer to Appendix Table 5.3.

7. Government of Pakistan, *Economic Survey*, Statistical Bulletin (2000, p. 144). The dollar traded by authorized dealers for about Rs. 52 in mid 2000, so that home-based work contributed just over $ 1 per day to household income, Government of Pakistan, State Bank of Pakistan, Statistical Annexure (2000, p. 91).

8. See Appendix 5.1 for the time children spent by sector in home-based work and other activities. The Pearson's correlation coefficient between age and hours worked for children was 0.24. While this was significant at the 1 per cent level, the correlation is low.

9. For sack stitching and prawn-shelling, the mean training is about two weeks, for incense-stick making 6 weeks and for carpet making 21 weeks.

10. A succeeding paragraph indicates that this was one form of fine imposed by the contractor.

11. The F-statistic of 9.97 per cent was significant at the 1 per cent level of confidence. The average household size in urban Sindh in the 1998 Population Census was 5.8, so that home-based work households were way above the reference group [Government of Pakistan, Economic Survey, Statistical Appendix, (2001, p. 132)].

12. The conversion factor for inflating the cut-off poverty line was computed using the general consumer price index, Government of Pakistan, *Economic Survey*, Statistical Appendix, (2001, p. 79).

13. The F-statistic of 49.1 is significant at the 1 per cent level.

14. While these two variables were highly significant and the model is successful in predicting who is likely to be engaged in home-based work, the overall fit of the model, as judged by the pseudo R bar square, is low.

15. The F-statistic is 3.65 and it is significant at the 6 per cent level of probability. In both cases, the number of non-resident relatives contributing to household income is negligible.

16. For a more detailed discussion of women's empowerment issues, see Chapter 7. Note here the limited notion of 'freedom': women are free to go outside but need permission to do so.

17. The generic form this takes is that a group of individuals, with mutual trust, agree to pool an equal amount each month and the lump sum accrues via rotation to each member of the group until all get the pooled funds once. The 'committee can subsequently be continued for more rounds.

18. Most of the earnings from home-based work was turned over to the parents by both girls and boys (over 90 per cent). A quarter of the children retained some of the earnings, and ninety per cent of them spent it all.

19. These rates of anemia are much higher than among the general urban population. Government of Pakistan (1998, p. 63) indicates anemia among urban 5-14 year old girls and boys to be 40 and 32.5 per cent respectively.

20. Anemia could have been even higher but for the high fish diet among most of the communities surveyed. Not surprisingly, the incidence of anemia, as observed by the doctor, is much higher than the children's own perception of whether they are anemic as reported in Table 6.9.

21. The intake of milk, vegetables, fruit, pulses and meat was much below the average dietary intake of these foods among the general urban population for persons 5 years and above for 1990-94, Government of Pakistan. (1998a, p. 47).
22. This result may be suggesting that parents put their stronger children to work.
23. The F-statistic is 21.3, which indicates a statistically significant difference at the 1 per cent confidence level. The incidence was identical for boys and girls in the control group where as in the HOME-BASED WORK group, the incidence at (5.77) for boys was significantly higher than that for girls (5.03) at the 5 per cent confidence level.
24. The F-statistic was 33.4 and the difference in the means in the two groups was significant at the 1 per cent level of confidence.
25. Not reported in Table 6.12
26. We explored threshold effects using both a logit model (1 if going to school, 0 otherwise) and with the household schooling ratio as a dependent variable. We used per capita household expenditures to classify the universally low expenditure households into the upper-low expenditure, middle-low expenditure, and low expenditure categories. We included two of the categories as dummy variables (one being the base) in both the logit and OLS (ordinary least square) regression models, but found neither to be significant. As such, we concluded that threshold effects were not important, and that the association of per capita household expenditure and schooling was linear.

References

Government of Pakistan, 2000, 2001, *Economic Survey 1999-2000, 2000-2001*, Economic Advisors Wing, Finance Division, Islamabad.

Government of Pakistan, 1998, *Compendium on Gender Statistics*, Federal Bureau of Statistics, Islamabad.

Government of Pakistan, 1998a, *National Health Survey of Pakistan 1990-94*, Pakistan Medical Research Council, Islamabad.

Government of Pakistan, 2000, *Annual Report*, State Bank of Pakistan, Islamabad.

Social Policy Development Center (SPDC), 2001, *Social Development in Pakistan: Annual Review 2000* (Karachi: Oxford University Press).

APPENDIX 6.1

Scoring method for living conditions index

We calculated the living conditions index by assigning weights to various facilities and consumer durables accessible to a household as indicated below. Weights were counted and households ranked according to the scores achieved. The range of scores varied from 2 to 14.

The weights for the living conditions index were as follows:

NATURE OF BUILDING OF THE HOUSE

0   Katcha
2   Pakka
1   Katcha-pakka

SOURCE OF DRINKING WATER FOR THE HOUSEHOLD
2   Tap in the household
0   Neighbourhood pump
0   Purchased from supplier
0   Public Pump

NATURE OF TOILET FACILITY
2   Private/flush
1   Private/septic tank
1   Shared
0   Public/outdoors
0   Open hole in ground

ELECTRIFICATION
1   Yes
0   No

WATER SUPPLY
1   Yes
0   No

OWNERSHIP STATUS OF THE HOUSEHOLD DWELLING
2   Owned
1   Provided free by employer
1   Subsidized by employer, either private or government/public
    ownership (amount paid per month)
1   Rented from private owner (amount paid per month)
1   Rented from government/public ownership (amount paid per
    month)
1   Pay *bhatta* (Form of rent paid to professional land grabber)

CONSUMER DURABLES
Radio
1   Yes
0   No

Cassette player
1   Yes
0   No

Fridge
2 Yes
0 No

TV
1 Yes
0 No

VCR
3 Yes
0 No

MODE OF TRANSPORTATION
1 Bicycle
2 Motorcycle
0 Public transport (bus)
0 Private transport (wagon)

Appendix 6.2.1
Binary logistic regression to identify predictors of home-based
work
(Dependent variable: Households engage in home-based work=1,
otherwise=0)

Independent variable	Co-efficient	Wald
Constant	0.731	0.291
PCHEXP	0.000	0.004
PCHEXPSQ	0.000	0.105
LCINDEX	-0.250*	14.839
DEBT	0.000	0.608
HHSIZE	0.288*	8.765
FEMRATIO	1.485	2.303
-2 Log likelihood	228.34	

Source: SDPI survey
Notes: Dependent variable definitions
    HHSIZE   = Household size
    LCINDEX   = Living condition index (see Appendix 4.1)
    DEBT   = Household debt
    PCHHEXP   = Per capita household expenditure
    PCHEXPSQ = Per capita household expenditure squared
    FEMRATIO = Ratio of females to total household size
    *   = Significant at least at the 1% level.
Overall correct predictions were 82 per cent and the Nagelkerke R
Square was .19. Sector dummy variables were all insignificant.

Appendix Table 6.2.2
Determinants of schooling
(Dependent variable: Ratio of school-going children
to school-going aged children) @

Independent Variables	Co efficient
Constant	-0.1890
	(-1.41)
PCHEXP	4.820 E-04**
	(2.11)
PCHHEXPSQ	-2.668E-07**
	(2.00)
LCINDEX	2.678 E-02
	(3.74)
DEBT	-2.675 E-06*
	(2.84)
HHSIZE	1.135 E-02
	(1.11)
HOME-BASED WORKHH	- 2.638 E-02
	(-0.51)
F–statistic	4.85*
R bar squared	0.08
n	273

Source: SDPI survey.
Notes: Independent variable definitions as in Appendix Table 6.2.1.
Home-Based Work HH = Households doing home-based work
The mean and standard deviation of the dependent variable are .23
and .36 respectively. Sector dummy variables were insignificant.
Parenthesis contain t-values
* = Significant at least at the 1% level.
** = Significant at least at the 5% level.
@ Ideally, the dependent variable should be the odds ratio.
Thus, if the dependent variable above is defined as SR (schooling
ratio) the dependent variable would be log (SR/1-SR). The problem
is that if SR is 1, as is the case for 42 households in our sample,
then 42 observations are lost as the division by 0 takes the odds
ratio to infinity.

Appendix Table 6.3

Food intake for women and children

Group/Food Category	Women doing Home-Based Work	Control group (Women)	Children doing home-based work		Control group (Children)	
			M	F	M	F
Daily milk consumption						
Never	44.2	22.3	36.5	45.4	22.0	20.8
Only in tea	48.8	54.3	53.8	48.6	46.3	62.3
One cup	6.6	19.1	7.7	4.4	24.2	17.0
Two cups	-	2.1	1.9	0.4	7.3	-
Vegetable consumption						
Daily	11.6	10.6	7.7	7.6	7.3	7.5
Several times a week	-	-	15.4	11.2	17.1	18.9
A few times a week	76.6	75.5	65.4	70.5	61.1	60.4
Once a week	7.6	9.6	5.8	7.6	7.3	11.3
Fruit consumption						
Never	28.1	17.0	15.4	24.8	9.8	18.8
Daily	1.3	9.6	-	1.2	9.8	13.2
A few times a week	12.9	19.1	23.1	16.0	34.1	22.6
Once a week	20.5	22.3	34.6	19.6	17.1	13.2
Less than once a week	23.1	20.2	7.7	7.6	22.0	15.1
A few times a month	13.9	10.6	13.5	14.8	-	-
Seasonal	13.9	10.6	3.8	12.0	7.3	13.2
Legume consumption						
Daily	1.7	-	0.8	0.7	2.4	-
Several times a week	20.1	-	1.9	6.4	4.9	9.4
A few times a week	66.0	-	78.8	74.5	63.4	73.6
Once a week	7.6	-	11.5	11.6	20.0	15.1
A few times a month	2.3	-	1.9	2.0	2.4	-
Meat consumption						
Never	3.0	3.2	1.9	3.6	2.4	7.5
Twice a day	-	-	1.9	0.8	.7.3	7.5
Daily	5.6	16.0	5.8	6.8	12.2	15.1
Several times a day	-	9.6	1.9	6.0	7.3	15.1
A few times a week	-	7.4	17.3	11.2	12.2	7.5
Once a week	45.9	27.7	46.2	49.0	46.3	26.4
Twice a week	11.2	19.1	-	-	-	-
A few times a month	9.9	4.3	17.3	16.7	4.9	9.4
About once a month	15.5	7.4	-	-	-	5.7
A few times a year	3.0	-	7.7	4.4	-	5.7
n	303	94	52	251	41	53

Source: SDPI survey.

Chapter Seven
AN EXPLORATION OF WOMEN'S EMPOWERMENT[1]

7.1 CONCEPTUALIZING EMPOWERMENT

This chapter explores questions arising from the conceptualization of empowerment in our study. It discusses why qualitative and quantitative data emerging from our fieldwork suggests no correlation between women's remunerative work and their personal empowerment in the home-based work context. We began with the assumption that economic earning lead to improved status for women and by implication, increased assertiveness. Since this was not the case, we re-visited our conceptualization of empowerment made at the start of the project.[2] We conclude that empowerment is context dependent; that it is not a commodity that one either has or does not have on the basis of a few variables, and that factors such as poverty, legal status and violence, the ideologies of work and gender, which are outside the control of individuals, families and local communities impact women's empowerment significantly.

To assess empowerment, or to operationalize the concept, we included questions related to the following broad categories: remuneration, conditions of work; mobility; health hazards, women's double burden; decision-making powers; access to and control over resources; and women's ability to organize. The underlying premise was that if their conditions of work meet certain minimum standards, if they had mobility, if their reproductive and community role was shared with them by a spouse or another household member, if they had access to state provided facilities and control over the resources they generate, then they could be considered to be empowered. In order to be able to assess these factors, we included various questions pertaining to different aspects within each category.

The categories of work conditions and the nature of women's home-based work included not only the hours and days per week of work, physical conditions of work, safety measures against hazardous work and remuneration, but also personal information pertaining to marital status, education, the number of years of paid work and household income and expenditure. These latter questions were included because we believe they impinge upon the conditions of work, remuneration and the ability to bargain and take initiatives.

Mobility is widely accepted as a measure of women's relative independence and autonomy since it indicates their access to the public sphere. We assumed that women might have become independent as a result of their economic earnings and therefore be confident about stepping out of the house, or, due to having to take/pick work from the contractor, they might have co-incidentally achieved greater mobility. We asked if they stepped out of the house and if so, whether they were accompanied/chaperoned by a male relative or if they could go alone. We also asked if they could step out of the house alone or accompanied, with or without permission of the household head, and the type of activity for which they could step out. The latter included leisure, shopping, to meet friends or relatives, work, or an outing.

The women's double burden was explored by looking into the extent of their household responsibilities including the care economy,[3] assistance with remunerative labour, assistance with household chores to free up their time for paid work, and if so, who (whether a male or female household member) had taken up the responsibility.[4] We also inquired about the number of hours they spent on household chores as well as the type of household chores they performed.

Women's decision-making powers provide insights into the autonomy and level of control they may exercise on their own life conditions as well as on those of their family. We were acutely conscious that many might interpret decision-making to mean the decision about what is to be cooked or bought for the household. Thus we included questions that are traditionally either under the purview of women or are shared with men in the household. These included questions regarding children's schooling, marriages, household expenditures and other family matters. We also included questions related to the reasons for doing home-based work, to find out whether the goal of financial independence or personal empowerment was pressing them into home-based work, after asking them whose decision it was that they should start doing home-based work.

Women's access to and control over resources provides crucial information on the degree of autonomy they can exercise to bring about a better quality of life. We asked about their access to food, to health clinics, community services, credit and whether they had any savings. In case they had savings, we inquired about the method of saving as well as the purpose i.e., what they intended to spend their savings on, e.g., dowry, education of children, buying jewelry or capital investment. We asked about their access to organizations that might help them improve their well being, their ability to attend meetings at such an organization as well as their interest in organizing for collective action. We also inquired about their relationship with the contractor, with the assumption that women would perceive him to be their oppressor and might be persuaded to bargain for better wages and work conditions, or for the provision of safety equipment, where needed, through collective action.

Based on the criteria discussed above, our data are not indicative of women's empowerment as a result of home-based work. The comparison with the control group of women demonstrates that women doing home-based work were over-worked, had less leisure time, did not have greater mobility, suffered from more physical ailments, had less access to healthcare, including less to spend on it, little by way of personal savings, were more indebted, and enjoyed similar decision-making powers as women in the control group.[5] A majority of the women involved in home-based work said that they were primarily working to supplement family income, or to pay off loans due to the disability or death of earning members in the family. Therefore, the motivation was not financial independence or personal empowerment but the need to survive under worsening economic conditions.

Qualitative data in the form of case studies (Annexure 1), field reports (Annexure 2) and focus group discussion (Annexure 3) also confirm that women were not empowered as a result of paid work.[6] For example, one case study states, 'Fahmeeda has been engaged in home-based work for 20 years. At first she was making carpets but left [that work] due to weak eyesight and now she makes *agarbattis* [incense sticks] at home. But she is not empowered. She is the victim of physical abuse. Patriarchy adapts itself to different cultures and communities in different ways. It creates an artificial division between the public domain that is for men and the private domain that is for women. It is one that affects women most profoundly' (Naz, Annexure 1.3). This case study highlights the fact that a woman who had been involved in productive work for 20 years continued to be a victim of physical abuse due to the particular circumstances that limit her choices and oppressed her so that her agency was null and void.

A field report states, 'Ironically though only those aspects of religion have been chosen for practice, which enslave and suppress women. This is inclusive of, but not limited to, strict pardah, so much so that women are not allowed to go out of the house and girls are not sent to school after the age of twelve. In most cases, the husbands are unemployed and home-based work is the only sources of income, which in other words implies that women are the sole earners in a number of cases. This however makes the husband no less authoritative and the wife no more 'empowered.' In fact...women have to grapple with double responsibilities, i.e., taking care of household chores and doing home-based work. The underlying notion being that whatever work goes on within the *'chardiwari'* [four walls] is women's work, whether it is an income generating activity or some household chore.' (Assad, Annexure 2.2). This observation indicates multiple factors at play in the lives of women including the ideology of work, gender relations, religion and poverty. Other reports also stress that home-based work does not contribute to women's empowerment as 'whatever they earn is spent on their food and medication. Their pay [sic] is hardly sufficient to keep body and soul together' (Fatima, Annexure 2.4).

These observations not only demonstrate the absence of empowerment, they also bring to light other issues that impact empowerment directly and deeply. These factors, discussed in greater detail later in the chapter, reveal that work alone is not a significant factor in improving women's status. In fact, women's secondary status is very deeply rooted; it is culturally and religiously sanctioned and ensured as an on-going process by the twin ideologies of gender and work.

What constitutes empowerment? One assumes that women achieve some degree of empowerment when they enter paid work and have an independent income. Some people assert that women become empowered even if they are pushed into paid work. However, our research demonstrates that there is no automatic linkage between paid work in the home and empowerment. In fact, such work can be debilitating if it is repetitive, underpaid and physically taxing. Therefore, we need to re-examine our assumptions about women's empowerment.

7.2 EMPOWERMENT RECONSIDERED

As earlier indicated, empowerment is not a unidimensional category that can be achieved if a certain pattern or combination of variables is put together, or that can be assessed if it is measured against certain indicators. This is not to say that no assessment is possible but to assert that the assessment needs to be context specific. In the present context, the interface between indicators such as access to resources, mobility, education, age, and culture, ethnicity, poverty and violence need to be underscored. This means that empowerment cannot be attained on the basis of access and control over resources in the narrow sense of the economic and the material. It is intangible and can only be observed in the manner in which women exercise control over their lives. In this regard, individual variations can exist so that some women are more empowered than others within somewhat similar sets of circumstances.[7] We examine below the different factors that impact empowerment and discuss if they led to any change in power relations that was advantageous to women.

7.2.1 POVERTY

Almost 77 per cent of home-based work households in the present study were assessed to be below the poverty line.[8] This was more than corroborated by the response of a majority of the women (82 per cent) who said that they were working to make ends meet. Furthermore, the reason that children were doing home-based work was also due to poverty and because they did not have the requisite fee to attend school.

On average, women in our survey had been working for twelve years. This coincides roughly with the time when the negative effects of structural adjustment policies (SAPs) began to be felt. Khattak and Sayeed (2000), quoting various sources, point out that simultaneously with the introduction of SAPs, especially the liberalization policies, poverty had increased in Pakistan.[9] This encouraged the trend toward women's incorporation into the market as women were forced to sell their labour at below minimum wage due to an increase in the supply of labour. The same policies have forced firms into subcontracting as a means of reducing production costs.

As mentioned earlier on, the level of poverty does not allow for savings. Focus group discussions reinforce the finding that women and their families would starve if they do not do home-based work. This is largely because there was a high level of male unemployment or underemployment. For example, one respondent said that her husband does not have a regular job, therefore, if she does not do home-based work, she asked how will she and her family eat? (Assad, Annexure, 1.1).

Another field report (Assad, Annexure 2.2) states, 'In the Gujrati community women are more mobile. They do not need permission of the head of the household to step out of the house. Girls are not prevented from studying and men do not mind helping women in their home-based work. Gujrati women are therefore better off than their Bengali and Burmese counterparts.' However, in the context of poverty, home-based work and empowerment, one cannot simply assert that just because the Gujrati women are faring better than those who are below the poverty line, they are empowered. According to Assad (ibid), perhaps home-based work can be more conducive to empowerment, if it is not the sole means of income for the family but a supplement to it. This is contestable as home-based work in its present form is able to expand because of the extreme exploitation (low wages sans legal protection) it entails. For any empowerment to begin to take place, women must begin to organize effectively for their rights and the state must enact and enforce legal protection.

7.2.2 VIOLENCE

Studies on work, wages, and labour issues usually analyze these issues in a vacuum, relegating the conditions prevailing in a community to the status of 'externalities' as these may affect the conclusions one may draw. While it is true that external conditions prevailing in a community may affect ones' analyses, ignoring these conditions will not yield accurate results, reflective of the complex interplay of multiple factors upon work, wages and living conditions.

How do the conditions prevailing in local communities affect home-based workers? Out of the four sites where the survey was conducted, three (Orangi, Korangi and Godhra) reported that violence had affected work. Ali and Parveen (1996) corroborate that the locale where workers live (determined largely by ethnicity) and the level of violence are crucial to the availability and determination of work and wages. The participants of the Focus Group Discussion in Orangi mentioned that during times of violence, dead bodies used to be sprawled everywhere and the stench was unbearable as no one, not even KDA (Karachi Development Authority) personnel, were willing to enter these areas. Curfews were imposed and it was difficult to get work and even more difficult to get paid. The participants of the FGD in Korangi stated that at times they and their children had to go without food due to the curfews. Women's and girl's mobility suffered tremendously as public transport was a particularly unsafe mode of transportation, and many families stopped sending their daughters to school.[10]

The intensity of the violence in Karachi, especially in the communities where the survey was conducted, put women back into their homes by foreclosing the possibility of stepping out. When no one, not even the state and its agencies can ensure anyone's physical security, and as it is dangerous for men and women to venture out, it is best to stay indoors. This phenomenon has also contributed to the expansion of home-based work as factories were closed for days and sometimes for weeks on end due to the violence and curfews. Parveen and Ali (1996, p.139) term this phenomenon the decentralization of work whereby work has shifted out of factories into homes.[11] Thus, violence had a negative effect upon the economic, social and psychological well being of these communities. Women were the worst affected in all these contexts so that empowering them means firstly to come up with coping mechanisms for the affected communities, and secondly, to address the particular needs of women especially in terms of their work and mobility.

7.2.3 ETHNICITY AND LEGAL STATUS

Ethnicity and legal status determines the type of work one can access, the level of wages one may receive and whether there will be police harassment or not. Ethnicity is directly linked with politics in Karachi, which has been the centre of ethnic conflict since the mid 1980s.[12] The localities where the fieldwork was carried out had a majority of Burmese, Bengalis and Gujratis.[13] As discussed previously, Burmese women were concentrated in incense-stick making in Orangi, Bengali women were a majority in carpet weaving and prawn shelling in Korangi and Machar Colony respectively, while Gujrati women constituted a majority in sack-stitching in Godhra.

The complex interconnections between ethnicity and legal status were evident in the manner in which different communities viewed themselves and each other as well as the type of work they were involved in and the remuneration they received. For example, Burmese women tried to present themselves as Bengali since Bengalis (many of who are also illegal immigrants but have effective networks) had more clout than the Burmese. This, in turn, can impact the kind of work and level of remuneration they receive.

Burmese women mostly got the lowest paid and most hazardous work (agarbatti making in our survey) because their bargaining power was extremely limited. Furthermore, as Burmese men cannot get outside work due to their illegal status and the risk of police harassment, Burmese women were forced into the lowest of the low-paid home-based work. It was to the advantage of contractors that Burmese women accepted extremely underpaid work due to restrictions on their mobility arising from legal and cultural reasons. In contrast, Punjabi and Sindhi women in Godhra complained that the contractor gave work and better remuneration to Gujrati women in Godhra due to their ethnic preferences since the contractors also belonged to the same Gujrati-speaking community (Assad, Annexure 2.2).

Some case studies of Bengali women from Korangi and Machar Colony indicated that many of these women were living in extreme insecurity. Their problems stemmed from being kidnapped or 'persuaded' by *dalals* (pimps) who brought them to Pakistan under the pretext of marrying rich men as demonstrated by Annexure 3.3 and 3.4.[14] Some of these women were sold off at least two to three times to men who married them but subsequently tried to force them into becoming sex workers. Their homes were like sub jails from where they were not allowed to step out and where they and their children were forced into home-based work to meet household expenditures, especially to buy food items. Their husbands physically abused them while their children were likely to be beaten or verbally abused by contractors. Sometimes, women also beat up their children when the latter did faulty work or refuse to work (Naz, Annexure 2.4).

The Burmese women were not aware that the government runs shelters where they could take refuge. In any case, they would be too frightened to seek government help lest their illegal status be discovered by the police who (after harassing them, which could mean sexual harassment to the point of rape), could put them in jail or send them back to Bangladesh to their alienated families. In short, they have nowhere to go. Given such circumstances, it is difficult to assess for empowerment or independence when women's subjugation is so deep. For these woman the important step would be breaking the cycle of being bought and sold. Despite their subjugation, the resistance of these women is manifest in their refusal to become sex-workers. This is why one needs to understand that empowerment and resistance are context dependent.

7.2.4 THE IDEOLOGY OF WORK

There are several ways in which the ideology of work impacts empowerment negatively or positively. The hierarchies within work confer status upon individuals so that certain types of work are held in high esteem (e.g. managerial work) while other types of work such as manual labour is considered low status. Within these broad categories, there are subcategories also based upon the level of skill, remuneration, locale, and whether it is perceived as being men's or women's work. All these factors impact a person's sense of empowerment.

Work is a gendered phenomenon so that men are generally regarded as the breadwinners and women as housewives without productive work. In the home-based work context, women's work, because it is relocated from the factory into the home, becomes all the more problematic as it blurs the boundaries between reproductive and productive work. Thus, home becomes the locus for both. Home-Based Work is, therefore, preferred by many men who can continue to exercise patriarchal control, and it is more oppressive for women since remunerative work merges with household chores so that there is no end to work. Home-Based Work oppresses women at the macro level as well because women fall outside the standard definition of 'worker'. Workers 'exist' in the public realm and not within the confines of the home, the private realm, the ultimate symbol and space for women's reproductive role. Since the home/the private realm has to be protected for privacy from incursions by the public realm, home-based work becomes all the more problematic. According to Chen, Sebstad and O'Connell (1999, p. 607), home workers '...are unsupervised wage employees tied through subcontracts to formal firms.' Both the law in Pakistan (discussed in Chapter 2) and the ideology of work do not treat these employees as workers to be protected by laws. Thus, home-based work in the present context pushes women back instead of leading to their empowerment.[15]

Women's home-based work is an indication of the economic crunch that the family is facing. The type of work that women do within the home-based work context indicates their level of poverty and their need for money.[16] In this regard it is important to distinguish work from drudgery. Much of what falls into home-based work in our survey may be termed as drudgery: it is back breaking with very low remuneration, it is not considered worthy of any social status and women who do it maintain that the moment they are able to, they will stop working. Thus, not all work (especially if it can be termed drudgery) provides women with a sense of autonomy. Some types of work have the opposite effect, i.e., it is oppressive. For many women, the fact that they are not working is a matter of prestige and a measure of how much their husbands cares for them. Some of those involved in home-based work feel that their husbands are harsh and force them into work. Thus, work in the home-based work context has negative social prestige.

Women were aware that they were being paid less than men and that their work conditions are unfair. As one of the field reports (Assad, Annexure 2.2) states, 'Women do realize that this [exploitation] happens because they are women and that their husbands would not have to undergo the same sufferings, since they are men, but there is little they can do about it because they are in too deep a financial mess to make do without home-based work.' The consciousness of exploitation on the basis of gender is not a sufficient condition for empowerment. In fact, under the present circumstances, it becomes debilitating because women suffer a dual oppression: first, they are underpaid workers who have to suffer through drudgery and second, they are more disadvantaged than underpaid male workers for being women.

The gendered ideology of work extends to the life of girls, an overwhelming majority of the children involved in home-based work and domestic work. All reports from the field underscore that mothers involved their daughters in home-based work rather than their sons. Some mothers explained that girls were easier to control, and were more diligent while the boys were careless. Sons were sent to school or the local *madrassah* for education but there is prejudice against sending girls to school as many felt that a 'girl cannot do anything after getting [an] education' (Habib, Annexure 2.1). Therefore, it was logical to restrict her to domestic chores and home-based work, since this would serve her in the future. Furthermore, this confirms the gendered phenomenon of work and the gendering of home-based work, which is generally considered to be women's work along with household work. In fact, women noted that their mothers and grandmothers were doing the same work. Burmese and Bengali men did not do any home-based work because they considerd it women's work.[17] However, 11.2 per cent of the men in our survey, mostly Gujrati and Punjabi men in Godhra, help women in home-based work.[18] Although field reports attribute this phenomenon entirely to culture, this also has an obvious linkage with the comparatively higher status of sack-stitching work within home-based work. As long as work is gendered and hierarchical, women will remain in an unequal power relationship in the social and remunerative context of work.

7.2.5 THE IDEOLOGY OF GENDER

Women's empowerment is directly connected to their self-perception, which is based upon gender constructions of their roles as women. In this regard, their incorporation into home-based work only reinforces their sense of helplessness and lack of status since most 'chose' to do it because of dire need. As one of them explained, her husband told her to '...work at home even if it is low-paid. I can't let you work outside the house' (Naz, Annexure 2.4). There was little space for negotiation with husbands or fathers since various other options that might allow better work conditions and remuneration were foreclosed due to women's secondary position within the household. The decision regarding where they would work was ultimately in male hands. This is widely accepted by women and is reported from the field in different words, for example: 'What is most distressing is the indifference exhibited by the women. Not only have they been brainwashed but [also] they themselves to a large extent support the treatment that is being meted out to them. They think that if their husbands help them with household chores or with home-based work, they will be committing some sort of a sin and will be held answerable for them' (Assad, Annexure 2.2). Focus group discussions also indicated that women believed that even if their husbands are unemployed, they should not be doing home-based work since this is women's work. Furthermore, they believed that women who go to factories are bad and that women should stay at home and work.

Such beliefs and constructions are made possible not only due to the community culture and belief systems but also because women themselves have internalized these norms and behave accordingly. This wins them social approval and sanction.[19] An example of the unchanging power relations between men and women is that the head of a household is always a man. This has nothing to do with his ability to earn, his age or status within the family. A widow reported that while she was earning money through home-based work, her young son would not allow her to step out of the house as he considered himself to be the head of the household (Khurshid, Annexure 1.7).

A case where individual initiative worked effectively was that of Hasina (Khurshid, Annexure 1.6). Despite living in a conservative community, she proactively took initiatives that sometimes raised eyebrows in the community e.g. using and advocating contraceptives. She wove carpets, but also volunteered as a nurse at a local hospital and taught children in the neighbourhood because she was educated. While openly critical of other men in the community, she expressed appreciation and gratitude toward her husband for being supportive. The community women criticized her for protecting her husband as they maintained that Hasina has much more potential and initiative and that her husband inhibited and prevented her from realizing it. This case is cited not to imply that open criticism of her husband would indicate Hasina's empowerment, but to assert that women buy into the patriarchal ideology through what may be termed as 'bonds of love.' Thus, one does not rebel or resist due to the sense of loyalty one feels toward the person who is the source of oppression in ones life. In Hasina's case, she is grateful to her husband for allowing her to realize some of her potential even though this is her right as a human being. Thus, education, personal initiative, a supportive husband or father can make a difference, yet, in every case, empowerment is context dependent.

7.2.6 THE NEXUS OF CULTURE, RELIGION AND GENDER RELATIONS

We have already discussed the socialization process whereby gender roles become naturalized. Girls are expected to and made to do domestic chores and home-based work, while boys go to school and are responsible for shopping. There were differences among the communities where the survey was conducted but, overall, gender relations were determined by stereotypical gender roles. The dominance of *Sipah e Sahaba*, an ultra right wing religious party, in Korangi and parts of Orangi further confirms the power of ultra conservative interpretations of religion. These interpretations are often detrimental to women's empowerment since they come from a closed mindset. Despite this unfavourable setting, there were women who successfully carved a space for themselves.

There were enterprising women who took bold initiatives (and therefore empowered themselves to some degree) in terms of economic independence. For example, Ayesha, after being widowed at a young age, made ends meet by cooking *biryani* (spicy rice and meat or chicken) and training her son to sell it on a cart. She saved money and was able to move into her own house. However, she refused to allow her daughter to attend school. She could afford the school fee as she was not below the poverty line, and despite being the head of her household, she steadfastly followed community norms and culture (Khurshid, Annexure 1.7).

Thus, even if a woman, as head of a household, acquired the authority that allowed her to go against the norms and culture of her community, she was unlikely to do so as the pressures to conform to these norms are extremely strong and rewarded by social acceptance whereas defiance is punished through social disapproval. Women heads of households are reluctant to risk social disapproval by going against the grain in a male dominated society that has granted them (under unusual circumstances) some powers similar to men.[20] Another way of viewing the same phenomenon is to refer to it as 'the convenience of subservience'[21] whereby Ayesha finds it convenient to adhere to and not challenge or defy local norms and culture as she can preserve her status and relative independence in this manner.

Women in our survey felt it was their obligation to help their husbands, especially when the husbands were unemployed. Furthermore, there was great premium placed on obedience as a quality in a good woman. Bengali women in the carpet making and prawn shelling sectors were restricted to their homes and told that stepping out of the house was tantamount to sinning against God since they would be defying their husbands if they did so. Another report also explains, '... the conditions in Korangi are exceptionally appalling. Here women ...do not go out of the house alone. So much so that one Bengali admitted that if he left his wife in the street across his house[,] she will not be able to find her way back. At a very early age gender roles are specified for the boys and the girls. They [girls] are taught that staying inside the house makes them 'izzatdar' [respectable and honourable] and that respect for women means staying indoors and doing what their husbands tell them' (Assad, Annexure 2.2).

It is very difficult if not impossible to fight the combination of culture and narrow interpretations of religion in an attempt to change gender power relations. As sources of social commendation and respectability, they serve as a powerful base for the maintenance of the status quo. To challenge these structures and ways of thinking in order to effect a change in favour of women is viewed as questioning male authority, which usually results in a harsh backlash. The path to empowerment is, therefore, not an easy one since it involves challenges at multiple levels such as a change in ones own way of thinking and also that of men and communities in their collective contexts.

CONCLUSION

We looked for women's empowerment in home-based work with the assumption that market-based work will empower them. We also assumed that their economic earnings would give them some degree of autonomy in the context of their domestic life. Our assumptions with regard to empowerment based on an increase in mobility, access to and control over resources and organizational abilities were ill founded. Therefore, there was a need to re-examine our assumptions about attaining empowerment.

Based on the qualitative data from the field, we conclude that a number of crucial factors impact empowerment. Our research reveals that violence, ethnicity, legal status, poverty, culture and religion, personal initiative and education are important variables of empowerment. For example, meager earnings cannot lift the oppressive conditions created by poverty, which determines where one lives (locality), which in turn is connected with the degree of violence one experiences in the Karachi context. In addition, the intensity or absence of violence determines the amount of work that can come to a particular locality/neighbourhood. Similarly, one's legal status, with respect to citizenship, is also a factor in the level of confidence one feels about challenging the status quo. The gendered ideology of work, whereby the type of work determines one's status, is also central to empowerment. Gender relations are at the heart of the lack of empowerment and are the most problematic area as both women and men buy into the same gender ideology that oppresses women.

Adopting the definition that empowerment implies a shift in power relations, the analysis of field data, in the light of the additional factors referred to above, leads us to assert that women have not been empowered due to home-based work. In fact, we conclude that, at present, home-based work, due to its inherently exploitative character, cannot be a conduit for empowerment. Women require fundamental structural changes in perceptions, in supportive policies and in their everyday lived realities in order to empower themselves. While some of the changes have to do with them as individuals, many are beyond their control.

Empowerment is not a tangible commodity that a person either possess does or does not so that one is either empowered or disempowered. Empowerment encompasses an intricate process of negotiation for changed power relations at several levels, all of which are interconnected and multilayered. Our research demonstrates pockets of resistance but does not provide evidence of empowerment resulting from remunerative but highly exploitative work within the home. As discussed earlier on, the degree of exploitation and marginalization is so intense that home-based women workers are preoccupied with questions of survival and existence; they do not have any space to begin to think of strategizing for more favourable power relations in the different contexts of their lives.

NOTES

1. This chapter draws on Chapters 5 and 6, and the case studies, field reports and focus group discussions (Annexures 1-3).

2. This is embedded in but not restricted to the questionnaire designed for women briefly described in section 3.4 and more fully described in this Chapter

3. The *UNDP Human Development Report* (1999, pp 77-83) defines and discusses the care economy. It includes not only caring for the elderly and the sick under the care economy but also discusses at length the psychological support that is extended by women to the healthy functioning of the family. The Report states, '...the essence of care is in the human bonds that it creates and supplies. Care, sometimes referred to as social reproduction, is also essential for economic reproduction' (p. 77).

4. We did not include women's third role —i.e. the community role—as it is extremely limited in the Pakistani context. Nevertheless, we asked about women's community activities and whether they were part of any voluntary organization in their community and whether they would be willing to engage in collective action.

5. See Chapter 6.

6. Field reports, case studies and focus group discussions in the Annexures were edited for language. However, at times the original language is quoted to make a point more forcefully.

7. According to Chaudhry (1997, p. 1.449), 'There is no one right path to empowerment; there is no one right way to enact resistance against oppressive power relations. The terms of resistance and bids for empowerment emerge out of specific circumstances of a particular life, and who is to say what terms and which bids are more efficacious? What matters is the challenging of power relations.' Quoting Foucault, she writes, 'Empowerment implies a change in power relations in a certain context. These power relations are multilayered and dynamic' [Foucault (1978, p. 452)].

8. Refer to section 6.4.

9. Also refer to section 1.3.

10. The transport business, controlled by the Pathans in Karachi, became particularly central to Karachi's ethnic conflict. The first incidence of violence was triggered in 1985 when a Pathan mini-bus driver ran over and killed Bushra Zaidi, a Mohajir (Indian Muslim migrants and refugees who came to Pakistan after the partition of India in 1947) girl. This led to clashes between the Pathans and Mohajirs. The latter felt they were being sidelined everywhere by the state and the dominant ethnic groups, namely Punjabis and Pathans.

11. It also shifted out of the province of Sindh into the Punjab.

12. Karachi has a multi-ethnic population with 54 per cent Urdu-speaking/Mohajirs, 14 per cent Punjabis, 9 per cent Pathans, 6 per cent Sindhis, 4 per cent Balochi and 12 per cent who belong to other ethnicities including Bengalis/Biharis and Burmese [Parveen and Ali (1996, p. 140)]. For more on Karachi as a context refer to section 3.5.

13. The Gujratis are referred to as Mohajirs, which is a more inclusive category.

14. Although official statistics are unavailable, the flesh trade in South Asia largely results from poverty. Bangladeshi women are trafficked into Pakistan and the Middle East mainly due to the same reason.

15. Khattak has argued in ed. Balakrishnan (2001) that the choice/ability to work from home can be an indication of empowerment since it gives women the flexibility to combine childcare and household chores with paid work. However, in

the home-based work context in Pakistan, this is not the case: women workers do not make autonomous decisions, and they cannot effectively negotiate their conditions of work and remuneration if they choose to work from the home. They are more victims of circumstance (in this case intensification of poverty) than individuals exercising their autonomy and rights.

16. There are gradations within home-based work so that for instance, in the context of our research, *agarbatti* making is considered to be at the lowest rungs of work while sack stitching is considered better since the remuneration is better. An expert worker can make around 100 sacks in two to three hours and earn Rs 30 while a family can make up to 4000 *agarbattis* in approximately six to seven hours and earn Rs 20.

17. Evidence from other countries such as Argentina, Germany, Hong Kong, Italy, Japan, Mexico and the Philippines reveals that a majority of home-based workers are women (Chen, Sebstad and O'Connell 1999, p. 606).

18. Refer to section 6.2

19. Foucault's conception of docile bodies (1977, pp. 135-169), and what he terms technologies of the self, makes clear how the body can be brought into harmony with what it is supposed to do, i.e., people internalize what is expected of them and play that out as if they were using their own agency. Thus, the subject produces itself as subject. This is how one should interpret the quantitative finding that 74 per cent of the women 'chose' to do home-based work on their own accord (section 6.2). This is the worst type of colonization as it indicates that colonization is so complete that the subject does not question the source of its oppression but imposes similar oppression upon itself.

20. Case study 1.7 demonstrates that it is possible for a man to take such a stand much more easily. A contributory factor might be that when a husband and wife unite, it is easier to fight for the rights of their children and attain equal rights for girls in that context. However, in this context, one upholds the ideology of the family and its sanctity, the role of the man as the protector who is fighting for his child rather than the rights of women or the issue of women's empowerment. Despite a degree of discomfort that this provokes within a community, the adherence to patriarchal norms makes it possible for the man or husband and wife to take a stand for their girls' education.

21. This is the title of an article on Pakistani women by Jalal (1991).

References

Chaudhry, L. N., 1997, 'Researching 'my people,' researching myself: fragments of a reflexive tale,' *Qualitative Studies in Education*, Vol. 10, No. 4.

Chen, M., J. Sebstad and N. O'Connell, 1999, 'Counting the invisible workforce: the case of home based workers,' *World Development*, Vol. 27, No. 3.

Foucault, M., 1977, *Discipline and Punish*, translated edition. (NY: Vintage Publishers)

Jalal, A. 1991, 'The Convenience of Subservience,' in ed. D. Kandyoti, Women, Islam and the State (London: MacMillan).

Khattak, S. and A. Sayeed, 2000, '*Subcontracted women workers in the world economy: The case of Pakistan*', SDPI Monograph Series #15, Islamabad.

Khattak, S. G, 2001, 'Subcontracted work and Gender Relations: The Case of Pakistan' in ed. R. Balakrishnan, *The Hidden Assembly Line: Gender Dynamics of Subcontracted Workers in a Global Economy* (New York: Kumarian Press).

Parveen, F. and K. Ali, 1996, 'Research in Action: Organizing women factory workers in Pakistan,' in Amrita Chhachhi and Renee Pittin (editors), *Confronting State, Capital and Patriarchy*, Macmillan Press Ltd. and St. Martin's Press, Inc in association with the Institute of Social Studies (ISS).

UNDP, 1999, *Human Development Report*, (New York and Oxford: Oxford University Press).

Chapter Eight

SUMMARY AND RECOMMENDATIONS

8.1 SUMMARY

Not much, based on qualitative and rigorous work, is known about subcontracted home-based work (home-based work) even though it is assuming increased importance in terms of the workforce it absorbs. The limited research done on this indicates that it is highly exploitative, entails low wages, long and irregular hours and is repetitive and some of it is quite hazardous.[1] Furthermore, there is a concentration of women and children, particularly girls, in the work force. This book adds to the conceptual and empirical base of this limited knowledge. Both qualitative and quantitative data were collected and analyzed and this book is based on both sets of analyses. We had 303 home-based work households in our sample and 94 households from the same neighbourhoods who did not engage in home-based work. The latter formed the control group for comparison.[2]

Our focus is both on macro and micro issues at the national level and also on the international value chain (linkage of stages of exchange relations between the home-based worker and final consumer). On a micro level, we investigate the reasons for engaging in home-based work, the contribution of the children to total family income, and the impact of the increased earnings on improving household education, nutrition and health. Other consequences are also explored, such as the possible neglect of children and a worsening of women's health as they attempt to shoulder a double burden of home-based work and housework and childcare. In particular, we focus on the hazardous nature of home-based work for women and children. The power dynamics within the household due to the start of home-based work are also explored.

On a macro level, we identify the determinants of the expansion of home-based work. Among other determinants, we explore the poverty and unemployment associated with structural adjustment policies that induce more households to engage in home-based work. In addition, we explore some inherent advantages of home-based work such as greater flexibility in responding to demand variations, pushing overheads on to contractors and the lack of enforcement of regulations. Finally, we attempt to locate household production within the international value chain. In order to understand the nature of bargaining power and exploitation, the allocation of revenue across the different tiers of the chain are also explored.

In a nutshell, this research is about the multi-tiered exploitation home-based work entails. Economic exploitation is not defined in the strict Marxian sense of appropriation of surplus value, although we come closest to this in Chapter 4 when reviewing the distribution of revenue across the national and international production or value chain. In the remaining chapters of the book, the reference is to social exploitation where the weaker party in a relationship is taken advantage off. This can occur in relations between contractors and home-based workers, between men and women within households and between adults and children within households.

This research focused on four hazardous home-based work sectors in various parts of Karachi i.e. carpet weaving, shrimp shelling, incense stick making and sack stitching. The criteria of sector selection were that women and children be involved in the work, that the work be hazardous to health and that some insight must be forthcoming at least from one of the selected sectors regarding exploitation across the international value chain i.e. that at least one of the sectors selected has its product exported. In the rest of this summary, we first briefly describe the contents of each chapter; next we summarize the main findings and end with a set of policy recommendations.

In Chapter 1, we set the stage with a conceptual framework and macroeconomic overview. We also locate home-based work into an informal sector context and present a literature review of home-based work. In Chapter 2, we review legislation pertinent to the protection of home-based workers. In Chapter 3, we describe the study design and survey method. Both quantitative data, via purposive sampling, and qualitative data, via focus group discussions (FGD), case studies and field reports, were generated. In Chapter 4 we review the extent of worker exploitation by documenting the distribution of revenue across the value chain.

In Chapter 5, we analyze the qualitative data including field reports, case studies and FGD reports. The approach is sectoral with a focus on work and socio-economic conditions and the cultural norms of the communities the work is located in. Quantitative data analysis is used to substantiate and provide support to the arguments. The findings in Chapter 6, based exclusively on quantitative data analysis, complement those in Chapter 5. We address issues of why the home-based work was opted for, work conditions, women's double burden, nutrition, health and child schooling and other activities. Gender comparisons for children and comparison of the home-based workers with a control group of non home-based workers provides important benchmarks and contrast throughout the chapter. It is often argued that women become more empowered from earned income. We explore this issue in Chapter 7 that takes into account the qualitative and quantitative findings of Chapters 5 and 6 in this regard and re-visit the concept of empowerment. We turn now to the main findings and recommendations.

In Chapter 1, we started by reviewing the conceptual framework of the neo-classical household model and use it only as a very broad framework within which to review the findings relating to sub-contracted home-based work in Pakistan. Two main findings emerge from the empirical literature across the board. First, that poverty drives women and children into home-based work. Second, that much of this work is hazardous to both women and children.

A review of the macro-economic conditions, starting with the intensive period of structural adjustment in 1988-89, shows high and increasing unemployment and sharply declining real wages. Thus, it is no surprise that real household incomes have declined and poverty rates [OK]. In view of the worsening macroeconomic scenario and its obvious micro consequences, home-based work is likely to continue to grow in magnitude as a household coping strategy.

Home-Based Work is a very neglected part of the neglected informal sector. Using the results of the first and the most recent surveys by the Federal Bureau of Statistics, we chart the dimensions of the informal sector. We indicate that the official definition, adopted from the ILO, is very 'enterprise' or 'unit' oriented and that scholars have been influenced by this definition, with some exceptions, in their research on the informal sector. Such analysis underestimates the extent of involvement of women and children in the informal sector.

Since the late 1980s, scholars have acknowledged the existence of home-based work as an important component of the informal sector. The findings, with regards to the conditions of work, and the extent of exploitation are frightening. A solution cannot be piecemeal and will need to address the 'causes', including poverty and the poor quality of state services, rather than merely the 'effects'. Policy solutions would also need to address the legal framework.

In Chapter 2, we review existing legislation pertaining to home-based work and conclude that the issue of legal protection is one of political will, which can only be induced by internal and external pressure. Until the state and international donor agencies display the political will to protect the marginalized, the existence of formal legal protection on paper will not make a difference. This suggests that the existence of laws without enforcement makes laws meaningless.

In Chapter 3, we describe our research design and survey method. We also describe Karachi, the large metropolitan city in which the four sectors of study are located. We show in Chapter 4 that, in all the four sectors we investigated, workers got low wages, worked for long hours, did repetitive work, were engaged in hazardous work and were not provided with any safety equipment to guard them against health risks. Economic exploitation is defined as the unequal distribution of revenue across the value chain. The share of home-based workers relative to the revenue of the sub-contractors, contractors and final distributors was extremely low ranging from 0.06 of domestic retail revenue per unit in incense-stick making to 18.2 per cent in carpet weaving. It ranged respectively from 0.2 per cent in incense-stick making to 2.0 per cent in carpet weaving as a percentage of what the consumers in the USA paid for these products.

The findings reported in Chapter 5 are based on qualitative information. The urban localities these communities lived in were highly polluted and deprived of adequate social and physical infrastructure. Women and girls mostly did this work and suffered multiple ailments like respiratory diseases, pains in the muscles and joints, and serious skin irritations and allergies. In many cases, despite the health impact of the hazardous work, they did not seek any medical attention because of unaffordable or inaccessible health facilities. Often they relied on local remedies or expired medicines dispensed by quacks.

Women across the board stated that they would have preferred for their children to be going to school and not doing such work if they could afford school and survive without such work. Thus, while they realized that home-based work was resulting in serious danger to health, the alternative was starvation. Similarly, children stated their desire for attending regular school, but confirmed that family compulsions forced them into home-based work and often kept them out of school.

Incense-stick making, carpet weaving and shrimp shelling was mostly taking place in the Bengali and Burmese communities of Orangi, Korangi and Machar colony. Our broader literature review of home-based work indicated that it is done across the country. However, the incidence, particularly of hazardous home-based work, may be higher among the migrant communities.

These communities were highly conservative in their religious interpretation of Islam and highly oppressive of women. Being immigrants, they felt insecure and became easy targets for many predators like the police, *jihadi* groups, political toughs of parties like the MQM and the contractors.

In turn, the men exploited the women. They severely restricted women's mobility, and contrary to conservative cultural norms, required them to work and often to be the sole breadwinner. Women were also responsible for all the household chores and childcare and hence had little time to themselves or for socializing. In any case, this was not an option for most of the women in the Bengali and Burmese communities who required women to be confined to their houses. Some of the women had been sold off into 'marriage' by pimps enticing them with better prospects away from their homes in Bangladesh. With no protection from kinship groups, they were completely at the mercy of their husbands who often had other wives. These women reported being beaten and forced into doing home-based work to earn an income.

labour Excess supply of labour and the lack of organizing ability or community unity prevented home-based workers from collectively getting better terms. Contractors took full advantage of their economic power. They paid late, cheated by providing fewer materials, and verbally and sometimes physically, abused the women and children. As expected, they generally treated the men with more respect.

Empowerment for women seems more a function of the cultural norms of the community than work and earnings. Thus, in similar circumstances, Gujrati women of Godhra who stitched bags were more mobile and on occasions managed to jointly get better rates for their work. Other enlightened practices included encouraging girls to study and men assisting the women with chores even though they generally held jobs.

The control group of households were often Punjabi or Urdu speaking. While they observed *purdah* also, the restraints on the women were not anywhere as rigid as those on the Bengali or Burmese women. They also attached a high premium to children's education. Interestingly, education did make a difference in how men treated the women, even in the Bengali community. It also appeared that an educated woman was capable of getting the respect of a contractor.

The findings in Chapter 5 from the quantitative data sets reinforced findings based on the qualitative data. As could be expected, poverty and related factors were the main motivation for engaging in home-based work for women and children. In over a quarter of the cases (26 per cent) in which the head of the household was a male, he was not doing any work and relying on the earnings of home-based work of the women and children. With regards to seeking less hazardous work outside the home, almost two-fifths of the women reported there were mobility problems in doing this and another two-fifths reported that family or neighbourhood pressures kept them at home. Bonded labour was going on in the carpet weaving sector whereby women and children tried to work off loans that the men had taken.

Both women and children identified negative health impacts or fatigue as the main disadvantage of home-based work. On average, children began to work at the age of seven and a half years of age and worked an average of about 5 hours a day on home-based work, six days a week. The doctor accompanying the field team assessed the work done by 83 per cent of the boys and 94 per cent of the girls to be 'hard.' Children paid a price for mistakes and in about a tenth of the cases were beaten by the contractor.

School enrollment among the non-home-based work household eligible children at 42.6 per cent was over twice that of the home-based work group (19.8 per cent). Interestingly, between two-thirds and three-fourths of the responses from both groups of children and women mentioned school expense as the main reason why children were not in school. Only 28 per cent of the children and a fifth of the mothers mentioned home-based work as the reason why children were not in school. Further, less than a tenth of the children doing home-based work thought that it interfered in schooling because the work made them too tired.

The desire for schooling was also very high in both groups. About two-thirds of those working and not going to school said that they would prefer to go to school and another quarter said that they would like to combine attending school with work or play. Similarly, over four-fifths of the children in the control group not enrolled expressed a desire to attend school. Children not engaged in home-based work had a better quality of life otherwise in terms of more time spent at play and less time spent at work or chores.

Almost three-quarters of the women felt that home-based work affected their ability to engage in childcare. After spending seven hours doing home-based work, they spent another four on household chores. Only one per cent of the women responded that men assisted in any way in lessening their work burden, and in fact, a third of the women reported that family members reacted negatively or harshly because home-based work meant less time for household chores. As expected, 87 per cent responded that daughters came to their assistance and 5 per cent responded that sons did so.

Judging by comparisons with the control group, the earnings from home-based work did not lead to any empowerment of the women when judged in terms of mobility, greater say in household decision making or independence in expending earned income. In fact, women and children in the control group enjoyed a better quality of life in terms of leisure time and health. Any positive change in the lives of women doing home-based work appears remote as gender roles are reproduced among children e.g. girls do more domestic work than boys. Similarly, women's conditions of work and bargaining and organizing abilities are weak, so that women's chances of empowering themselves are low.

Children in the control group had a better immunization record, diet and suffered much less from anemia and other traditional ailments. Almost all the children in the home-based work group complained of some work related ailment. Pain in the back, joints, blisters and skin problems occurred with the greatest frequency. These children also had much less access to health care than children in the control group. The incidence of pain in the back, limbs and joints was much higher for women doing home-based work compared to the control group. Also, the incidence of illness, averaging more than once a month, was much higher. They also found health care to be much less accessible and affordable than did women in the control group.

The contractors generally paid late for the work done and in some cases did not pay at all. They had assisted only one per cent of the women and under five per cent of the children in the treatment of ailments that resulted from the home-based work. Despite this, only a quarter of the women felt their relationship with the contractor was not good. There was no organization working with women to assist them to better their pay and working conditions. Over half the women indicated a willingness to be part of some kind of collective action to improve their working conditions if provided some kind of leadership and assistance.

Based on the findings of Chapter 5 and 6 and the primary qualitative data, the gender empowerment is re-conceptualized in Chapter 7. The simplistic notion that globalization is positive for women because it creates work opportunities for women and that earnings empower women is questioned and examined in detail.

The conclusion is that empowerment is a highly complex and contextual issue and not amenable to change based on simple indicators or checklists.

8.2   RECOMMENDATIONS

8.2.1 DATA COLLECTION

Ultimately, the problem of home-based workers is acute poverty that drives them to extremely hazardous and low paying work. Their welfare, therefore, can be addressed in the broad rubric of a government's anti-poverty strategy. However, in order to be able to deal effectively with the problem, the government will need to know the magnitude of home-based work underway. In this regard, the Federal Bureau of Statistics will need to revise its definition of the informal sector to include home-based work. This would be a move away from its current unit or enterprise orientation. The *Household Income and Expenditure Survey* or the *Pakistan Integrated Household Survey*, rather than the *Labour Force Surveys*, are the appropriate surveys to gather such information. Alternatively, the FBS could rely on registration boards discussed as recommendation 8.2.3. Once the magnitude of home-based work is ascertained, it would be possible to find the appropriate solutions. Pakistan, as a signatory to the ILO Labour Statistics Convention, is obliged to collect, compile, and publish such labour statistics.

8.2.2 CREDIT AND DEBT ELIMINATION

One component of the current poverty alleviation strategy is the provision of micro-credit via the *Khushali* (well-being) Bank that provides micro-credit. Credit provision should be flexible about what enhances well-being. In view of the debt induced oppression of home based workers, a good use of the funds would be to buy out the debt of bonded labour and other workers indebted to contractors, and hence subject to exploitation, via loans on easy terms.

8.2.3 REGISTRATION BOARDS[3]

We recommend that the provincial or district governments set up registration boards such that all labour, contractors and employees engaged in a particular activity would need to register. Apart from being a source of information for the number and size of home-based work sectors, which could be conveyed to the FBS, it would also be a clearing-house of information on other issues such as rates. It could also establish a welfare fund and manage the activities of this fund.

8.2.4 WELFARE FUNDS[4]

Our research has indicated that home-based workers get an extremely small percentage of the total value generated by their work; hence there is a large margin owners operate with. Interfering in the market place is dangerous and often results in negative unanticipated outcomes. However, in view of the large margin, a levy should be imposed on the owners, collected by the relevant local government institution, and utilized to establish a welfare fund for each sector to finance several activities.[5] The federal, provincial or district governments could provide matching grants for the fund that could finance the following kind of activities:

- Safety equipment (gloves, masks);
- Safety training courses for workers (attendance mandatory for those registering);
- Labour legislation awareness courses for owners and contractors (attendance mandatory for owners and contractors, since our findings showed no awareness currently), particularly with regards to ILO Convention 182 of 1999 on Worst Forms of Child Labour that the Government of Pakistan ratified in August 2001.
- Other skills training for workers;
- Establish an employment exchange with information provided on work matters like work opportunities and rates;
- Provide schooling and health facilities (children across the board expressed a desire to be in school and our results show that expense rather than home-based work is what keeps the children out of school. Similarly, the welfare fund could address the issue of the lack of access to health facilities).
- Legal counseling

Promoting the above stated objectives would also be in line with Pakistan's international commitments, since it is a signatory to the ILO Conventions on social security, worst forms of child labour and equal remuneration (refer to Chapter 2). We found that work at home further burdens and oppresses women rather than empowering them, given the social, cultural and productive context of their existence. There is some evidence that educated women dealt with the contractors and the world with more confidence and commanded more respect, and hence there is enhanced importance one can attribute to the social investment in girl's education.

8.2.5 REGULATION

There will be a need to regulate the proper implementation of the duties and responsibilities of the registration board. The state is currently concerned about downsizing its role in the productive sector and cutting off fat in the public sector. In a country like Pakistan, downsizing needs to be about the more efficient utilization of existing human resources rather than a loss of jobs. Thus, surplus staff could be part of the local government effort to ensure the proper delivery of services at the grassroots level, and these efforts checked and complemented by Citizens Monitoring Boards being established by the Local Government Plan, 2000.

8.2.6 AMNESTY

There are two important issues to keep in mind. First, home visits by women government servants may be necessary in communities that observe strict *purdah*. Cultural change, to one in which women are treated more fairly and humanely by men, such as was the case to some extent in' the Gujrati community, is a slow process and often accompanies economic growth. Inducing change forcibly can backfire and may not be warranted. However, in view of the extreme oppression of women, particularly of those sold into home-based work, the full force of existing legal protection should be available to them via state supported legal counseling. This work, in the short run, could be complemented by civil society organizations.

Second, since many doing home-based work are illegal immigrants, they would be unlikely to want to register because harassment and denial of a work permit may be a likely outcome. Thus, the government would have to change its current policy to one of blanket 'amnesty' policies[6]. Once individuals enter a country, they have acquired rights as humans. These individuals are very unlikely to return, and forcing them to live on the exploitative margins of existence is a shameful default policy. Poor countries have an opportunity here to show the way to the rich ones.

The 'illegal status' they currently live in also results in exploitation by contractors and the police. This sense of insecurity also seems to push them into extreme forms of religious practice to gain social acceptability.

8.2.7 COLLECTIVE ACTION

Both the quantitative and qualitative information showed that there is virtually no organization working with women to assist them to enhance their pay and improve their working conditions. Over half the women indicated a willingness to be part of some kind of collective action to improve their working conditions if provided some kind of leadership and assistance. Several factors like excess supply of labour and fear of job loss, lack of information and awareness, lack of mobility and relationship with the contractor hindered collective action.

There is a role for civil society organizations like PILER and Aurat Foundation to mobilize workers. Since power is so unequal in the labour market equation, and since the margins at the higher ends of the production chain are so high, some redress, initially in the form of district government mandated rates until collective bargaining is established, is called for. Over time, efforts of civil society organizations and information made available by registration boards may lead to workers' associations that would enable them to secure decent rates. The right to free association, based on the Constitution and conventions Pakistan is a signatory to, will need to be ensured by the state.

8.2.8 RATIFYING CONVENTIONS

Given the nature of the tenuous relationship home-based workers have with the state, in view of their citizen status, the notion of support from the state was a puzzling question for them. Of those who responded to the question of what kind of assistance they would like from the government or some other organization, technical training, credit (earlier mentioned) and framing better policies accounted for the bulk of responses. However, the low response rate on this question indicates the pessimism women felt about the likelihood of anything concrete being done for them or their children. The state has a fundamental responsibility to those living within its borders and this should be fulfilled within the broad framework of the ILO Home Workers Convention of 1996 that Pakistan should ratify and implement as a starting point.

NOTES

1. One could argue that the same is true for most industrial work. While comparing home-based with industrial work was not the purpose of this analysis, based on casual observation, we are quite confident that the conditions of home-based work are far worse than formal sector industrial work.
2. The fieldwork started in mid-January and was completed in end- February 2001.
3. While the latest Labour policy suggests the EOBI and SSIs to remove irritants and encourage registration, these measures are not comprehensive enough. More importantly, the discouragement/denial of the right of association effectively makes registration almost impossible.
4. The Labour Policy 2002 suggests that, 'Workers Welfare Funds and Education Cess Funds may be utilized to establish quality educational facilities in all districts of the country for providing free education up to matric and intermediate levels to worker's children.' This policy also underscores the strengthening of the tripartite character of the management boards. However, these policy formulations are limited in scope.
5. Such a fund has been successfully set up by the *beedi* HOME-BASED WORK sector in India, and this is precisely the kind of activity that falls in the domain of the newly created local government institutions.
6. The National Aliens Registration Authority (NARA) established in 2001, a government initiative to register illegal immigrants (largely Bengalis, Burmese and persons of Arab descent are included while Afghans are excluded from this list) can have limited success due to its mandate that can potentially be used against registering aliens. Aliens have to first register and then are eligible to receive a work permit or permission for own business. Further, a registered alien will not have the right to shift and settle in any other city of Pakistan without permission of the Authority. Such restrictive clauses do not encourage women to register themselves and their minor children. In any case, the male household head is often unemployed, thus foreclosing the option of registration. Also, many aliens are weary of NARA because it is staffed by persons formerly or currently with the police and intelligence services. Due to fears of harassment rather than access to legal protection, most aliens are unwilling to register.

ANNEXURES

ANNEXURE 1: CASE STUDIES

PROCEDURE

Households were selected for more in-depth case studies if they were either much worse off or much better off than the average i.e. there was some interesting distinguishing factor.

Case study 1.1
(Nadia Maleeha Assad)
Sector: Carpet Weaving
Location: Korangi

Haseena, was 20 years old, a mother of two and lived in Korangi. Her husband was unemployed and uneducated. Carpet weaving was the sole means of income that they had for making ends meet. Haseena, her husband and her six-year-old daughter wove a carpet all day. She did not have any extended family to turn to and owed about Rs. 6000 to the contractor. Despite weaving all day, she had not been able to pay off her debt for the past two years. The contractor visited her house after almost a week, and after counting the *phairas* (rounds) completed, gave her half the money and deducted the remaining half from her debt. Although two long years had gone by, her debt remained virtually unchanged from the day she took it because of the interest. The contractor not only abused her verbally, but, time and again, he beat her little daughter. Once, he came to demand the money that she owed him, and while arguing, he started beating her up. Her husband tried to stop him, but the contractor dragged him out of the house and beat him up too. They did not report the incident to the police, since they do not trust the police. They had no idea who they could turn to for help or how to pay off the contractor's debt. Haseena's little daughter had swollen finger joints because of carpet weaving. She also complained of fatigue and dizziness. Haseena herself had a skin infection with blisters all over her legs. She too complained of dizziness and irritation in the skin. Her husband suffered badly from chronic cough and breathing problems. They did not get any medical assistance from the contractor. Haseena's case is one of many. Contractors took undue advantage of these families because they were indebted. Lives went to waste trying to pay off an un-payable debt.

Case study 1.2
(Nadia Maleeha Assad)
Sector: Carpet Weaving
Location: Korangi

Zain-ul-Abideen was a retired Bengali army officer residing in Korangi. He had six children and his eldest son was studying in class 10. Zain came from an educated family. His brothers and sisters were all educated and his parents were aware of the importance of education. Zain did not have permanent employment, but he, along with his sons, engaged in labour to meet their expenses. Despite financial constraints, his children, including his daughters, were going to school.

Zain believed that educating girls is as important as educating boys. He wanted his daughters to study so that they could be better people. He thought that educating a mother was tantamount to educating a generation, and only an educated mother would be able to make the children aware of the importance of education. He lamented that his community members did not allow girls to go to school due to distorted religious beliefs. He thought that Islam has laid stress on educating children, and that it is the parents' duty to give the children a good life. Zain did not let his wife engage in carpet weaving at home because he viewed it as hazardous and time consuming. He preferred his wife to give sufficient time to the children and not be subject to too much pressure. He was also aware of the hardships of the families who had undertaken home-based work, particularly, the contractor's exploitation, and did not want the same to happen to his family. He had tried, in his own way, to convince community members to send their children, and especially the girls, to school. He actively participated in setting up a small primary school for children in the locality where they could receive formal education, and his own children attended this school.

His case is an example of the perceptible difference in the living standards of the households where husbands are considerate and enlightened as compared to where they are not.

Case Study 1.3
(Sadaf Naz)
Sector: Carpet Weaving
Location: Korangi

Fahmeeda was 50 years old and had three sons and five daughters.
She mentioned that, at first, her husband was all right and was
engaged in wage labour. He also constructed a house for the family.
However, for the last eight years, he had been a heroin addict and
had started beating her.

Some six months back, her daughter, Kulsoom, along with her
husband, came to stay with them. Alam, Kulsoom's husband, was a
sugarcane juice vendor. Jaafer, Fehmeeda's husband, demanded rent
for the room occupied by Kulsoom and Alam. Fehmeeda opposed
this and Jaafer got angry and beat her with a stick. No one came to
help her from within the family. She left her house that day, but
since she had no other shelter, she came back the same evening.
Her husband also beat her another time and injured her head and
badly cut her hand.

Fehmeeda had been weaving carpets for the last 20 years.
However, she had to give up carpet weaving due to weak eyesight
and took up making incense sticks instead.

Case Study 1.4
(Sadaf Naz)
Sector: Carpet Weaving
Location: Korangi

Zohra Bibi, originally from Bangladesh, was weaving carpets in
Korangi Town. Her father died before her birth. She had two
brothers and three sisters. Her father was a farmer, but, after his
death, her family turned to woodcutting to make ends meet.

She got married for the first time at the age of 12 with a
woodcutter. Her first husband died after two years of marriage, and
she came back to her parent's house. A person named Qasim, who
according to her was a *dallal* (pimp), used to come to their house.
He convinced Zohra to leave Bangladesh for Pakistan and promised
to marry her to some rich Pakistani. She came to Pakistan, with a
group of ten females, under Qasim's supervision. According to her,
she did this against everyone's advice.

Qasim sold her in marriage to a Punjabi for Rs. 8000. She said
her husband wanted to take her to Multan and sell her there but
she refused to go. Consequently, he divorced her within seven

months of marriage and also demanded the Rs. 8000 he had paid
for her. Since she had no money, she appealed to the local *Punchayat*
(council of elders) to resolve the issue, and it ruled in her favour.

She then started working in a hotel where the owner of the hotel
proposed to her even though he already had three wives and was
70 years old. She decided to get married because she thought it
better to have a husband in a male dominated society. She wove
carpets to run her kitchen. She knew of the hazardous nature of
carpet weaving but felt she had no other choice.

Case Study 1.5
(Sadaf Naz)
Sector: Sack Stitching
Location: Godhra

Parveen was married at 13 with Habib, a contractor in a towel
factory. She mentioned that she was kidnapped at 12 from her
house in Bangladesh and was brought to Pakistan by a *dallal*,
along with other girls. Interestingly, this *dallal* was herself a
woman. She sold Parveen for rupees Rs. 18,000 to a Bengali family.
She stayed with this family as a domestic servant for one year.
After that, she got married to Habib, who already had married
thrice before, once in Bangladesh and twice in Pakistan. The two
wives in Pakistan had divorced him, but he still sent money to his
wife in Bangladesh every month.

Her husband abused her physically and her neighbours know
about their domestic fights. Since she was alone in Pakistan, he
took advantage of this and beat her at will. She often escaped to the
neighbours' house, but returned to her house because of her children.

She even refused the interview money, because she feared that
her husband might become suspicious. He never gave her money,
and she had no clue about his income. Perveen stitched sacks and
earned Rs. 30 per 100 sacks. She felt that it was not a very hard
job, but was hazardous due to the jute fibers.

Case Study 1.6
(Ayesha Khurshid)
Sector; Carpet Weaving
Location: Orangi

Hasina, a 22-year-old Bengali woman living in Orangi, had a
different attitude from the rest of the women living in that locality.

She had matriculated and her husband was also earning a decent living. Besides that, she wove carpets at home to supplement the family income. Hasina also did volunteer work at the nearby clinic as a nurse and as a tutor for the neighbourhood children. Her living standard was much better than the people living around her, and it was the outcome of the couple's hard work and planning. Their only child was very well mannered and clean, unlike most of the children observed during the fieldwork. She was the only woman we met in that locality who practiced birth control. Hasina and her husband were of the opinion that they will have their second child only when they can provide the child enough time and attention as also the necessities of life.

Unlike most of the other people interviewed, she did not complain about the behaviour of the contractor. She thought the contractor always treated her with respect and gave her wages on time. However, she also recounted her health problem due to the home-based work. She was very responsive on most issues and criticized men very openly in the focus group discussion. According to her, women were also responsible for their misery, since they do not make enough effort to bring about a change. Hasina said that they themselves had given their husbands the freedom to ill-treat them.

It was an eye-opener meeting a woman like her in that locality where religious extremism seems to determine every norm of life. Her different attitude towards life was probably the result of several factors including her family's education, her exposure to the outside world and a supportive husband.

Case Study 1.7
(Ayesha Khurshid)
Sector: Sack Stitching
Location: Godhra

Ayesha, was a forty-year old widow living in the Gujrati community of Godhra. She had four children and her husband died when the eldest child (son) was only eleven years old. Her husband used to work in the vegetable market. After his death, there was no money to support her and her children so she had moved in with her in-laws. Her eldest son, Jamil, had to quit his studies and look for work to support the family. Ayesha had to do something in which she and her son could work together without her having to leave the house. Since she was a good cook, she decided to cook *biryani* (fried rice) and her son sold it on a mobile stall. This worked well for them, and she was able to support her family independently. Later on, Ayesha shifted into her own house that she built from the savings from this micro-enterprise.

Despite her self-sufficiency, Ayesha still followed all the traditions of her community religiously. For example, she did not let her fifteen-year-old daughter go to school because she thought that it was inappropriate for young girls to go out of the house. She told us that while she was earning money through home-based work, her young son would not allow her to step out of the house as he considered himself to be the head of the household. It seemed that the underlying reason for the decision to stay housebound was the enormous amount of social pressure on her.

Case Study 1.8
(Ayesha Khurshid)
Sector: Sack Stitching
Location: Godhra

This case study is based on the personal initiative taken by a woman, which succeeded in part because of the supportive attitude of her husband. Rashida was a forty-five year old woman, with three daughters, of the Gujrati community living in Godhra. She saw her family as one that brought about a social change in the neighbourhood and persuaded others to send their daughters to school as she was doing.

Safia, her eldest daughter, had matriculated, and was working as a teacher in an NGO school. Her second daughter, Zaitoon, had done her Bachelors and had also learnt to apply *mehndi* (henna) designs and was using this skill to earn a living. The youngest daughter, Surraya, had also done her Bachelors and also taught in the NGO school. Besides this, all the three sisters, as well as Rashida, stitched *boris*. This household was different from most other households in the locality. The home environment seemed very relaxed and open. All the girls were allowed to go outside the house to work or socialize and they themselves were very confident.

Rashida had no regrets in not having a son, and did not seem worried about the future or the marriage of her daughters, whom she took pride in. Rashida told us that she and her husband were the first parents in their community to send their daughters to school about eighteen years ago. All the other families opposed this decision. Though the Gujrati community was more forward looking, it is only recently that parents had taken an interest in the children's education. It also appears that economic reasons were.

driving the change. Rashida, however, said that her reasons for educating her daughters were based on the intrinsic value of education rather than the economic returns that might accrue from them.

This family took the field team around during the survey, without caring for the contractor's reaction. They talked very openly about the contractor's unfair practices. They had tried to look for other better paying home-based work but could not find any. Rashida and her daughters had the same health problems as most of the other home-based workers in this sector. Her daughter, Zaitoon, told us that all the girls from the neighbourhood get together to do the *bori* stitching, and it has become more of a social activity now.

As earlier indicated, Rashida came from a family where education was considered important both for males and females. She persuaded her husband, who came from a family in which girls did not go to school, about the importance of education for girls. She told us that their current life would have been impossible for them if her in-laws were still alive.

ANNEXURES

ANNEXURE 2: FIELD REPORTS

PROCEDURE

Each of the three field teams was assigned a task of writing a field report at the end of the fieldwork. Aside from the introductory and concluding remarks, they were provided with the following format within which to report their observations:

1. Extent of exploitation visible in the contractor/worker relationship[1]
2. Impact of HB work on health of women and children
3. Impact of HB work on overall well-being
4. Impact of HB work on women's empowerment
5. Other issues

The following tips were provided to the field teams based on the pre-tests.

BEFORE THE START OF FIELDWORK

1. Time yourself during the pretest.
2. Don't go in with pre-conceived notions.
3. Don't lead/prompt the respondent.
4. Dress appropriately/don't stand out.
5. Don't make respondent feel inferior.
6. Make sure you have no biases against any community/occupation/gender/age group/activity.
7. Develop a community profile

AFTER THE FIELDWORK STARTS

1. Introduce yourself to respondents (female fieldworker should introduce the male interviewer)

2. Be polite to all respondents (avoid queries diplomatically from people who gather around)
3. Try to diplomatically limit the crowd development if possible.
4. State briefly the objective of the survey.
5. Let respondents know that they will be paid Rs. 150 per household as a compensation for their time.
6. Be sensitive.
7. Avoid taking a position on any issue.
8. Don't pose questions in a way that may generate suspicion..
9. Pose questions in easily understandable language.
10. Conversational style:
    a) Looking at questionnaire should prompt you.
    b) Talk to the respondent.
    c) Make eye contact
11. Gently steer respondent back to the point. Don't cut them off.
12. Children should be present, and questions from the child questionnaire, directed to them when possible.
13. Maintain daily journal for daily report
14. Note all interesting observations. Flag every interesting household, since you may need to return for a case study.
15. Tell respondents you are doing this for improving govt. policy.
16. No personal benefit should be promised as an outcome of the research.
17. Tell them that objective is to improve the condition of home-based workers in general.

We anticipated there would be repetition, but we felt it was nonetheless important to have independent reporting from each team to avoid a loss of insights. We also anticipated that there may be conflicting views, which would require subsequent discussion and clarification. The integrity of the sections has been maintained and the order in which the teams chose to do the reporting has also not been altered in the first two reports. The third report, for which the reporting is by sector, did not conform to the provided format. These edited reports (edited for language and repetition within the report), along with the case studies and focus group discussion reports, were the primary data sources for chapters 5 and 7.

Field Report 2.1
(Aamir Habib)

2.1.1 LOCALITIES

2.1.1.1. Orangi

Orangi is situated in North Karachi (see Appendix 3.1). Mutahida Quami Mahaz (MQM), an offshoot of a political party comprising of Muslim refugees from Northern India (resulting from the partition of the Indian sub-continent in 1947), have political dominance in the area. While Bengalis and Burmese were the majority communities in Orangi, both these communities comprised mostly of illegal migrants who had difficulty in going outside the locality.

Both the Bengali and Burmese communities were very religious. Generally, based on their understanding of Islam, women and girls only went outside the home with the permission of a male member of the family. Women perceived it to be their religious responsibility to obey husbands and perceived it to be a sin to bother their husbands, their only master after God.

Working outside the home was generally not permitted for women, thus the women and children worked at home making *agarbatti* (incense sticks). They earned only Rs. 5 per thousand pieces of agarbatti. Males did not assist with home-based work even if they were not engaged in any other activity. Women and children woke up early in the morning and worked until late at night. The children attended *madrasah* (traditional religious schools) from 8 to 11 a.m. and then again from 2 to 5 p.m. and engaged in home-based work in between. Some children also attended NGO run informal schools. More children were viewed as a means of increasing revenue from home-based work in view of the low rates received for the work.

2.1.1.2. Korangi

Korangi is situated in the sout-heast coastal area of Karachi. Bengalis were in a majority in this locality, which was politically dominated by MQM, Haqiqi (a splinter group of MQM). The community had strong affiliations with religious parties, and the radical Sipah-e-Sahaba had a discernable effect over the social life of the community. The community males were predominantly engaged in fishing, and the main home-based activity for women and girls was carpet making.

Korangi had similar social values as Orangi, but was a more backward area, in terms of both infrastructure and social norms, because it is much farther from the main city. Poverty was more visible, and many children were only partially clothed. Here, children, generally five and older, also went to the factory for carpet making. The households had contracted loans based on their children who worked at the factory to pay them off. Women and children woke up early in the morning and worked until sunset. Children went to the *madrasah*, and assisted with home-based work when they returned. The rate was a meager Rs. 2 per one completed row (*phaira*).

2.1.1.3. Godhra

Godhra is situated in the north-west of Karachi near the industrial area. The MQM politically dominated this area. Although Sipah-e-Sahaba had a presence, they did not have much impact over the social life of the community. The main home-based work was sack sewing. The migrant Gujrati community, who migrated from a town named Godhra in India, was in a majority, but Sindhi and Urdu-speaking families were also resident in the community.

The Gujrati community gave the impression of being well organized. Men helped the women in doing home-based work when at home during the sack-sewing season. However, women did the bulk of the home-based work, while children assisted on a part time basis. They earned Rs. 30 for 100 stitched sacks.

The Gujrati community placed a high premium on education and most of the children, including girls, attended regular school. This is likely to have been the result of the higher educational attainment of Gujrati men. This higher education level also made them less susceptible to the obscurantism of the local 'mullah' (*imam* or guardian of the local mosque) than Bengali and Burmese men.

2.1.1.4. Machhar Colony

Machhar Colony is situated in Lyari, Karachi's south-west coastal area. The Bengali community was in the majority in this locality, but some Punjabi and Sindhi families also resid here. The Pakistan People's Party (one of the two main national political parties) was politically dominant. The men were mainly engaged in fishing, while prawn shelling was the main home-based activity.

The Machhar Colony community again had a similar life style and values as the Bengali communities of Orangi and Korangi. Women and children woke up at 4 a.m. and worked until sunset when prawn shelling work was available (during the season). Children, few of whom went to school, often went to a *wara* (factory type place) in the locality to work.

A pot, referred to as a *gala*, containing 4 kgs. of prawn would be reduced to about 2 kgs. after shelling. A token worth Rs. 10 per *gala* was given them when they picked up the work and this could be cashed in when they returned the shelled prawns.

2.1.2 EXPLOITATION

Incense stick (*Agarbatti*) making is simple work once mastered, but very hazardous. The contractor verbally abused the children on account of very minor mistakes and also fined them. At times, the contractor also beat the children. Children and women avoided talking about the contractor's attitude due to the fear of losing their work. In Korangi, the exploitation was more intense than in Orangi. The children on whom loans had been taken were the butt of the contractor's verbal and physical abuse. I was able to personally observe the wounds in a couple of cases. Men seem to have more concern for the money than the children do. Children working in the factory worked at home during the holidays.

The contractor-worker relationship was comparatively better in Godhra. Most of the women and children seemed to be satisfied with their relationship with the contractor. While a few children complained that the contractor verbally abused them, this was very rare. In case of poor quality work, the contractor returned it for re-stitching. While I got the opportunity to meet with very few women (only 4 or 5), their homes were well maintained and clean. These women seemed well aware of their rights, and not subject to the abuses evident in the other localities.

The worse cases of worker abuse by contractors occurred in Machhar colony. The children who went to the *wara* were the most vulnerable. The contractors routinely verbally and physically abused them for very minor mistakes. Machhar Colony was the only community where no one complained of having been fined; the main complaint was regarding the harsh treatment of the contractor.

2.1.3 HEALTH

The chemicals used in *agarbatti* making are toxic and almost all of the women and children had skin problems. Inhaling sawdust causes bronchial problems and women complained of pains in the chest and watering eyes. Exhaustion was common for both women and children. The common complaint of carpet makers in Orangi and Korangi was back pain, pain in the joints, legs and chest. Children complained of exhaustion, watering eyes, cough and pain in the legs, joints and limbs. Children also had cracks in their fingers and breathing problem. The wool dust of the sacks also resulted in bronchial problems. Children in Godhra complained of coughs, pain in legs, due to prolonged sittings, and watering eyes. Women complained of general body pains. Prawn shelling is mainly done in icy water. Women and children suffered from skin problems including swelling, nausea from the smell and exhaustion. Children also suffered from exhaustion.

2.1.4 HOME-BASED WORK AND OVERALL WELL-BEING

One could argue that agarbati making contributed little to welfare given how little households earned from this activity. While more household income was generated from weaving carpets, making payments on loans offsets this. Sack stitching was less remunerative; it constituted an income supplement, since the men generally earned the income for the household. The earnings from prawn shelling were barely enough for the household's food needs.

2.1.5 WOMEN'S EMPOWERMENT

Home-Based Work seems to have no bearing on women's empowerment, which is virtually non-existent in the Bengali and Burmese communities of Orangi, Korangi and Machhar Colony. As earlier indicated, women required permission to go out and had to be escorted by someone even a child. According to the community's norms, a seven-year-old girl is an adult and hence is not allowed to go to regular school. In Machhar Colony and Korangi, women would be lost outside their houses on their own. In Godhra, women could go outside when they needed to, but even here required permission of the males. In some ways, the Gujrati women of Godhra appeared to be heads of their households, but this was more a cultural phenomenon rather than a result of the home-based work they engaged in.

Field Report 2.2
(Nadia Maleeha Asad)

2.2.1 INTRODUCTION

It is generally believed that women's empowerment is influenced by their working status. A working woman is believed to be an 'empowered' woman but interaction with home-based working women of Karachi revealed otherwise. This survey, spanning different locations and incorporating different sectors of home-based work, revealed that cultural background has a larger role to play in this context. The extent to which a woman can assert herself or follow her will depends largely on the community she belongs to and the social norms of that community. Work and earnings seem to have little effect in this regard.

2.2.2 WOMEN'S EMPOWERMENT

The communities associated with home-based work were mostly Bengali, Burmese and Gujrati. While the Gujratis were concentrated in Godhra, the former two were residing in Orangi, Korangi and Machhar Colony. In each locality, we studied one particular kind of home-based work i.e. *agarbatti* making in Orangi, carpet weaving in Korangi, sack stitching in Godhra and prawn cleaning in Machhar Colony.

The Bengalis and Burmese were staunchly conservative. However, only those aspects of religion were practiced that, in their interpretation enslaved and subdued women. This was inclusive of, but not limited to, strict *purdah* (segregation of the women's domain and presence from men), so much so, that women were not allowed to go out of the house and girls were not sent to school after the age of twelve. In most cases, the husbands were unemployed and home-based work was the only source of income i.e. women were the sole earners in a number of cases. This, however, made the husband no less authoritative and the wife no more empowered. In fact, in such cases, we observed that women had to grapple with the double responsibility of taking care of household chores and doing home-based work. The underlying notion was that whatever work goes on within the char-diwari (the four walls of the house) is women's work, whether it is an income generating activity or some household chore.

The Gujrati community, however, was different. Here, women were fairly mobile. They could go out of the house without having to take the husband's permission. They visited each other's houses and were well aware of their surroundings unlike their Bengali and Burmese counterparts. Again, unlike in the Burmese and Bengali communities, girls were encouraged to study. The men were mostly working and did not consider it shameful lend to a helping hand to their wives in the home-based work. Once again though, this behaviour was due entirely to the greater broad-mindedness of the Gujrati men. Engaging in home-based work had no effect on women's empowerment.

2.2.3 EXPLOITATION

The scale of exploitation varied in all cases, depending upon the nature of the work and whether the material was delivered to the home or collected from the contractor. In Orangi, where *agarbatti* making was the major activity, the contractor was a relative in most cases—one main reason why there were very few instances of major exploitation. Material was supplied to the households, and women dealt with the contractor themselves. Since the women observed strict *purdah*, there was little opportunity for the contractor to abuse the women either physically or verbally. The *agarbattis* were tied in bundles of a thousand, which fetched about Rs. 5.50. Workers were, however, not paid on time, and they were fined for faulty work.

In Korangi, carpet weaving was the major activity and it entailed an alarmingly high rate of exploitation. Children worked in the home as well as at factories. Parents took loans on the children who were subsequently bonded to work in the factories until the loan was paid off, a remote possibility. Since the men did not have a permanent job, home-based work was the main source of income for the household. The contractor paid according to the completed rows of the weft (*phairas*). Most households, with hard work, managed to complete ten or twelve rows in a day. This amounted to about Rs. 30.00 out of which they had to meet the daily expenses and pay off the contractor's debt. Hence the debt kept on accumulating. The parents' indebtedness provided the contractor with unbridled authority to abuse and beat up the children, and there was little the family could do about it.

In Godhra, women and children had to go and get work from the contractor. Since a number of contractors provided the sack (*bori*) work in the area, people got work from a different contractor each time. The level of exploitation, therefore, depended on which contractor they dealt with. No major complaints of exploitation were reported except that the workers felt that the wages were too low. It was interesting that in Godhra, Sindhi and Urdu speaking minorities complained that the contractors, who were Gujrati, discriminated in favour of their own community members in distributing work and determining rates. No such complaints were observed from minorities in areas where the Burmese and Bengalis were in a majority. This was perhaps because the latter were mostly illegal immigrants and kept to themselves, or perhaps that work was not in as much demand by other communities.

In Machhar colony, the children got work from the *waras* where most of the prawn shelling is done. The kids suffered the wrath of the contractors or *munshis* in case of defective work. Again, since a different contractor provided work each time, the treatment meted out to the children naturally depended on the person. The *galas* or baskets of prawns were weighed before giving them to the children for cleaning and were weighed once again when they were brought back. If they weighed less than expected or if there was some fault in cleaning the prawns, the children were beaten by the contractors. Another mishap that occurred, more often than not, was when the contractors got the work done by the household and then ran away without paying them for their labour. The women are helpless in these situations and their attitude is that such matters are in God's hands.

Thus, in all cases, women and children were exploited, although the degree and nature varied. In no case were they paid on time. Women realized that this happened because they were women and that their husbands, as men, would not have to undergo the same sufferings. There is little they could do about such exploitation because their financial vulnerability made them dependent on home-based work. They also acknowledged that collective action could be useful, but they felt that strong motivation and leadership was needed for this and that, on their own, they were not organized enough to put up a successful strike.

2.2.4 HEALTH

All the four kinds of home-based work had an adverse impact on women and child health. General body aches and exhaustion were observed in all cases due to prolonged working hours and little rest. Women making *agarbatti* complained of cough and flu due to the sawdust. In certain cases, nose bleeding was also observed. In Korangi, carpet weaving caused women and children to suffer from cough and breathing problems. They also suffered from chest and joint pains, and in some areas, skin infections were also reported. Prawns are highly perishable and hence have to be kept in ice cold water. Women complained that having to constantly put their hands into freezing water resulted in flu, fever and cough. Cleaning the prawns also resulted in skin infection and rashes. Sack stitching caused cough and irritation in the throat. The fibers also resulted in congestion, skin infections and itching. Due to long working hours, most women and children suffered from joint pains, dizziness, watering eyes and weak eyesight.

2.2.5 ECONOMIC WELL-BEING

In this context also, home-based work has different effects on different communities. In the Bengali and Burmese communities, where the men either did no work or engaged in fishing which did not yield a regular income, the income from home-based work met the daily requirements of the family. Households had no savings and also did not have enough money to send the children to school if they wanted to. Home-based work therefore, only assured a meager living. The Gujrati women used their earnings for the children's tuition fees and some spending money. They also saved via a 'committee' system. Thus, home-based work was a useful income supplement, but not adequate as the sole income source.

2.2.6 CONCLUDING COMMENTS AND OTHER OBSERVATIONS

It is clear that cultural norms have a major impact on women. Men belonging to the Bengali and Burmese communities were highly religious. However, their distorted religious principles have reduced women to mere slaves. Though this is generally the case, the conditions in Korangi were exceptionally appalling. Here, women were completely oblivious of their surroundings and did not go out of the house on their own at all. One Bengali man mentioned that if he left his wife in the street across his house, she would not be able to find her way back. At a very early age, gender roles are specified for the boys and the girls. Girls are taught that staying inside the house and doing what their husband tells them makes them *izzatdar* (respectable).

The Korangi community was exceptionally backward, perhaps as a result of being located on the outskirts of the city that isolated them from the rest of Karachi. They were also hostile towards the field team and towards NGOs, possibly because a number of human rights organizations had visited the area but little had been done so far to improve their living standards. Moreover, factories where children made carpets had in the past been raided and shut down, resulting in a loss of work for quite some time. Since these households depended on their children's earnings, they were afraid to cooperate with the field-team fearing that it might result in something similar.

Even the work that the men were associated with depended largely on the community they belonged to. Bengalis and Burmese were generally associated with fishing, although the income fluctuated highly in this trade, whereas the Punjabis residing in the same locality were mostly carpenters.

Most of the households belonging to the control group comprised of Punjabi and Urdu-speaking communities. They were observed to be much more aware of their surroundings. Their women observed *purdah*, but they did not have to follow strict rules like the ones set for the Bengali women. The Punjabis did not mingle with the Bengalis and were of the opinion that it is not financial compulsion but 'habit' that caused the Bengalis to make their children work rather than send them to school. They believed that they had got used to living off the income earned by the children. The Punjabis and Urdu-speaking community realized the importance of education and sent their children to school. In general, they showed no intention of taking up home-based work in the near future. However, they indicated that even if they did take up home-based work, it would be sewing, stitching or embroidery and not the hazardous work that the Bengalis and Burmese do. They also viewed work like *agarbatti* making or prawn cleaning as messy and time consuming.

Religion can be viewed as the backbone of Bengali culture. For them, sending the children to the *madrasah* was more important than sending them to school, even though it is was sometimes more expensive. Women were kept inside the house for religious reasons, but when it came to providing them with their rights, as have been defined by Islam, religion was put on the back burner. On average,

Bengali women had seven children, because they believe, or rather their husbands believe, that birth control is not endorsed by Islam.

What was most distressing about this particular practice of religion was the indifference exhibited by the women. Not only had they been brain-washed, but they themselves, to a large extent, supported the treatment meted out to them. They thought that if their husbands helped them with the household chores or with home-based work, they would be committing some sort of a sin and would be held answerable for that.

Households were better off when the husband was educated and recognized the importance of educating his children. Only those children had the privilege of attending school whose father had the wisdom to realize that without education they will not be able to accomplish a great deal in life. Once again, it turns out to be a man's world where the fate of the whole household depends on his discretion. Perhaps the panacea would be to educate the men of these communities and to make them realize that their daughters and their wives are as much human as they are and therefore, they deserve to be treated as such.

Field Report 2.3
(Azmat Ali)

2.3.1 AGARBATTI MAKING

Agarbatti is mostly used at religious places like mosques, graveyards or *mandirs* (Hindu temples) and also used in houses for fragrance. *Agarbatti* making home-based work in Korangi, Karachi, was mostly engaged in by the Burmese and Bengalis. The Burmese and Bengali communities migrated to Pakistan after 1971 and started to live in various areas of Karachi like Orangi, Korangi, Muhammadi or Machhar Colony.

The Government of Pakistan allotted plots for their shanty houses, but they were deprived of other facilities. Because they were not nationals, there was a high incidence of home-based work such as *agarbatti* making in these communities. Women worked in their homes only, because their husbands did not allow them to go out to work. Children, mostly girls between 6 to 12 years, worked with them.

Women doing the home-based work were mostly illiterate. The men were idle and preferred not to work, mostly indulging themselves in unproductive activities. They also supported various addictions like cigarettes and *pan*. The women also engaged in these addictions, which, therefore, consumed much of the income earned from the home-based work.

A household earned about Rs. 5.00 for a bundle containing 1000 *agarbatti* that entailed at least two to three hours of joint work. A family working jointly could at best produce four bundles in a day. Most of what was earned was consumed on the same day. The contractors passed these bundles on to the factories for packing.

Agarbatti making is quite a long and difficult process. The process entails wetting the sawdust and then sun-drying it. A chemical paste is cooked on the fire using a large pot. Then wooden sticks are dipped in the paste and rolled on the sawdust. Inhalation of the fumes from the chemical mixture as well as the sawdust is very hazardous. Also, the chemical paste injures the skin, especially of young children. The field team observed that most of the workers had scars on their hands that were blackened as they worked.

The practice of receiving advance payments from contractors and the inability of paying these loans back put them at a disadvantage and wedded them to this hazardous activity. Being illegal immigrants also limited their ability to seek other occupations in the urban areas. Thus, they were compelled to work without protest and at very low wages despite being aware of the hazardous nature of the work they did.

The Bengali and Burmese communities were not eager to send their children to formal schools due to the expense, but most of the children attended a *madrasa* for acquiring a religious education. Girls, who were much less mobile than boys, did much of the home-based work.

2.3.2 CARPET WEAVING

Carpets were being made both at factories and in homes, although in Korangi, where we did our fieldwork, it was mostly a home-based activity. Carpets were being woven predominantly by the women and children of the Bengali and Burmese communities.

Carpets were woven on large wooden frames lodged in some corner of a room. A design was embedded horizontally and vertically on the frame, using thick threads of attractive colors, in various sizes including 3x6, 4x6, 5x8 and 3x12 ft. It takes up to three to six months to complete one carpet at home, depending on the specifications, with a payment of Rs. 700.00 to Rs. 2,000.00 resulting from this work. Women and children, generally between the ages of 6 to 12 years, do the work.

Contractors were, thus, able to circumvent Labour Laws prohibiting children aged less than ten years from working. Once again, the desperation of the Bengali and Burmese communities comes into play, since it is difficult for them to find alternative employment.

Compared to the men, women were steadfast and hard workers and used the income for home expenses. Again, more girls than boys were involved in this work. Boys and girls attended *madrasa* for Qur'anic education, and wove the carpet on their return. Men often worked in factories near their homes.

2.3.4 PRAWN SHELLING

Seven types of prawn were caught in Karachi, with the biggest size exported to Japan and USA after shelling. Shelling took place in homes in Machhar Colony. One kilogram of second quality shelled prawn fetched Rs. 150 to 700. Women and children in the Bengali and Burmese households did the work.

Prawn shelling is difficult because prawns are kept in iced water to preserve them. In addition to braving the discomfort of the cold water, the softened skin is easily cut.

One basket (*gala*) of peeled prawn, weighing 5 kg., fetched Rs. 10.00 and a household can peel about five *galas* per day. Once again, their vulnerability makes them accept poor rates. Many families doing this work had no other source of income, although some men managed to get work doing deep-sea fishing. However, this income was not well utilized which partly accounted for the poor standard of living of the households.

2.3.5 SACK STITCHING

Sack stitching was the home-based work engaged in by the Gujrati community of Godhra (new Karachi), which migrated to Pakistan in 1947 from Gujrat, India. This community was more prosperous than the others and had a higher mean education level. The men of this community were generally hardworking, and while the children did home-based work, they also attended school.

Sack stitching was seasonal work, available for about four months in the year. The contractors provided the cloth and needles and then collected the sacks once they had been stitched. The sacks were used for exporting potatoes and onions to the Middle East. An expert worker could sew 50 sacks in about two hours and this earned Rs. 30.

Apart from the problems caused by the long sittings in uncomfortable positions, this work was hazardous because of the inhalation of wool fibers.

Field Report 2.4
(Sadaf Naz)

2.4.1 ORANGI TOWN

In Orangi Town, we interviewed women and children making *agarbatti* in their homes. The majority of the population of this area was Bengalis and Burmese. They were illegal immigrants who migrated from Bangladesh and Burma in the 1970s. Inter community *purdah* was very strong but there was no intra-community *purdah*.

Males were considered household heads even if the female was the sole breadwinner. The family size was big because women considered family planning to be against Islam. Women and children engaged in *agarbatti* making in their homes because it enabled them to also do the domestic work. *Purdah,* the insecurity of being illegal immigrants or illness or death of males meant plenty of cheap female labour for the sub-contractors. The sub-contractors were fully aware of the cultural and other constraints of the communities and took full advantage of this by paying them very low wages. The workers complained about these low wages.

There was also a high level of exploitation in contractor-worker relationships. If the workers did not complete their contracts within a specified time, the contractors verbally abused them. Workers were also fined for producing faulty work. However, there was no evidence of the contractors physically abusing female workers. The contractors provided the material and the workers got paid for their labour only. Due to the long work hours, women had problems from inhaling sawdust, muscular pain, exhaustion and general body pains. Children were forced to do this work by their parents and were beaten for faulty work. Female children were involved in home-based work in much larger numbers than male children. They suffered from muscular pains and nosebleeds. The girls, in particular, learnt at a very young age to do domestic as well as home-based work and they had no choice in the matter. The majority of males were wage labourers, while women did productive work along with household chores and childcare. They did not not seem to be aware of their productive contribution.

2.4.2 KORANGI

The majority of the Bengali and Burmese populace in this area were engaged in weaving handmade carpets. Women wove carpets with the help of their young children because the income of the men was insufficient to cover household expenses. There were also small-scale factories for carpet making, called *karkhanas*, where children wove carpets. The conservative views of men meant that the mobility of women was restricted, based on concepts of *purdah, Izzat* (honor) and *sharam* (shame). One male respondent boasted that if his wife goes out even two to three streets away, she would not be able to find her way back.

The majority of the children worked in *karkhanas*, because their parents had taken loans from contractors and the children were working off these loans. The level of exploitation in the contractor-children relationship was very intense. Children were abused both verbally and physically.

Men in Korangi worked as fishermen and did not like to depend only on their women's income from home-based work. They preferred to work instead of sitting at home, if possible. However, men did not acknowledge the economic contribution of women, and even the women themselves did not recognize their own economic contribution towards the household. Both men and women believe that it is the responsibility of women to run the kitchen. Females were not being empowered due to home-based work; rather they were being exploited by doing domestic unpaid labour and productive labour.

Women suffered from common diseases such as cold, fever and cough and also, due to sitting for long hours, from muscular pains, general body pains and pain in the tips of the fingers. Working women and children also suffered from chest diseases. The children got cut while snipping thread with the help of knifes, but they did not go for medical treatment.

2.4.3 GODHRA

The majority of the population was of Gujrati origin. All interviewed households had a nuclear family, but the average family size was as high as ten to twelve. The practice of *purdah* in this community was not very strong compared to the Bengali and Burmese communities. This community was not as conservative, and they allowed their girls to go to school until primary class. After primary, they stopped their girls from going to school due to cultural pressure. At twelve, girls were viewed as mature, and therefore, meant to remain indoors. Also, they had difficulty in bearing the school expenses. In some households, children took tuition from neighbours instead of going to school.

Women collected the raw material for stitching sacks and had to stand for long periods in queues, to get work. They also delivered the finished work after it was completed. In case of faulty work, the worker had to repair the piece, and in case of major damage, the expenses were to be borne by workers. The contractor stopped the flow of work for an indefinite period of time if there was repeated faulty work.

Early marriages were not in practice, so the young daughters helped their mothers not only in domestic chores but also in home-based work. Thus, many hands meant shorter working hours, an average of four to five hours, compared to other home-based work activities. Women had regular interaction with other females of the same locality. Sometimes they got together at one place for doing home-based work and chatted while working. Boys were not engaged in this activity and it was easier for mothers to control their daughters as compared to the sons.

School-going children stitched sacks after returning from school. In some of the households, the income of the household head was sufficient to cover daily expenses. Nonetheless, women and children stitched sacks because women viewed it as giving them some financial independence. They purchased items for their own use from the money so earned and also saved some money to contribute towards the dowry of their daughters.

This home-based work led to cough, breathing problems, chest and muscular pain for the women. They also suffered from intense pain in deliveries due to not having proper rest. The long periods of sitting while doing home-based work sometimes led to abortions. Children also suffered from breathing problems, cough and general body pains.

2.4.4 MACHHAR COLONY

Machhar Colony is a landfill area and is inhabited by Bengalis. Women and children are engaged in home-based work. Women took prawns from *waras,* workplaces where women and children worked.

Prawns were measured in *galas* containing five kilogram. There were many *waras* located in this area.

Women were not allowed to go out of their houses due to strict *purdah*. The main occupation of males was catching fish and they also worked as wage labourers. However, since this income was not adequate for household expenses, women and children engaged in home-based work.

Children in this community were physically abused by the contractor for not shelling carefully and for breaking the tips of the prawns. Some families took work from contractors to their houses. Due to poverty, there was much cheap labour available. Many respondents mentioned that contractors ran away without paying for their labour. Wages were not given on a daily basis; workers were issued tokens worth Rs. 10, on which the name of the contractor was written. Workers accumulated these tokens and payment was expected after a fortnight. Shopkeepers were willing to accept these tokens in exchange for items of daily use.

Children were not going to school and worked in *waras* due to the opportunity cost of children's work. They also did not get pocket money from their parents, if they refused to do home-based work. The health of women and children was adversely affected by this work. They suffered from fever, cough and posture related pains in the feet and body. In addition, they suffered from finger pains and skin problem like rashes.

Field Report 2.5
(Taqdees Fatima)

2.5.1 BACKGROUND

This report starts with the impact of home-based work on the health of women and children. Malnutrition, food impurities, environmental pollution and unhygienic living conditions, stress and excessive physical labour were the fundamental characteristics of poor communities living in the areas visited.

2.5.1 HEALTH HAZARDS

The following occupation related diseases were the common health hazards reported by home-based workers in the fours localities visited: nose bleeding, headache, cough, cold, flu, asthma, respiratory tract infection, backache and pain in the shoulders, leucorrhoea (for women), gastric problems, skin allergy, bronchitis, tuberculosis, weak eye sight, stillbirths and itchy skin.

2.5.2 EXTENT OF EXPLOITATION IN THE CONTRACTOR-WORKER RELATIONSHIP

One of the objectives of the study was to assess the extent of exploitation of home-based workers by sub-contractors. The sub-contractors exploited the workers by paying very low wages with which workers could not make ends meet. For example, Rs. 5 was paid for making 1000 *agarbattis*, Rs. 10 for pealing one *gala,* Rs. 3000 for spending three months on a 5x8 carpet and Rs. 30 for stitching 100 jute bags. These statistics indicate the unprecedented and high degree of exploitation by the sub-contractors. Owing to the low wages paid by the contractor, women in one of the localities resorted to working as vendors selling various things in the neighbor-hood besides doing home-based work.

Sub-contractors threatened work stoppage if the workers demanded an increase in wages. There was an incidence of verbal and physical abuse of children on the part of sub-contractors. They also imposed fines for any defect in the quality of goods. Sometimes, the sub-contractors withheld payment to the workers for indefinite periods and workers become desperate, as they did not have any other earning alternative available to them. Women were of the view that it was only women and children who were subject to exploitation, they believed that men were treated with more respect.

2.5.3 IMPACT OF HOME-BASED WORK ON OVERALL WELL-BEING

Poverty compelled women and children to do home-based work. Another factor pushing women and children to home-based work was when men in the household did not work. The surroundings of all these localities were very filthy and the municipal administration did not have any plans to solve the problems of housing, solid waste disposal, drainage, sanitation and provision of clean drinking water supply. The unhygienic environment was very conducive to the spread of diseases and thus health expenditure of these households was very high.

2.5.4 IMPACT OF HOME-BASED WORK ON WOMEN'S EMPOWERMENT

Women were not empowered even if they were earning. They were subjected to ill-treatment and were sometimes beaten, and were considered by men as reproductive machines. Women's empowerment has a direct impact upon literacy and education only if and when they play an effective role in decision-making within the household. Women's empowerment was, however, only evident in those women who were widows or whose husbands were working abroad or whose husbands were open-minded. Our survey revealed that husbands were usually so orthodox that they did not permit their wives to go out of their homes or to work with male strangers or to work in a factory.

NOTES

1. Exploitation is used here in a loose sense including verbal and physical abuse, delayed payments and poor rates rather than in the Marxian sense of the extraction of surplus value. Of course, exploitation in the Marxian sense is also likely to accompany exploitation based on unequal power as defined above.

ANNEXURES

ANNEXURE 3: FOCUS GROUP DISCUSSIONS (FGD)

PROCEDURE

The following outline was utilized to train the field-teams for the focus group discussions and for use in the pre-test FGD:

Choosing focus group participants:

Invite 10-12 participants from the household respondents, assuming that up to two will not show up. Explain to invitees the purpose of the FGD, and specify time and place. Reconfirm if possible.

Role of the focus group moderator/team

- One person from the team (moderator for the session) can introduce the team and convey the purpose of the project. Role of tape-recorder should be mentioned.
- The team should be non-authoritative and non-judgmental.
- The team must always respond to discussion in a friendly and unbiased way.
- The team must facilitate the whole group participation, encourage lively discussion, and manage to cover the research agenda within the one-to-one-and-a-half hour session while letting the participants take the lead.

Conducting the session

- Participants should be seated in a circle in a neutral, relatively undisturbed space.
- The discussion may be warmed up with a few neutral questions, e.g. 'how odd the weather is this year, isn't it?' or 'How many children do you have?' General group introductions should take place.

- Team should establish group norms:
  - Everyone should get a chance to talk.
  - We should try to speak one at a time.
  - We want to encourage everyone to share their comments comfortably.
  - We will stick to the topic under discussion. The topic can be introduced here as a general discussion on how women in this locality obtain home-based work or how home-based work is organized in this locality.
- The focus group guidelines should follow a funnel format, with questions ranging from the general to the specific. It is necessary, however, for the team to remain flexible, and use his/her sensitivity to estimate when it is appropriate to probe further into an issue or to come back to it later. The team must take quick notes to keep track of the multitude of issues for discussion that will be raised in order to make sure they are all covered.
- If the subject matter becomes sensitive, one technique to address this may include bringing up a case study for discussion.

Role of the note takers

- Note-taking is the key to the recording of the discussion.
- One person can manage the audio equipment as well. The verbatim notes should be supported by the tape-recording of the interview, and should help to produce an authentic transcript of the focus group discussions.

During the focus group

- The team should attempt to take verbatim notes of the focus group discussion. Naturally, comments on irrelevant subjects, such as if someone comments on the heat outside, may be left out. Respondents from the focus group will be identified as 'A', 'B', 'C' etc.
- Observations of the mood, change in tempo, level of enthusiasm, and other relevant aspects of the focus group need to be noted, because they will assist in interpreting the discussion for analysis afterwards.

AFTER THE FOCUS GROUP SESSION

- The team will summarize the focus group by filling out the attached summary sheet. This should be done immediately after the FGD. It is an essential part of the data collected from the session.
The team should prepare a brief summary sheet for submission as part of the data collected in focus group.

The following key themes were provided to the field-team for guiding the discussions:

GUIDELINES FOR CHILDREN'S FGD

- Is home-based work keeping you out of school?
- If going to school, is it difficult for you to do well?
- Would you rather not work and just concentrate on schooling?
- What would you prefer to do?
- Is home-based work adversely affecting your health?
- Are you punished by parents for not working well?
- Do you have contact with the contractor?
- Is the contractor harsh?
- Do you get enough playtime?

GUIDELINES FOR WOMEN'S FGD

Try to get priority rankings. They should be asked if they feel they are better or worse off because of the home-based work compared to others in their neighbourhood that do not do such work in terms of the following:
- Youth health
- Children's health
- Children's education
- Free time
- General prosperity and well-being
- Other (specify)
- What are the main reasons they work at home?
- Do they feel that the work that they do is dangerous/hazardous?
- Do they think that the work that they do is tedious, repetitive and boring?
- Do they think that their children should be doing this kind of work?

- Do they think that the contractors take advantage of them or give them a fair deal?
- What could be done to improve their situation?
- Is there something specific the government could do to improve their situation?
- What do they think they could do to improve their situation?
- When did this work start in their community?
- Incidence of activity by locality. Has it changed over time? If yes why?
- Has the violence in/around community affected their work?

Other issues
- A profile of subcontracting process
- Locality/community profile
- Ethnic issues

While the key themes mentioned above were covered in all the reports, not all the teams utilized these themes as sub-headings.

METHOD UTILIZED FOR THE FGDS

The method adopted in conducting these FGDs was as follows:

For the women's FGD, the three women in the field team sat with the women in a room in the locality. One person asked the questions and others took notes and intervened if clarifications or explanations were needed. Since one or two assertive people can dominate discussions, all participants were individually addressed. In the case of contradictory opinions, the field-team probed deeper to see if a consensus could evolve.

The three men handled the three child FGDs. They gathered ten to fifteen working children from the immediate neighbourhood and introduced the themes for the discussion. The children talked about their views regarding work, whether they liked working, whether they had enough time for rest and recreation and whether they liked to go to school. Since the team spent more than a week in a locality for fieldwork, they established contact with working children through key informants. They also invited some of the children who were not engaged in home-based work for their perspective.

There were two FGDs held per sector, one for women and one for children. The summary of the discussions are reported below:

3.1 INCENSE STICK MAKING, ORANGI

3.1.1 WOMEN'S EMPOWERMENT

There was no uplift in the status of women in this sector due to their home-based work earnings. Women simply followed in the footsteps of their mothers and grandmothers in doing this work. They did not question that, within the traditional framework that is imposed on them by their husbands, they are not supposed to be breadwinners. In most households, men did not earn regularly for several reasons including illness or unemployment. Men in this locality did not help the women with either home-based work or with household work. Women told us that if they refused to do the home-based work for any reason, the husbands subjected them to verbal and physical abuse, in most cases forcing them to take on home-based work again. Even so, they do not raise their voice against the men because they think that such opposition is unacceptable on religious and cultural grounds.

The women found their home-based work boring and monotonous, but had no option but to do it. They were unable to save anything due to low income and high inflation. The money they earned was just enough to meet their daily requirements. Most of the women we spoke to do not spend any of the money on themselves. Women were confined to their houses and sought the consent of their husbands', who completely dominated them, even on issues that did not involve them.

3.1.2 EXPLOITATION

Women were not satisfied with the rates and the delayed payments. In most cases, the contractor was a relative and so, while they were not viewed as outsiders or as *seths* (big bosses), they still complained about them. Women did not indicate that there was any physical abuse, but verbal abuse, particular of children, was routine. Most of the children went to *madrasas*, since regular schools were not affordable. Children worked almost as much as adults.

3.1.3 ECONOMIC WELL-BEING

As mentioned above, women did not manage to save anything out of their earnings and the home-based work was needed for survival. Women did not think that engaging in home-based work brought any substantial change in their financial status. They also felt that their hard work was neither appreciated by their husbands nor by society.

3.1.4 HEALTH

The main health problems confronted by women and children due to the home-based work included breathing problems, cough, body ache, fatigue, joint pains, asthma and nosebleeds.

3.2   CARPET WEAVING, KORANGI

3.2.1 WOMEN'S EMPOWERMENT

Women in Korangi were in a much worse condition than in Orangi. Many women had not stepped out of their houses in years. They were reluctant to attend the FGD, and those attending were not very responsive or open about discussing their problems. Their working hours were very long, especially when combined with household chores. Men in this locality were even more conservative than those in Orangi and treated women like a commodity. Women complained of physical beating and told us that they were forced to weave carpets. They had no decision-making powers regarding any issue and were confined to the homes. Women did not socialize with each other or have any free time for themselves. Only those women looked more confident whose husbands were supportive of them. Almost all the women were married off at a very young age and their consent was not solicited, despite this being their religious right.

3.2.2 EXPLOITATION

Exploitation was again more intense in this sector. In most of the cases, parents had taken a loan on their children. To pay off this loan, children often worked in factories while women worked at home. The incidence of physical abuse, especially of children, was very high. Women again complained of low rates and late payments. However, they thought that the big factory owners, rather than contractors, were the ones enriching themselves at the worker's expense and appropriating the profits.

3.2.3 Economic Wellbeing

Again, women and children did not think that their earnings had brought any substantial change in their economic well-being. No savings were reported and this work was simply viewed to be necessary for survival. Most of the children wanted to go to school but knew that their parents could not afford that or to give them pocket money out of their earnings.

3.2.4 Health

Women and children suffered from cough, cold, pain in the whole body, especially in the back and fingers, skin problems and fatigue. Children going to school complained that they could not concentrate on their homework due to home-based work.

3.3.1 Sack stitching, Godhra

In this community, most of the children went to school and also to the *madrasah*. In most cases, children fetched the material from the contractors, but sometimes women did so. Since children were in direct contact with the contractor, they were often exposed to verbal abuse, but no physical abuse was reported.

Children started work after coming from school and women after other household chores were done. It took two to three minutes to sew a sack and, on average, a household sewed 300 to 400 sacks per day for about Rs. 30 to Rs. 33 per hundred. Defective pieces were returned, and in case of continuous poor quality work, the household lost the work. Women spent their earnings to finance the education of their children and also to buy dowry items for their daughters.

Both women and children suffered from inhalation of the jute fiber and body aches, due to posture and long work hours. The sacks were used for the export of onions and potatoes and so the work was seasonal. There was other home-based work available in this locality such as stitching children's garments, ribbon making and textile factory waste cloth sorting. However, since the rates for sack stitching were higher, households preferred this work despite the health hazards.

Gender stereotyping was evident during the focus group discussion. Girls mentioned that they did the home-based work because sewing is for females. According to the mothers, girls were more easily controlled than boys.

Women in this community were very enterprising and some of them were shopkeepers, a sight not observed in the rest of the country. Women were also cheerful, and by engaging in collective sewing sessions in the alleys, they interacted with other women in the neighbourhood while working. There were instances of collective action in which they were successful in compelling contractors to increase the piece rate. Women felt exploited because, in their opinion, had this work been done by men, they would have secured higher rates. Moreover, contractors also delayed payments. Women were also conscious of their poor surroundings and held the City Metropolitan Corporation responsible for this.

Women got very excited at the idea of an organization of their own that could discuss their problems. They mentioned that communal violence had reduced the work available but that matters were returning to normal.

3.3.2 PRAWN SHELLING, MACHAR COLONY

Children worked both in the *waras* (shed) and at home. They worked in *waras* when home-based work was not available or, because the women and elder sisters could do work given for the homes. The contractors preferred getting the work done at the *wara* since it was easier for them to control the kids, push them into working faster and monitor to ensure there was no theft.

They also fetched prawns for shelling at home. Starting at a very early age, the children worked for long hours. The children reached the *waras* as early as 4 a.m. and continued working until 11:30 a.m. Children worked similar hours at home because there were no storage facilities and delay was not an option for the highly perishable product.

The contractors and his aides physically abused the children. Since prawns are very delicate, there is a possibility of breaking of the tails during shelling. Children were severely beaten for such mistakes.

Skin problems resulting from this work were reported and observed by the field teams. Pain due to bad posture and long working hours were common, as was the case for other home-based work.

One *challi* (a basket) contained one *gala* weighing 4 to 5 kgs. It took one to one and a half hours to peel one *gala*. Children peeled 3 to 4 *galas* per day and a household peeled 10 to 15 galas per day on average, when the work was available.

Most of the people in this community were illegal immigrants from Bangladesh. There were reports of domestic violence. Some of the women were brought here and sold to men of different ethnic origins. Men in this locality were very strict and their narrow interpretation of Islam about *purdah* prevented women from socializing and visiting even neighbours.

People realized that prawn shelling is hazardous, but they do not have a choice since no other work was available in that locality. Even prawn shelling did not provide regular work throughout the year. Women said that though their husbands do not generally let them go out of their houses, but if some employment were available in the area, they would be allowed to work due to financial difficulties.

ANNEXURES

ANNEXURE 4: QUESTIONNAIRES

The control group questionnaires are not included since they are draw on the questionnaires for the women, child and households of families engaged in home-based work.

QUESTIONNAIRE (FOR WOMEN)

GENERAL INFORMATION

Marital Status
1   Single
2   Married
3   Divorced
4   Separated
5   Widowed

Age of respondent _____ Years

W1   Are you the household head?
1   Yes
0   No

Education
W2   Have you ever attended school?
1   Yes
0   No   *If No, Skip to W4*

W3   If Yes, then:
Can you read?
1   Yes
0   No

Can you write?
1   Yes
0   No

WOMEN'S EMPOWERMENT

Mobility
W4 Do you go outside the house on your own when you need to?
1 Yes
0 No   *If No, Skip to W6*

W5 If Yes, do you need permission of your brother/parents/ husband?
1 Yes
0 No

Access to Resources/Saving/Consumption
W6 Who keeps the earning from HB Work? (%)
1 Husband/Guardian _____ %
2 Retained _____ %
7 Others (specify) _____ %
(Note: Total should add to 100%)

W7 Do you save money through *bachat* committee (BC) system?
1 Yes
0 No

W8 Do you have personal savings from the income?
1 Yes
0 No   *If No, Skip to W10*

W9 If Yes, are any savings kept for daughter's/your own future? e.g. dowry
1 Yes
0 No
7 Others (specify) _____

W10 How much of your income do you keep for personal expenses (%)?
1 _____ %
0 No   *If No, Skip to W12*

W11 If some, identify where the money is spent?
1 Clothes for self
2 Jewellery for self
3 Food
4 Support habit/paan-cigarette, tobacco, naswaar, hukka, gutka
5 Health

6   Presents for children
7   Presents for relatives
8   On husband
9   Children's education
10   Other children
11   Other children's needs
12   HH in general
77   Others (specify) _____

Decision-making
W12 Do you know of any welfare organization or NGO/CBO in your
     locality or any such organization from outside?
1   Yes
0   No   *If No, Skip to W18*

W13 If Yes, what is the nature of the organization's activities?
1   Welfare
2   Education
3   Health
4   Religion
5   Women's organization
6   Legal services
7   Civic services
77   Others (specify) _____

W14 Do you access the services of the organization?
1   Yes
0   No

W15 Do you participate in the activities of this organization?
1   Yes
0   No   *If No, Skip to W17*

W16 If Yes, why did you join?
1   Consider it very socially worthy
7   Others (specify) _____

W17 If No, why not?
1   Not approved by the family
2   Not interested
3   No time
4   Not approved by neighbourhood
7   Others (specify)_____

W18 Who made the decision that you should work?
1   Self
2   Your husband
3   Family member
4   Joint family decision

W19 Do you have a say in decisions regarding?
a)   Schooling
     1   Yes
     0   No

b)   Marriage
     1   Yes
     0   No

c)   Family matters
     1   Yes
     0   No

d)   Household expenditure
     1   Yes
     0   No

e)   Others (specify) _____

     1   Yes
     0   No

W20 Would you prefer factory work/regular employment outside
     the home to Home-Based Work?
1   Yes
0   No   *If Yes, Skip to W22*

W21 If No, then why?
1   Family uncomfortable
2   Neighbours/relatives talk
3   Too far
7   Others (specify) _____

W22 If Yes at W20, then what are the reasons for preferring factory
     work?
1   Home-Based Work is too hard
2   Home-Based Work is too hazardous
3   Home-Based Work is too tedious

4   Pays better than HOME-BASED WORK
5   Won't have to deal with the contractor
6   Like to leave house for a while
7   Others (specify) _____

WORK RELATED QUESTIONS

W23 How long have you been engaged in this activity?

_____Years_____Months

W24 How old were you when you began to work?
_____ Years

W25 Who taught you the skills for HOME-BASED WORK?
1   Self
2   Contractor
3   Family
4   Vocational training
5   Friends/neighbours
7   Others (specify) _____

W26 What are the reasons that you are doing this work?
1   Inflation/poverty
2   Dowry
3   Independence
4   No other work available
5   Adds to family income
6   More profitable than other activity
7   To collect money for own use
8   To pay off loans
9   Because of the death/disability of some other earning member
     of the household
10   Because of the illness of some other earning member of the
     household
11   Unemployment of husband
77   Others (specify) _____

W27 Is your child (being interviewed) in school?
1   Yes
0   No   *If Yes, Skip to W29*

W28 Why is your child not in school?
1 School does not provide a better job
2 School is of poor quality
3 School is too far
4 School is too expensive
5 Child prefers to stay at home
6 Need income from child's work/poverty
7 School is worthless
77 Others

W29 Why does your child do Home-Based Work?
1 To add to family income
2 No other work
3 Other work too dangerous
4 Other work does not pay well
5 Prefer they stay at home
7 Others (specify) _____

W30 What are the advantages of working at home?
1 Less commuting time
2 Mobility problems
3 Inadequate clothes to work outside
4 Lack skills for outside work
5 Feel unsafe going out
6 Neighbourhood does not approve of our going out
7 Male family members do not approve of our going out
8 Can watch over them
77 Others (specify) _____

W31 What are the disadvantages of the Home-Based Work?
0 None
1 Makes the house messy
2 Less time for family
3 Less time for friends and community
4 Very tiring
5 Low income
6 Health problems
7 Long hours
8 Take up limited living space
9 Contractor bothersome
77 Others (specify) _____

W32 How did the Home-Based Work start in your family/household?
1   Approached by contractor
2   Approached by neighbour
3   Being done in the neighbourhood
4   Approached by friends
5   Approached by family member
7   Others (specify) _____

Time Organization
W33 During what time and how many hours do you work?
1   Daytime for   _____ hours per day
2   Night-time for _____ hours per night
     Total   _____ hours

W34 How many days do you work in a week?

_____Days

W35 Do you do this work all-year long?
1   Yes
0   No   *If Yes, Skip to W37*

W36 If No, why?
1   Work only available during some times of the year
2   I do other work
7   Others (specify) _____

Payment
W37 What is the payment rate?
Rs   /piece

W38 How much work done in a day by all family members?

Activity	Unit
Activity 1	
Activity 2	
Activity 3	
Activity 4	

W39 Have rates ever been increased?
1   Yes
2   No   *If No, Skip to W41*

W40 If Yes, how often?
1   Once
2   Twice
3   Thrice
4   More than thrice

W41 Have rates ever been reduced?
1   Yes
0   No   *If No, Skip to W43*

W42 If Yes, state why?
1   Competition from others
2   Less work available
7   Others (specify) _____

W43 Do you keep a record of the work done in the household?
1   Yes
0   No   *If Yes, Skip to W46*

W44 If No, has there ever been a difference of opinion with the
     contractor regarding how much work was done?
1   Yes
0   No

W45 If Yes, what was the outcome?
1   Contractor prevailed
2   Our view was accepted
3   Compromised
7   Others (specify) _____

W46 Are you paid on time?
1   Yes
0   No   *If Yes, Skip to W48*

W47 If No, how many days after delivery are you normally paid?
1   Up to 15 days
2   Up to 30 days
3   Up to 60 days
4   Over 60 days

W48 Has it ever happened that you were not paid at all?
1   Yes
0   No   *If No, Skip to W50*

W49 If Yes, what did you do?
1   Went to owner
2   Discussed with community elders
3   Went to police
7   Others (specify) _____

W50 Does contractor make your work difficult due to various mal-
     practices?
1   Yes
0   No   *If No, Skip to W52*

W51 If Yes, state the nature of these malpractices
1   Supplies poor quality material
2   Arbitrarily rejects products
3   Miscounts/mismeasures
7   Others (Specify)

Contract (women)
W52 What is the nature of your contract?
1   Oral
2   Written

ORGANIZATION OF THE PRODUCTION

W53 What is the name and address of your contractor(s)?

Contractor 1 (Activity _____)
Name   _____
Address   _____

Contractor 2 (Activity _____)
Name   _____
Address   _____

Contractor 3 (Activity _____)
Name   _____
Address   _____

W54 What happens if deadline is not met?
1   No deadline
2   Fine/rate reduced
3   Operations terminated

4   Not paid
7   Others (specify) _____

W55 What happens in case of faulty work?
1   Product rejected—cost borne by you
2   Product rejected—cost borne by employer
3   Product repaired
4   Fined
7   Others (specify) _____

Market Information
W56 How do you dispose of your finished work?
1   Contractors collect
2   Deliver to contractor

W57 How is your working relationship with the contractor?
1   Good
2   Bad
3   Indifferent   *If 1 or 3, Skip to W59*

W58 If bad, give the main reason:
1   Wants too much work done
2   Wants work done for long hours
3   Pays poorly
4   Does not pay on time
5   Abuses physically
6   Abuses verbally
7   Engages in malpractices
77   Others (specify) _____

WOMEN'S NON-ECONOMIC ACTIVITIES. HOUSEKEEPING ACTIVITIES/HOUSEHOLD CHORES

HOUSEHOLD RESPONSIBILITIES

W59 What kind of household chores do you perform?
1   Childcare
2   Shopping
3   Cleaning
4   Washing dishes
5   Washing clothes
6   Mending
7   Cooking

8   Pressing clothes
9   Caring for the sick/elderly
10   Repairs/maintenance of dwelling
11   Repair/maintenance of HH durables
12   Caring for HH members
77   Others (specify) _____

W60 At what time did you wake up yesterday? _____

W61 At what time did you go to sleep yesterday? _____

W62 How many hours did you spend yesterday on the following?
1   Home-Based Work   _____ Hours
2   HH chores   _____ Hours
3   Leisure   _____ Hours
4   Others (specify) _____ Hours
                              All working hours to be accounted for

W63 Has someone in the household taken over the domestic
     workload now that you are working?
1   Yes
0   No   *If No, Skip to W65*

W64 If Yes, who?
1   Daughters
2   Sons
3   Husband
4   Other relative
5   All share with me now

W65 Do family members (brother/husband/in-laws) get angry
     because you don't have time for chores?
1   Yes
0   No   *If No, Skip to W67*

W66 If Yes, what do they do?
1   Fight with you
2   Verbally abuse you
3   Physically abuse you
4   Help you when you are tired
5   Leave you alone
7   Others
(Note: The possibilities for a case study should be looked for)

W67 Do you feel your children are as well cared for as before despite your work?
1 Yes
0 No   *If No, Skip to W69*

W68 If Yes, what are the reasons?
1 Other family members are pitching in
2 You are now working much harder
7 Others (specify) _____

Home-Based Women Workers Organization
W69 Have you ever negotiated a better rate via collective action (working together with fellow HB Workers)?
1 Yes
0 No

W70 Is there any organization you rely upon?
1 Yes
0 No   *If No, Skip to W72*

W71 If Yes, which one? (Specify) _____

W72 Would you be willing to engage in collective action to negotiate wages rates/better condition if any organization were to assist you?
1 Yes
0 No

W73 What kinds of assistance do you need for this Home-Based Work from government and/or other organizations to improve your welfare?
1 Training in marketing
2 Technical training
3 Training-assistance with accounting
4 Credit
5 Assistance with forming movements/organizations
6 Framing better policy/laws
7 Others (specify) _____

W74 Do male adults in the household engage in Home-Based Work?
1 Yes
0 No   *If No, Skip to W78*

W75 If Yes, how many hours?
1
2
3

W76 Do they complain of Home-Based Work related health problems?
1   Yes
0   No   *If No, Skip to W78*

W77 If Yes, state nature of medical problems
1   General (fever, cold, etc.)
2   Eye infection/itching
3   Ear infection
4   Watery eyes
5   Difficult in seeing/eye strain
6   Cough
7   Asthma
8   Skin problem
9   Breathing problem
10   Stiff neck
11   Backache
12   Anaemia
13   Pain in legs
14   Pain in some limb
15   Pain in joints
16   Swelling knees
17   Swelling in other parts of body
18   Pain in chest
19   Stomach/belly pain
20   General bodily pains
21   Dizziness/nausea
22   Blisters
23   Skin-cracking/discoloration
24   Muscular pain
25   Exhaustion
77   Others (specify)

Nutrition
W78 How much milk do you consume?
0   Never
1   Only in tea
2   One cup/glass

3   Two cups/glasses
4   More than three cups/glasses

W79 How often do you eat vegetables?
0   Never
1   Every day
2   A few times a week
3   Once a week
4   Less than once a week
5   On seasonal basis

W80 How often do you eat fruits?
0   Never
1   Every day
2   A few times a week
3   Once a week
4   Less than once a week
5   On seasonal basis

W81 How often do you eat legumes?
1   Once a day
2   Once a week
3   Twice a week
4   A few times a week
5   A few times a month
6   About once a month
7   A few times a year

W82 How often do you eat meat?
0   Never
1   Once a day
2   Once a week
3   Twice a week
4   A few times a week
5   A few times a month
6   About once a month
7   A few times a year
8   When guest(s) come

W83 What did you have yesterday?

For breakfast
1   Roti
2   Paratha

3   Tea
4   Milk
5   Leftover
7   Others (specify)_____

For lunch
1   Roti
2   Paratha
3   Tea
4   Milk
5   Fish
6   Dal
7   Vegetable
8   Fruit
9   Curry
77   Others (specify)_____

For dinner
1   Roti
2   Paratha
3   Tea
4   Milk
5   Fish
6   Dal
7   Vegetable
8   Fruit
9   Curry
77   Others (specify)_____

QUESTIONNAIRE (FOR CHILDREN)

Schooling
C1   Do you attend school?
Yes
No   *If No, Skip to C4*

C2   If Yes, does Home-Based Work make school work difficult for
     you?
1   Yes
0   No   *If No, Skip to C7*

C3   If Yes, state why?
1   Get very tired doing Home-Based Work and can't concentrate
      on school work.
2   Home-Based Work/chores leave little time for school work
7   Others

C4   If No at C1, why are you not in school?
1   School does not provide a better job
2   School is of poor quality
3   School is too far
4   School is too expensive
5   Prefer to stay at home
6   Family needs income from work/poverty
7   Parents think school is worthless
77   Others (specify)

C5   If not attending school, did you ever attended school?
1   Yes
0   No   *If No, Skip to C7*

C6   If Yes, why did you drop out?
1   Home-Based Work/chores left little time for school work
2   Felt exhausted after Home-Based Work
3   Didn't like the school
4   School too far
5   Bad school
6   Parents didn't have enough money
7   Parents think schooling is useless
77   Others (specify)

WORK RELATED QUESTIONS

C7   How long have you been engaged in this activity?
      _____ Years _____ Months

C8   How old were you when you began this work? _____ Years

C9   Did you receive any job training for this work?
1   Yes
0   No   *If No, Skip to C12*

C10 If Yes, then from whom?
1 Contractor
2 Family
3 Vocational training
4 Friends/Relatives
5 Neighbours
7 Others (specify)_____

C11 Number of weeks of training: _____weeks

C12 What are the reasons you are doing this work?
1 Don't like school
2 Inflation/poverty
3 Independence
4 No other work available
5 Adds to family income
6 More profitable than other activity
7 To collect money for my own use
8 To pay off family loans
9 Because of the death/disability of some other earning member of the household
10 Because of the illness of some other earning member of the household
77 Others (specify) _____

C13 What are disadvantages of the Home-Based Work?
0 None
1 Makes the house messy
2 Less time for play
3 Less time for family
4 Less time for friends and community
5 Very tiring
6 Low pay
7 Health problems
8 Long hours
77 Others (specify) _____

C14 Do you shift regularly to other kinds of work during the year?
1 Yes
0 No   *If No, Skip to C16*

C15 If Yes, what kind of work?
1 Domestic
2 Own account work

3   Shop
4   Factory
5   Apprenticeship
6   Other home base work
7   Others (specify)_____

C16 How is your relationship with the contractor?
1   Good
2   Bad
3   Indifferent
4   No contact with the contractor   *If 1, 3 or 4, Skip to C18*

C17 If bad, give the main reason:
1   Wants too much work done
2   Wants work done for long hours
3   Pays poorly
4   Does not pay on time
5   Abuses physically
6   Abuses verbally
7   Others (specify) _____

Time organization
C18 During what time and how many hours do you work as Home-
     Based Work?
1   Daytime for   _____ Hours per day
2   Night time for _____ Hours per night
     Total   _____ Hours

C19 How many days you work in a week?   _____ Days

C20 Do you do this work all-year long?
Yes
No   *If Yes, Skip to C22*

C21 If No, why?
1   Work only available during some times of the year
2   I do other work
7   Other (specify) _____

C22 Has it ever happened that you did not perform your work
     well?
1   Yes
0   No   *If No, Skip to C24*

C23 If Yes, what were the consequences?
0   None
1   Scolded by family
2   Scolded by contractor
3   Fined by contractor
4   Beaten by family
5   Beaten by contractor
6   Not allowed to play
7   Not allowed to go to school
77   Others (specify) _____

C24 At what time did you wake up yesterday? _____

C25 At what time did you go to sleep yesterday? _____

C26 How many hours did you spend yesterday on the following?
1   Home-Based Work   _____ Hours
2   HH chores   _____ Hours
3   School or homework   _____ Hours
4   Meals   _____ Hours
5   Play   _____ Hours
7   Others (specify) _____

Household Chores
C27 What kind of household chores do you perform?
0   None
1   Childcare
2   Shopping
3   Cleaning
4   Washing dishes
5   Washing clothes
6   Mending
7   Cooking
8   Pressing clothes
9   Caring for the sick/elderly
10   Repairs/maintenance of dwelling
11   Repair/maintenance HH durables
12   Caring for HH members
77   Others (specify) _____

Earnings

C28 What happens to your earnings?
1   % goes direct to parents/guardian: _____
2   % keep: _____
7   % Other   _____.   *If only 1, Skip to C 31*

C29 If you keep some, do you spend it all?
1   Yes
0   No   *If Yes, Skip to C31*

C30 If No, do you save some?
1   Yes
0   No

Social/Family

C31 What do you do for fun when not working?
1   Play some game
2   Watch TV
3   Play with friends
4   Read books/magazines
5   No time available
7   Others (specify) _____

C32 If given a choice, what would you prefer to do in the future?
1   Go to school full-time
2   Work for income full-time
3   Help full-time in household enterprise or business
4   Work full-time in household chores or housekeeping
5   Go to school part-time and working part-time for income
6   Part-time in household enterprise or business
7   Part-time in household chores or housekeeping
8   Complete education/training and start to work
9   Find a better job/work than the present one
10   Play and go to school
77   Others (specify) _____

C33 Do you feel your family has enough time to take care of you?
1   Yes
0   No

Nutrition

C34 How often do you consume milk?
0   Never
1   Only in tea

2   One cup/glass
3   Two cups/glasses
4   Three cup/glasses
5   More than three cups/glasses

C35   How often do you eat vegetables?
0   Never
1   Every day
2   Several times a week
3   A few times a week
4   Once a week
5   Less than once a week
6   Several time a month
7   A few times a month
8   On seasonal basis

C36   How often do you eat fruits?
0   Never
1   Every day
2   Several times a week
3   A few times a week
4   Once a week
5   Less than once a week
6   Several times a month
7   A few times a month
8   On seasonal basis

C37   How often do you eat legumes?
1   Every day
2   Several times a week
3   A few times a week
4   Once a week
5   Less than once a week
6   Several times a month
7   A few times a month

C38   How often do you eat meat?
0   Never
1   Twice a day
2   Once a day
3   Several times a week
4   A few times a week
5   Once a week
6   Several times a month

7   A few times a month
8   When guest(s) come
9   A few times a year

C39   Do you get enough rice to eat?
1   Yes
0   No

C40   What did you have yesterday?

For breakfast
1   Roti
2   Paratha
3   Tea
4   Milk
6   Leftover
77   Others (specify)_____

For lunch
1   Roti
2   Paratha
3   Tea
4   Milk
5   Fish
6   Dal
7   Vegetable
8   Fruit
77   Others (specify)_____

For dinner
1   Roti
2   Paratha
3   Tea
4   Milk
5   Fish
6   Dal
7   Vegetable
8   Fruit
77   Others (specify)_____

QUESTIONNAIRE (FOR HOUSEHOLD)

INFORMATION OF THE HOUSEHOLD'S ACTIVITY

General
Living conditions
Nature of building of the house
Katcha
Pakka
Katcha-pakka

Source of drinking water for the household
Tap in the household
Neighbourhood pump
Purchased from supplier
Others (Specify)

Nature of toilet facility
Private/flush
Private/septic tank
Shared
Public/outdoors
Others (specify)

H1   Does the household have electricity?
1   Yes
0   No

H2   Does the household have running water?
1   Yes
0   No

H3   What is the ownership status of the household dwelling?
1   Owned
2   Provided free by employer
3   Subsidized by employer (private or Government/public
     ownership) (amount paid per month)
4   Rented from private owner (amount paid per month)
5   Rented from Government/public ownership (amount paid per
     month)
6   Pay bhatta
7   Other (specify) _____

H4 Which of the following are present in the household?
a) Radio
    1   Yes
    0   No

b) Cassette Player
    1   Yes
    0   No

c) Fridge
    1   Yes
    0   No

d) TV
    1   Yes
    0   No

e) VCR
    1   Yes
    0   No

H5 Which mode of transportation does the household have?
0 None
1 Bicycle
2 Motorcycle
3 Public transport (bus)
4 Private transport (wagon)

H6 Number of people residing in the house above 14 years

Male   _____

Female   _____

Total   _____

H7   Number of children less than 14 years:

	Child 1	Child 2	Child 3	Child 4	Child 5	Child 6	Child 7
Gender	1. M	1. M	1. M	1. M	1. M	1. M	1. M
	2. F	2. F	2. F	2. F	2. F	2. F	2. F
Age							
Currently attending school	1. Yes	1. Yes	1. Yes	1. Yes	1. Yes	1. Yes	1. Yes
	0. No	0. No	0. No	0. No	0. No	0. No	0. No
Highest class completed							
Doing HOME-BASED WORK	1. Yes	1. Yes	1. Yes	1. Yes	1. Yes	1. Yes	1. Yes
	0. No	0. No	0. No	0. No	0. No	0. No	0. No
Height*							
Weight*							

Child 1=Self   *** will be done by the doctor**

H8   How many household members work on this HOME-BASED WORK?

HH Member	Number	Male	Female
Adults			
Children			

H9   Is the head of household working?
1   Yes
0   No

H10   Does the household incur any expenses for Home-Based Work?
1   Yes
0   No   *If No, Skip to H12*

H11 If Yes, give values for an average month when working:

Type of material	Activity 1	Activity 2	Activity 3	Activity 4
1				
2				
3				
4				
5				
6				

H12 What is the current value of the assets the household owns for this activity?

Activity 1
Fixed capital:
Machinery   Rs _____
Tools   Rs _____
Other   Rs _____   **Total capital   Rs _____**

Activity 2
Fixed capital:
Machinery   Rs _____
Tools   Rs _____
Other.   Rs _____   **Total capital   Rs _____**

Activity 3
Fixed capital:
Machinery   Rs _____
Tools   Rs _____
Other   Rs _____   **Total capital   Rs _____**

H13 What were the main sources of funds for your capital when you started this Home-Based Work?
1   Government assistance
2   Bank loan
3   International organization
4   NGO finance
5   Private loan
6   Another business
7   Friends
8   Relatives
9   Wages/job of self or household member/other sources
10   Contractor provided funds

H14 Monthly household expenditure:

Details	Expenditure
Items of daily use	
House rent	
Medicine/Doctor's visit	
Schooling	
Transportation	
Gas	
Electricity	
Water	
Others (specify)_____	
Total	

HOUSEHOLD'S PRODUCTION PERFORMANCE

H15 Number of non-residing members who contribute in household income on a regular basis:

0
1
2
3
Total amount Rs _____

H16 Total number of non-Home-Based Work earning members in the household

H17 Household monthly income of non-Home-Based Work earners
1   Rs _____
2   Rs _____
3   Rs _____

H18 Have you taken any loans in the last six months?
1   Yes
0   No   *If No, End*

H19 How much debt has your household incurred?
Rs _____

H20 Whom was the loan contracted from?
1   Relatives
2   Neighbors
3   Professional moneylender
4   Bank
5   Welfare society (NGOs, etc.)
6   Employer/contractor
7   Shopkeeper
77   Other (specify) _____

H21 What is the nature of the loan?
1   Interest (%)
2   Interest free

H22 How will the loan be repaid?
1   Work it off in the Home-Based Work
2   From saving

HEALTH QUESTIONNAIRE
(To be filled in by the doctor)

Name of child   _____
Gender   _____
Age   _____
Height   _____
Weight   _____
Size of biceps   _____

IMMUNIZATION HISTORY OF WORKING CHILD (*To be asked from adult*)
1   Not vaccinated
2   Partially vaccinated
3   Fully vaccinated (by card)
4   Vaccination status unknown

Type of Labour
Light
Normal
Hard
Extra hard

HQ1 Is the child anaemic?
1   Yes
0   No

HQ2 Does the child currently have a disease/ailment?
1   Yes
0   No   *If No, Skip to HQ4*

HQ3 If Yes, is it
1   Congenital
2   Community disease
3   Home-Based Work related
7   Other (specify) _____
                    If not Home-Based Work related, Skip to HQ8

CHILDREN'S HEALTH (*To be asked from child, preferably*)

HQ4 If Home-Based Work related, what was/were the nature of
    your illness/injury/ailment?
1   General (fever, cold, etc.)
2   Eye infection/itching
3   Ear infection
4   Watery eyes
5   Difficult in seeing/eye strain
6   Cough
7   Asthma
8   Skin problem
9   Breathing problem
10   Stiff neck
11   Backache
12   Anaemia
13   Pain in legs
14   Pain in some limb
15   Pain in joints
16   Swelling knees
17   Swelling in other parts of body
18   Pain in chest
19   Stomach/belly pain
20   General bodily pains
21   Dizziness/nausea
22   Blisters
23   Skin-cracking/discoloration
24   Muscular pain

25   Exhaustion
77   Others (specify)

HQ5 How serious was the injury/illness?
1   Did not need any medical treatment
2   Needed treatment but could not afford it
3   Medically treated and released immediately
4   Stopped work temporarily
5   Hospitalized
6   Prevented work permanently
7   Other (specify) _____

HQ6 How often have you been ill in the last six months due to
    Home-Based Work?
0   Nil
1   Once
2   Twice
3   Three times
4   Four times
5   Five times
6   Six times
7   More than once a month
8   More than twice a month

HQ7 Did contractor assist with treatment?
1   Yes
0   No

WOMEN'S HEALTH (TO BE ASKED FROM HB WORKER WOMAN)

HQ8 Do you have any health problems as a result of this HB Work?
1   Yes
0   No   *If No, Skip to HQ13*

HQ9 If Yes, what was/were the nature of your illness/injury?
1   General (fever, cold, etc.)
2   Eye infection/itching
3   Ear infection
4   Watery eyes
5   Difficulty in seeing/eye strain
6   Cough
7   Asthma
8   Skin problem
9   Breathing problem

10   Stiff neck
11   Backache
12   Anaemia
13   Pain in legs
14   Pain in some limb
15   Pain in joints
16   Swelling knees
17   Swelling of other parts of body
18   Pain in chest
19   Stomach/belly pain
20   General bodilyy pains
21   Dizziness/nausea
22   Blisters
23   Skin-cracking/discoloration
24   Muscular pain
25   Exhaustion
26   Gynaecological problems
77   Others (specify)

HQ10 How serious was the injury/illness?
1   Did not need any medical treatment
2   Needed treatment but could not afford it
3   Medically treated and released immediately
4   Stopped work temporarily
5   Hospitalized
6   Prevented work permanently
7   Other (specify) _____

HQ11 How often have you been ill in the last six months due to HB
     work?
0   Nil
1   Once
2   Twice
3   Three times
4   Four times
5   Five times
6   Six times
7   More than once a month
8   More than twice a month   *If Nil, Skip to HQ13*

HQ12 Did contractor assist with treatment?
1   Yes
0   No

HQ13   Is there any health-related safety equipment issued by the
        contractor?
1   Yes
0   No   *If No, Skip to HQ16*

HQ14 If Yes, specify   _____
                               _____

HQ15 Are the following facilities close enough?
Government dispensary
Yes
No

Private doctor
Yes
No

Hakeem
Yes
No

Homeopath
Yes
No

Government hospital
Yes
No

Private hospital
Yes
No

HQ16 Are the following facilities affordable?
Private doctor
Yes
No

Homeopath
Yes
No

Hakeem
Yes
No

Private hospital
Yes
No

QUESTIONNAIRE (FOR INTERVIEWER)

Does the household have electricity?
1   Yes
2   No

Nature of building of the house
Katcha
Pakka
Katcha-pakka

HEALTH
How will you evaluate the workspace in the home for each of the following?

Categories	1	2	3	4	5
Space					
Light					
Dust					
Air quality/Fumes					
Temperature					
Smell					
Noise					
Others					

Rating:
Excellent
Good
Acceptable
Poor
Bad

QUESTIONNAIRE (FOR SETH/OWNER)

S1   What are the main reasons for recruiting HB workers?
01   Possibility to recruit from a much larger area
02   Possibility to hire workers in accordance with variations in demand
03   Minimization of the risk of unionization
04   No labour problems
05   Can pay labour less to beat the competition
06   No problems with government regulations as in the formal sector
07   Freedom to vary the volume of the production
08   Greater opportunity to vary the nature of the work
09   Reduction of costs since most costs are borne by household
10   Greater flexibility in responding to the fluctuations and irregularity of the market
77   Others (specify) _____

S2   Where does this product go after it is collected from contractor?
1   Retailer
2   Wholesaler
3   Exporter
7   Others (specify) _____

S3   At what price is it delivered at the different tiers?
1   Retailer
2   Wholesaler
3   Exporter
7   Others

INDEX